Risk:
Analysis, Assessment and Management

Dedicated to
Wenda Ramby Ansell
and
Wilf Wharton

Risk:
Analysis, Assessment and Management

Edited by
Jake Ansell
University of Edinburgh, Scotland

and

Frank Wharton
University of Hull, UK

JOHN WILEY & SONS
Chichester · New York · Brisbane · Toronto · Singapore

Other Wiley Editorial Offices

John Wiley & Sons, Inc., 605 Third Avenue,
New York, NY 10158–0012, USA

Jacaranda Wiley Ltd, 33 Park Road, Milton,
Queensland 4064, Australia

John Wiley & Sons (Canada) Ltd, 22 Worcester Road,
Rexdale, Ontario M9W 1L1, Canada

John Wiley & Sons (SEA) Pte Ltd, 37 Jalan Pemimpin #05-04,
Block B, Union Industrial Building, Singapore 2057

Library of Congress Cataloging-in-Publication Data

Risk: analysis, assessment and management / edited by Jake Ansell and
Frank Wharton.
p. cm.
Selection of contributions made to a series of seminars held
during 1989/90 at the School of Management, Hull University.
Includes bibliographical references and index.
ISBN 0-471-93464-X (ppc)
1. Risk management. 2. Risk perception. 3. Risk. I. Ansell,
Jake. II. Wharton, Frank.
HD61.R556 1992
658.15'5—dc20   92–5256
                                                          CIP

British Library Cataloguing in Publication Data:

A catalogue record for this book is available from the British Library

ISBN 0-471-93464-X

Typeset in 10/12 Times by APS, Salisbury, Wiltshire
Printed and bound in Great Britain by
Biddles Ltd, Guildford and King's Lynn

Contents

List of Contributors

Dr J. Ansell (Editor)
Department of Business Studies, University of Edinburgh, William Robertson
Building, 50 George Square, Ediburgh EH8 9JY

Dr G. M. Ballard
Atomic Energy Authority Technology, Risley, Warrington WA3 6AT

Dr C. Boyd
Department of Management and Marketing, University of Saskatchewan,
Saskatoon, Saskatchewan, Canada S7N 0WO

Ms P. Carter
Department of Management Systems and Sciences, University of Hull,
Cottingham Road, Hull, HU6 7RX

Professor C. B. Chapman
Department of Accounting and Management Science,
University of Southampton, University Road, Highfield,
Southampton SO9 5NH

Sir Richard Doll
ICRF Unit, Gibson Laboratories, Radcliffe Infirmary, Oxford OX2 6HE

Mr J. Donaldson
Centre for Service Management Studies, 14 Charvil House Road, Charvil,
Reading RG10 9RD

Dr S. S. M. Ho
Department of Accounting, Chinese University of Accounting, Shatin NT,
Hong Kong

Dr N. Jackson
Management Division, University of Newcastle upon Tyne,
Newcastle NE1 7RU

Professor A. M. Lee
7 Parkland Crescent, Ferriby, Humberside HU14 3EZ

Professor R. H. Pike
The Management Centre, University of Bradford, Emm Lane, Bradford
BD9 4JL

Professor L. Thomas
Department of Business Studies, University of Edinburgh, William Robertson
Building, 50 George Square, Edinburgh EH8 9JY

Mr F. Wharton (Editor)
Department of Management Systems and Sciences, University of Hull,
Cottingham Road, Hull HU6 7RX

Dr B. Wynne
Centre for the Study of Environmental Change, Lancaster University, Lancaster
LA1 4YF

Preface

Risk is an unavoidable feature of human existence. Neither man nor the organizations and societies to which he belongs can survive for very long without taking risks. On a personal level every decision or action carries risks which range in severity from loss of face, status, money, employment, health, and liberty to the loss of life itself. At another level we are confronted by threats from infectious diseases, fatal accidents, economic disasters, famines, political upheavals, nuclear war, and the possible consequences of the irreparable damage being done by man himself to the environment and the very ecological system which supports his existence.

As mortality rates have fallen in developed economies there has been a dramatic growth of interest in improving the quality of life with a shift in attention from the cause and prevention of premature death to the identification of risk factors associated with chronic disease. The risk factors often concern behaviour, diet, occupation and the environment. The associations are often weak and difficult to detect. Organizations struggling to survive in today's increasingly sophisticated and competitive economies must of necessity be concerned about problems of business risk management. To survive they must constantly reinvest in the development of new products and the use of new technologies. However, such decisions are often fraught with uncertainty and risk not only for the shareholders, employees and customers but also, perhaps, for the population at large.

Public and governmental interest in problems of technological risk management has been stimulated in recent years through media attention, pressure group action, numerous disasters and the evidence of science concerning threats to society and the environment. There is pressure for governments to assume greater control of risks albeit at the expense of more restricted opportunity for further economic and technological advancement.

This volume on aspects of risk management consists of contributions made to a series of seminars held in the School of Management at Hull University during 1988/90 together with invited contributions from other authors. There are contributions on aspects of risk analysis, assessment and management which range from methodology to ethics with examples drawn from finance, industry, transport, health and the environment.

Clearly the book is not a comprehensive treatise on risk. It does, however, address some of the more important and difficult aspects of risk management in a variety of contexts. In so doing it may perhaps contribute to the development of a conceptual framework for thinking about risk which is more generally applicable than those used in more focused or specialized texts.

The editors are grateful to the other authors for their contributions and to Diane Taylor, Management Science Editor, John Wiley & Sons Ltd for her encouragement and advice.

J. ANSELL
F. WHARTON
December 1991

Chapter 1

Risk Management: Basic Concepts and General Principles

F. Wharton
Hull University

ABSTRACT

Through improved communications and media attention, the management of risk has become the subject of growing concern to individuals, organizations and society at large. It is a subject area which now attracts contributions from economists, engineers, environmentalists, biologists, epidemiologists, mathematicians, philosophers, psychologists, sociologists and management and political scientists. As a consequence the word risk itself is used to imply different concepts and measures, the terms risk analysis and risk assessment are used in various and sometimes interchangeable ways and there exists no unified approach to the problems of risk management. Some basic definitions, concepts and principles are proposed.

THE EVOLUTION OF RISK

It is estimated to be some 4 billion years since the first stirrings of life on earth and some 4 million years since the human species began to emerge. Relatively speaking, therefore, man has not yet survived for very long. On a time scale of, say, 40 years since the earliest life on earth man would have appeared only 2 weeks ago, the earliest civilizations would have been formed only 20 minutes

Risk: Analysis, Assessment and Management. Edited by J. Ansell and F. Wharton.
© 1992 John Wiley & Sons Ltd.

ago and the industrial revolution, which transformed his way of life and now threatens the survival of man and his environment, would have started during the last minute.

Primitive man was at one with his environment. It is only more recent generations, encouraged by western philosophers and Christian religions, that have tended to set man apart from his environment and to foster the notion that somehow the world and its resources had been created for man's exclusive use (Ashby, 1978). As was quite recently observed 'Despite Darwin we are not, in our hearts, part of the natural process. We are superior to nature, contemptuous of it' (White, 1967).

It is only during the last few decades and through the evidence of science that man has once again begun to identify with his environment.

That man has not only survived but also become so dominant a species is largely due to there have evolved in him two important attributes—an ability to communicate and a highly developed intelligence.

Through the ability to communicate man has been able to act collectively. Whilst man as an individual is a relatively defenceless and ineffectual creature, organized man is a quite different proposition. Organized man has been able to defend and feed himself more effectively and extensively exploit the earth's resources than any other species.

It has been argued that too much is made of 'man the tool user' and not enough of 'man the language user'. It is also believed that the increase in cranial capacity and intelligence of man is largely associated with the gradual elaboration of language (Boughey, 1971).

Through his intelligence, the ability to learn by observation and experience, to understand cause and effect, to form conceptual models of his own and the environment's behaviour, man has been able to anticipate and to an increasing extent control his environment and destiny.

The deliberate and systematic pursuit of knowledge led to the emergence of science and technology resulting in the significant socio-technical developments of the last century. Man now occupies every corner of the earth and has demonstrated his unique ability to survive in different or changing circumstances by a process of adaptation of behaviour and the use of technology rather than by having to rely upon the relatively slow process of physical evolution. His form and physiology have changed little over more than 100 000 generations (Boughey, 1971).

The human population is expected to double over the next two generations. Man need no longer be threatened with premature death through starvation, fatal diseases, or hostile predators. In more advanced societies, where mortality rates have been reduced to very low levels except in old age, there is now more concern about improving the quality of life than with avoiding premature death. Advances in agricultural and industrial technologies have provided some societies with levels of sustenance, shelter and education which, with the assistance of medical science, have quite dramatically reduced mortality rates over the last century (Doll, 1987).

Unfortunately the considerable material and social advantages that have accrued from the use of technology have been accompanied by a whole new host of largely man-made hazards and threats to the quality of life if not to life itself (Meadows, 1972).

Man now uses tools, machinery and vehicles which cause fatal accidents, manufactures materials, products and foodstuffs which are potentially dangerous and in the process absorbs the earth's resources and creates toxic by-products and radioactive waste on a scale which threatens the environment and the whole ecosystem (MIT, 1970).

The continuing use of modern agricultural and industrial technology could have catastrophic effects on ecological life support systems—land erosion and deforestation, the pollution of rivers and oceans, the disturbance of the thermal balance in the atmosphere and possible damage to protective ozone layers in the stratosphere.

And yet paradoxically the whole process is driven by the survival instinct. Individuals pursue security through increased material well-being whilst organizations fight for survival by increasing their net cash flows. In a capitalist economy, companies engaged in the provision of goods or services must constantly invest in the development of new products and services and new manufacturing technologies if they are to generate the cash flows and confidence necessary to avoid failure or takeover by stronger industrial predators. This inevitably involves taking risks which may affect not only the shareholders' investment but also the well-being of employees, customers and society at large. And yet the risks that they take can and ultimately do precipitate the very outcome they seek to avoid. As the leading industrialist Harvey-Jones (1988) has observed 'There is an intrinsic impermanence in [industrial] organizations'.

Risks pervade all human activity. Neither man nor the organizations he creates can survive without taking risks. At one level every decision or action carries some risk of a loss of face, status, money, health or liberty whilst at another level man is threatened by infectious diseases, fatal accidents, economic disasters, political upheaval, famines and the effects of environmental degradation.

It is simply not possible to avoid taking risks. In every human decision or action the question is never one of whether or not to take a risk but rather which risk to choose. Individuals, organizations and governments confront essentially the same problems in risk management.

Through improved communications and media attention, risk has become an issue of growing concern both to society at large and to the individual. Problems of risk management are now receiving serious attention by governments, organizations and academic institutions. Unfortunately the subject area is interdisciplinary and one to which economists, epidemiologists, mathematicians, biologists, environmentalists, psychologists, sociologists, philosophers and political scientists all have a contribution to make. Inevitably there are problems with the fundamental concepts, basic definitions and terminology.

In this book there are contributions on aspects of risk analysis, assessment and management which range from methodology to ethics with examples from finance, industry, transport, health and the environment. In this chapter, the fundamental concepts and definitions are discussed. Some difficulties with orthodox theory are described.

THE CONCEPT OF RISK

The origin of the word *risk* is thought to be either the Arabic word *risq* or the Latin word *risicum* (Kedar, 1970).

The Arabic *risq* signifies 'anything that has been given to you [by God] and from which you draw profit' and has connotations of a fortuitous and favourable outcome. The Latin *risicum*, however, originally referred to the challenge that a barrier reef presents to a sailor and clearly has connotations of an equally fortuitous but unfavourable event.

A Greek derivative of the Arab *risq* which was used in the twelfth century would appear to relate to chance outcomes in general and have neither positive nor negative implications (Kedar, 1970).

The modern French *risque* has mainly negative but occasionally positive connotations as for example in '*qui ne risque rien n'a rien*' or 'nothing ventured nothing gained' whilst in common English usage the word risk has very definite negative associations as in 'run the risk of...' or 'at risk' meaning exposed to danger.

The Concise Oxford Dictionary (1976) refers to '... the chance of hazard, bad consequences, loss, etc. ....' and *Webster's Dictionary* (1981) also emphasizes the negative aspects by reference to 'the possibility of loss, injury, disadvantage or destruction'.

Clearly over time and in common usage the meaning of the word has changed from one of simply describing any unintended or unexpected outcome, good or bad, of a decision or course of action to one which relates to undesirable outcomes and the chance of their occurrence.

In the more scientific and specialized literature on the subject the word risk is used to imply a measurement of the chance of an outcome, the size of the outcome or a combination of both. There have been several attempts to incorporate the idea of both chance and size of outcome in the one definition.

Rowe (1977) defines risk as 'The potential for unwanted negative consequences of an event or activity' whilst Lowrance (1976) defines risk as 'A measure of the probability and severity of adverse effects'.

Rescher (1983) explains that 'Risk is the chancing of a negative outcome. To measure risk we must accordingly measure both of its defining components, the chance and the negativity.' The way in which these measurements might be combined is described by Gratt (1987) '... estimation of risk is usually based on the expected result of the conditional probability of the event occurring times the consequences of the event given that it has occurred'.

It follows then that in the context of for example a potential disaster, the word risk might be used either as a measure of the magnitude of the unintended outcome, say, 2000 deaths, or the probability of its occurrence, say, one in 1000 or even the product of the two—a statistical expectation of 2 deaths.

Over time a number of different, sometimes conflicting and more recently rather complex meanings have been attributed to the word risk. It is unfortunate that a simple definition closely relating to the medieval Greek interpretation has not prevailed—one which avoids any connotation of favourable or unfavourable outcome or the probability or size of the event. This author would suggest: 'A risk is any unintended or unexpected outcome of a decision or course of action.'

THE PERCEPTION OF RISK

Before consideration is given to techniques for risk analysis, assessment or management, it should be acknowledged that the risks at issue are perceived risks and not necessarily actual risks.

Individuals, organizations and governments make decisions based on perceptions about the likely consequences of their actions. Some of the inevitable consequences may not be recognized, there may be gross misconceptions about the likelihood or magnitude of those that are recognized, and yet other perceived consequences may be more imagined than real. In short, there may not be much overlap between the set of real and the set of perceived potential outcomes.

Missed and misconstrued perceptions of the consequences of decisions are of themselves a major, arguably the greatest, source of risk in decision making and any responsible decision maker will make every effort to obtain a complete and accurate perception of the risks faced before attempting to undertake an analysis and assessment.

Whether real or imagined, however, perceived risks have to be taken into account in decision making and there is an inescapable need for methods of analysis and assessment.

The identification of possible outcomes of decisions is the purpose of risk analysis whilst the estimation of probabilities and the size of the outcomes is the subject of risk assessment.

RISK ANALYSIS

'Analysis is the separation of a whole into its component parts: an examination of a complex, its elements and their relationships' (*Concise Oxford*, 1976).

The basic risk paradigm (Maccrimmon and Wehrung, 1986) can be represented in the form of a decision tree as illustrated in Figure 1.1. It is a decision problem in which there is a choice between just two options, one of which will have only one possible outcome whilst the other option has two possible outcomes. The first option leads to a certain outcome (this is often the no change or status quo option), and the other has two probabilistic outcomes, one being a gain and the other a loss.

Simple and obvious examples of the basic problem would include the decision by a bachelor as to whether to continue with the life he knows or to take a chance on marriage; the decision by an investor as to whether to leave his savings in a secure bank account or invest them in a new share issue; the decision by the doctor as to whether to prescribe a known drug or to experiment with a new drug; the decision by the farmer as to whether to continue with the existing pesticide or try a new one; the decision by the manufacturer to continue to market an existing product or to replace it with a newly developed product; the decision by the oil company to sell drilling rights in a particular location or to drill itself, etc.

In all these situations the possibility of gain is accompanied by the risk of loss and possibly disaster. Although actual problems may have many more options and outcomes, the structure illustrated above has the essential elements. Extensions and variations to the basic structure might include the possibility of a sequence of connected decisions, several options or a continuum of possible outcomes for some options (French, 1986; Moore and Thomas, 1976).

The structure of the problem may be extremely complex as for example in the design of a new chemical plant comprising numerous interconnected processes each one of which could cause the whole plant to fail or in the management of

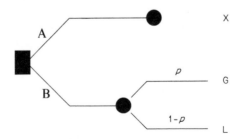

Figure 1.1 The basic risk paradigm

large-scale construction projects involving perhaps thousands of interrelated activities any one of which could cause the project to overrun its expected duration or cost.

Adding to the complexity of the analysis is the need not only to anticipate unintended eventualities and determine appropriate responses but also to contemplate unintended outcomes from the responses. Clearly there is no limit to the potential depth of the analysis in contingency planning and risk reduction (Cooper and Chapman, 1987; Hamburger, 1990).

At each decision point, however, the essence of the problem is the same—the need to compare two or more options with probabilistic outcomes.

The process of estimating the probability and size of possible outcomes, and then evaluating the alternative courses of action is one of risk assessment.

RISK ASSESSMENT

The Economics

The evaluation and comparison of risks is often assumed to be some form of cost–benefit analysis. The estimation of the probabilities and value of an outcome are obvious prerequisites in the exercise but some means of combining these measures is required to yield an overall measure for the purposes of comparison.

In decision theory the expected value or certainty equivalent concept can be defined as the sum of the product over all outcomes of their probability and value, i.e. the probabilistically weighted average value.

In the case of our basic model the expected or certainty equivalent value for option B, $EV[B]$, would be calculated as follows:

$$EV[B] = p \cdot G + (1 - p) \cdot L$$

More generally, if a decision could lead to n possible mutually exclusive outcomes then

$$EV[v] = \sum_{i=1}^{n} p_i \cdot v_i$$

where p_i = the probability of the ith outcome

v_i = the value of the ith outcome

and

$$\sum_{i=1}^{n} p_i = 1.0$$

The use of statistical concepts can be extended to using the statistical measure of dispersion or variability as a measure of risk.

In our example the variance of the possible outcomes resulting from choosing option B would be calculated as:

$$V[B] = p \cdot (G - E[v])^2 + (1 - p)(L - E[v])^2$$

or in the more general case:

$$V[v] = \sum_{i=1}^{n} p_i(v_i - E[v])^2$$

The expected value obtained can be interpreted in two ways. The simplest interpretation is that of the mean average value of the outcome when the decision is taken many times. The more difficult concept is that of the maximum price a 'rational' man would pay for the opportunity to play a game in which the outcomes had the given probabilities and values. The second interpretation, however, can itself only be explained in terms of average results and is essentially based on the same reasoning as the first.

This is a simple and straightforward measure which is undoubtedly a useful basis for comparison in many risk situations.

In practice the concept has numerous limitations, not the least of which stems from the fact that most decisions or actions are taken in situations which do not repeat themselves. In terms of our basic model the outcome can only be either the gain or loss depicted and could not possibly be the 'expected' value.

The variance of the outcomes has become synonymous with risk in much of the writing on financial management and investment appraisal (Levy and Sarnat, 1986). In so far as this measure of risk deals with the whole range of outcomes, whether favourable or adverse, it is consistent with the author's preferred concept of the meaning of risk.

Whilst useful in the development of portfolio and capital investment theory, as a measure of risk it conveys little of practical value in relation to one-off decisions in general.

In one-off situations an adverse outcome could have implications more serious than are conveyed by the mere size of the loss that is measured.

Indeed some 200 years ago Bernoulli observed that given the opportunity to play a game in which there is an equal chance of either winning or losing, say, £1000 the majority of people would not play (Bernoulli, 1738). Furthermore as the potential loss (and gain) increases, the proportion who will not play increases. In general terms, humans seem to avoid the risk of losses and are said to be 'risk-averse'.

Bernoulli's explanation was that there existed a 'utility of money' which was a positive but decelerating function such that the loss in utility represented by the utility equivalent of a loss of £1000 was greater than the gain in utility represented by the utility equivalent of winning £1000.

It is interesting to note that other species have been observed to be similarly risk-averse. In a recent paper, Real cites numerous examples and describes how in carefully designed experiments with bumblebees it became abundantly clear that given the choice between flowers containing a constant amount of nectar and flowers containing a variable (but the same average) amount bees prefer to visit flowers of constant yield. Furthermore, increasing the range of the yield in the flowers of variable yield confirmed that the bees' risk aversion increased with variance and it is not until the average amount contained in the flowers of variable content exceeds that of the flowers with a constant yield by a significant amount that the bee is tempted to take the risk and go for the more variable yield (Real, 1991).

Thus where two options offer the same mean payoff but one has a greater variance it is the option with the lesser variance which is preferred. Correspondingly, if the options had the same variance it would be the one with the higher mean payoff which was preferred.

Since Neumann and Morganstern (1945) used Bernoulli's expected utility model their development of game theory has been the dominant model of human economic decision making.

The Psychology

In recent years there has been a shift from reliance on economic and statistical models towards concepts drawn from psychology and more particularly cognitive psychology (Wallsten, 1980). It has been recognized that decision making is a complex cognitive task, frequently situation dependent, in which human beings perform in a manner determined by their limited memory, retention and information processing capabilities.

To assess perceived risks it is necessary both to estimate the probability of outcomes and to evaluate the magnitude of the outcomes. These are not observable measures, they are the result of evaluative judgement.

In the case of an individual the evaluation will depend on his own value system whilst if a group decision is required then political considerations will have a bearing.

Whilst for the mathematician or statistician it would be wrong to exclude any option or outcome from the analysis and assessment, in practice there is a tendency to exclude low probability outcomes on the basis that they are 'remote' possibilities which can be ignored 'for all practical purposes'. They are in effect accorded an 'effectively zero' probability.

Perhaps the main motivation for limiting the analysis in this way is that if every conceivable outcome were accounted for there would be too many to be taken into account (there would always be a potentially endless list of very low probability outcomes).

But this introduces the concept of the 'effectively zero' probability and the question of how low a probability needs to be for it to be considered negligible. Where human life is at stake, for example, there has been a tendency to take as the thresholds of significance the chance of death from a natural disaster. In the United States this would be of the order of one in a million.

The problem is exacerbated by the difficulties associated with the estimation of low probabilities. The nature of the associated eventualities is usually such that the estimates are based on several questionable assumptions and may be subject to estimating errors of a considerable order of magnitude.

It would appear, for example, that people tend to underestimate the probability of events that are relatively undramatic and frequent but overestimate the probability of those that are dramatic, infrequent or have not happened for some time (Lichestein, 1978).

The need to include low probability outcomes will also depend on the estimated size of the potential gains or losses. Clearly if the potential outcome is a possible disaster or catastrophe which threatens the very existence of the individual, organization or country then it cannot be ignored no matter how low the probability of the event.

Indeed the possibility of an outcome of catastrophic proportions might in practice rule out a possible option irrespective of the estimated probability of a disastrous outcome. The rational, expected value approach may indicate that the option should be considered but in practice those involved may feel that they 'cannot take the chance' no matter how small the estimate of that chance.

This raises the concept of 'the unacceptable risk' based on the perceived size of the potential loss.

Clearly there are non-trivial problems in practice, however, in dealing with low probability disasters in which taken separately the probability of the outcome might on the one hand be perceived to be 'effectively zero' but on the other the potential loss is thought to constitute 'an unacceptable risk'. The possibility of low probability disasters raises questions which pose judgemental issues which no amount of rational analysis will resolve.

Another serious difficulty in evaluating possible outcomes is that the evaluations tend to be time dependent. An eventuality which is imminent will receive a higher evaluation than one which can only occur at some time into the future particularly if the time scale involved is of the order of a lifetime. 'It might never happen.' 'A cure will be found.' 'Alternative sources will be discovered.' The tendency is, in effect, to discount the evaluation of the potential loss or gain in much the same way that an economist or accountant will discount the value of future cash flows.

This human behaviour characteristic may explain (a) the reluctance of people to change their life style even when confronted with evidence that it will probably lead to serious health problems later in life; (b) the preference of companies for investment criteria such as payback period which emphasize the short-term returns in investment or project appraisal; and (c) why environmentalists are having difficulties persuading organizations and governments to assume a more responsible attitude to the protection of the environment and ecological systems of the world.

The Politics

In evaluating risk, a decision maker must surely be influenced by considerations of who is to be affected by each particular outcome. Is it the decision maker himself, a group including the decision maker, some other group entirely or a future generation? In many situations the assessment of risk is very much subject to the consideration of moral and ethical values in which a fundamental principle is that whilst an individual may take a calculated risk on his own account he must proceed more conservatively where the interests of others are at stake (Rescher, 1983). The weight that an individual attaches to the risk to others of his actions will clearly vary from individual to individual.

Where groups of individuals share responsibility for decisions—committees, boards, governments—and the decisions affect other groups or the population as a whole then decisions must assume a largely political dimension. In theory a company board of directors will select capital projects on the basis that their main objective is to maximize the wealth of the shareholders but in doing so may put at risk their employees' jobs, the customers' safety or the state of the environment. Attitudes will vary between board members.

In health and social services, decisions by authorities to allocate limited resources to the care and treatment of one client group necessarily mean there are fewer resources available for other groups. Reducing the risks for one group must increase the risks for another. Given the full facts no two professionals would make exactly the same assessment.

In government, many decisions serve to curtail the extent to which individuals or organizations are allowed to put themselves or others at risk by their own decisions. The pressure for governments to assume responsibility has grown with public concern about the need for control. But the assessment of where the balance lies between a relatively safe society which stifles opportunities and a freer society in which there are greater risks will undoubtedly be weighted by political considerations.

RISK MANAGEMENT

Classical decision theory proceeds on the assumption of strict adherence to expected value calculations as the sole basis for evaluating decisions or courses of action.

In every sector of risk management, however, there is an unavoidable need to incorporate subjective and judgemental contributions in the process. In some management situations, subjective judgement will be of overriding influence. That is not to say, however, that the resulting decisions are any less 'rational'.

Rescher (1983) has suggested that rational management of risk calls for adherence to three cardinal rules:

(1)   The maximization of expected values.
(2)   The avoidance of catastrophe.
(3)   The ignoring of remote possibilities.

Clearly the application of these rules will call for judgemental decisions as to what severity of outcome constitutes 'catastrophe' or what probability of occurrence might be reasonably dismissed as a 'remote possibility'.

It is possible, however, to establish an order of priority in application of these rules. Clearly, avoiding catastrophe must take precedence over maximizing expected values if there is any real prospect of disaster. On the other hand, there is always at least the remote possibility that somehow any course of action will lead to disaster. If all human action is not to be stifled, therefore, it is necessary that ignoring remote possibilities should be allowed precedence over avoiding low probability disasters.

In modern society it is open to individuals and organizations to reduce the potential disaster to manageable loss through insurance, although in terms of expected value insurance deals are unlikely to be attractive. For obvious reasons the cost of the premium will be greater than the expected loss. By reducing the potential loss, however, the individual or organization can avoid catastrophe—an unmanageable and disastrous loss.

There is evidence (Slovic et al, 1977), however, that people are not prepared to insure against low probability disasters—behaviour consistent with the principle of ignoring remote possibilities—preferring instead to insure against smaller losses which are more likely to occur.

Since the formation of joint stock companies and the introduction of limited liability, it is now possible for the individual to invest in large companies without fear of financial ruin. The worst that might happen to the shareholder is that he loses some of his investment. Through the operation of the stock markets, however, the managements of organizations are compelled to achieve as good a return on the shareholders' investment as similar companies or face collapse or takeover.

Although ownership and management are effectively divorced, the need to generate high earnings per share drives management to constantly seek new products and employ new technologies which may carry greater risks for employees and society at large than for the company shareholder. The management of technological risks may be thought of as being largely a matter of adequate safety and reliability engineering. But clearly there are serious problems in foreseeing and assessing all possible outcomes and of defining what constitutes an acceptable risk.

Failures to cope with uncertainty in the management of technological risk abound. Their causes include overconfidence in scientific knowledge, the underestimation of the probability or consequences of failure, not allowing for the possibility of human error and plain irresponsibility concerning the potential risk to others. And yet to avoid such risks by adopting an overly conservative attitude to technological innovation may be to deny the potential benefits to shareholders, employees and society. Clearly there is a need for more rigorous analysis and assessment of risk coupled with a stronger sense of social responsibility.

It is for governments to decide where the balance is to lie between providing for too much and too little control. They have an increasing role to play in controlling the extent to which people are allowed to put either themselves or others at risk. In an article entitled 'No risk is the highest risk of all', however, a leading political scientist maintains that an overcautious attitude may paralyse scientific endeavour and leave humanity less secure than before (Wildavsky, 1979).

But opinions will be sharply divided as to how much public money should be allocated to risk management as a whole, how it might be distributed between potential sources of risk and where the balance should lie between expenditure on prevention and expenditure on compensation.

And there is not just the present generation to be considered. Society must decide to what extent the behaviour of individuals and organizations in current society can be allowed to put at risk the well-being of future generations.

These are political issues to which a purely scientific approach cannot be applied and for which there are no generally applicable principles. Risk analysis, assessment and expert evaluation may inform the debate but the resolution of these issues and risk management at this level will be determined by essentially political processes and considerations.

> For better or for worse, it is through the processes of political determination, and through these alone that a society can decide how it rates liberty against security, how it sets the value of human life, for example, or where it stands on the choice between material well-being and the pursuit of its ideals.
>
> (Rescher, 1983)

REFERENCES

Ashby, E. (1978). *Reconciling Man with the Environment*, OUP, London.
Bernoulli, D. (1738). *Commentar. Acad. Sci. Imp. Petropaolitanae*, 175. English translation by L. Sommer, 1954, *Econometrica*, 22, 23.
Boughey, A.S. (1971). *Man and the Environment*, Macmillan.
Concise Oxford Dictionary (1976). University Press, Oxford.
Cooper, D. F. and Chapman, C. B. (1987). *Risk Analysis for Large Projects: Models, Methods and Cases*, John Wiley & Sons, Chichester.

Doll, R. (1987). Major epidemics of the 20th century: from coronary thrombosis to AIDS, *Journal of the Statistical Society, A,* **150,** Part 4, 373–95.

French, S. (1986). *Decision Theory,* Halstead Press, NY.

Gratt, L.B. (1987). Risk analysis or risk assessment: a proposal for consistent definitions, in *Uncertainty in Risk Assessment, Risk Management, and Decision Making,* Plenum Press, NY, pp. 241–9.

Hamburger, D. (1990). The project manager: risk taker and contingency planner, *Project Management Journal,* **21,** June, 43–8.

Harvey-Jones, J. (1988). *Making it Happen,* Guild Publishing, London.

Kedar, B.Z. (1970). Again: Arabic Risq, Medieval Latin Risicum, Studi Medievali, Centro Italiano Di Studi Sull Alto Medioevo, Spoleto.

Levy, H. and Sarnat, M. (1986). *Capital Investment and Financial Decisions,* Prentice-Hall.

Lichestein, S. (1978). Judged frequency of lethal events, *Journal Experimental Psychology,* **4,** 551–78.

Lowrance, W.W. (1976). *Of Acceptable Risk,* William Kaufmann, Los Altos, CA.

Maccrimmon, K.R. and Wehrung, D.A. (1986). *Taking Risks: The Management of Uncertainty,* Collier Macmillan, London.

Massachusetts Institute of Technology (1970). *Man's Impact on the Global Environment,* MIT Press.

Meadows, D.H. (1972). *The Limits to Growth,* Eath Island Ltd.

Moore, P.G. and Thomas H. (1976). *The Anatamy of Decisions,* Penguin Books.

Neumann, J.V. and Morganstern, O. (1945). *The Theory of Games and Economic Behaviour,* Princeton University Press, Princeton.

Real, L.A. (1991). Animal choice behaviour and the evolution of cognitive architecture, *Science,* **253,** Aug, 980–6.

Rescher, N. (1983). *Risk: A Philosophical Introduction to the Theory of Risk Evaluation and Management,* University Press of America.

Rowe, W.D. (1977). *An Anatomy of Risk,* John Wiley and Sons, NY.

Slovic, P. *et al.* (1977). Preference for insuring against probable small losses, *Journal of Risk and Insurance,* **44,** 237–58.

Wallsten, T.S. (1980). *Cognitive Processes in Choice and Decision Behaviour,* Lawrence Erlbaum, New Jersey, pp. ix–xv.

Webster's Third International Dictionary (1981). G. and C. Merriam Co., Springfield, MA.

White, L. (1967). The historical roots of our ecological crisis, *Science,* **155** 1204.

Wildavsky, A. (1979). No risk is the highest risk of all, *American Scientist,* **67,** 32–6.

Chapter 2

A Risk Engineering Approach to Risk Management

C.B. Chapman
Department of Accounting and Management Science
University of Southampton

ABSTRACT

This chapter outlines an approach to the management of risk which was initially developed for planning offshore North Sea projects and subsequently adapted for a range of projects in the United States, Canada and elsewhere. It has been used for assessing issues like reliability, preferred technical choices, economic and financial viability, but the context used here is project planning and associated costing.

INTRODUCTION

The basis of this chapter is the development of project planning and costing procedures for offshore North Sea oil and gas projects in the late 1970s (Chapman *et al.*, 1983). It has been used elsewhere in various forms (Chapman and Cooper, 1985; Cooper and Chapman, 1988; Chapman, Cooper and Page, 1987). The approach employed here closely follows Chapter 30, Risk Engineering, from *Management for Engineers* by Chapman, Cooper and Page (1987), with the kind permission of John Wiley & Sons. While not original, the author hopes those who have not seen earlier versions will find it useful. As the author's colleagues Dale Cooper, who co-authored earlier versions, is too far away (Australia) and too busy (as director of a stock broking firm) to get involved in

Risk: Analysis, Assessment and Management. Edited by J. Ansell and F. Wharton.
© 1992 John Wiley & Sons Ltd.

this chapter he does not appear as a co-author; he can escape any criticism but share any praise.

'Risk engineering' is a term associated with the use of the approach outlined here to identifying and measuring risk to the extent that is useful to do so, and developing the insight to change associated risks through effective and efficient decisions. It has been applied in many contexts, and the principles are relevant to a wide variety of decisions. A project planning context is the relevant one for this chapter, but experience with others may be of interest (Cooper and Chapman, 1987). Project planning allows a comparatively simple treatment of the basic risk engineering notion of alternative views and representations of any given situation, with a variety of associated models, and a need to select that view which is most appropriate to the particular circumstances.

The particular context used for illustrative purposes is the analysis of risks associated with a target schedule (programme or timetable) for constructing an offshore pipeline. This provides a convenient example because it allows a very simple initial analysis of activity durations to be followed by increasingly complex approaches. However, it is a realistic example, based upon a composite of actual risk analysis studies associated with North Sea oil and gas projects.

The next section introduces the example problem. Following sections consider five sequential activities involved in the example problem, increasing the complexity of the associated model framework and perspective in each section. Methods and computer software used to implement such models are then discussed, followed by brief consideration of project risk management method design, other considerations, and a concluding section which addresses the benefits of a risk engineering approach.

PROBLEM DESCRIPTION

A project team has a base plan for a 200 km offshore pipeline. This includes a target schedule (programme or timetable) and associated contingency plans. Five activities are central to the plan: design of the pipeline, procurement of a pipe supplier, delivery of the pipe, coating the pipe, and laying the pipe.

Design is straightforward, but the project team must compete with other projects for staff. Procurement has a predictable duration, if it is known whether or not particular suppliers will be chosen for reasons of corporate policy. Pipe delivery has a predictable duration for some suppliers, but the duration may be very uncertain for others.

The pipe is steel, 80 cm in diameter. Before it can be laid, it must be coated with 15 cm of concrete and anti-corrosive materials. Coating involves three main sources of uncertainty: when a yard will be available, how productive the yard will prove on a normal shift basis, and whether or not overtime or second-shift working will be required.

Laying involves a number of sources of uncertainty because of the nature of the task and its physical environment. Pipe sections are welded together on a lay barge and strung over the back of the barge, maintaining a smooth 'S curve', even in several hundred metres of water, via tension on a large number of leading anchor lines. As the barge approaches an anchor, a tug lifts the anchor and carries it out in front again. There is a nominal maximum wave height for laying, which may be from 1.6 m up to 5 m, depending upon the barge and the anchor-handling tugs. In March a 1.6 m barge may be unable to lay any pipe, or it may achieve 31 lay-days, with an expectation of about 5 days, depending upon the sea area. Conditions improve to midsummer, with an expectation of about 25 lay-days, then decline to a November low comparable to March. As 1.6 m barges and associated equipment can cost about £100 000 per day, the shoulder seasons are expensive per kilometre of pipe laid, and the winter is non-viable. The latest generation of barges are significantly more productive during the shoulder seasons and such barges have been used during the winter, but their daily rate, including support facilities, can be closer to £200 000.

During laying, a single pipe buckle is likely, and two or more are possible. When the pipe buckles, it drops to the ocean floor and fills with water, sucking in mud and other debris. Repair usually takes 20–30 working days. Although starting again used to be the only alternative in these circumstances, submarine repair and hook-up is now feasible.

New barges involve uncertain lay rates in the 1–5 km per day range. If a barge gets into trouble on a prior contract it may not be available on the planned start date. Unless substantial retainers are paid, a barge may not be available for unplanned additional seasons, and replacements may not be easy to find. If a pipeline is completed a season earlier than necessary, the opportunity cost of the idle capital is about £400 000. If a pipeline is a season late, the opportunity cost of non-productive platforms and wells may be very much greater.

The normal (and rather restricted) objective of the risk analysis in this example is to determine the probability of completing the five sequential activities on time.

ADDITION OF INDEPENDENT DISTRIBUTIONS

Design and procurement might be assumed to be independent activities, with unconditional probability distributions defined by Table 2.1. $P(D_i)$, $i = 1$ and 2, are interpreted as subjective estimates based on all relevant available data and experience, as agreed by the project team, associated with durations which are central classmarks for values over the intervals 3.5–4.5 months, 4.5–5.5 months, and so on.

The variability in $P(D_1)$ might reflect the uncertain availability of design staff. The variability in $P(D_2)$ might reflect two possible suppliers with very different

Table 2.1 Design and procurement distribution

Design		Procurement	
D_1	$P(D_1)$	D_2	$P(D_2)$
5	0.2	3	0.2
6	0.5	4	0.1
7	0.3	5	0.7

track records, implying two different underlying distributions giving rise to the bimodal nature of $P(D_2)$. A simple probability-tree model distinguishing these two suppliers' duration distributions and the probability of each being selected might be used to obtain $P(D_2)$, or $P(D_2)$ might be estimated directly, the explicit approach being preferable in most circumstances.

For illustrative simplicity, here and subsequently in this chapter, the same interval widths have been used for both distributions, and very few classes. In practice, more intervals are normally used. Alternatively, three-point estimates of the PERT type (Chapman, Cooper and Page, 1987) are used, or other distributions are specified via parameters, with computer software automatically generating 'controlled-interval' probability trees of a similar kind. 'Controlled interval and memory' (CIM) computer software computational procedures can handle different interval widths for each component distribution and the result, but they normally employ a constant interval width within each distribution. 'Common-interval' procedures used here are very basic special cases of a more general controlled-interval approach, but they provide the conceptual framework required for this chapter: they are important as a basis for understanding for all those involved in actual studies, and they provide a simple basic approach which can be implemented with a pocket calculator or very simple computer software if CIM software is not available. The 'controlled memory' aspect of the CIM approach can be used in a common-interval framework, and will be illustrated in an introductory way in this chapter.

A simple tabular representation of the associated two-level probability tree is provided by Table 2.2, D_1 defining three branches, each of which is associated with three D_2 branches.

Implied values of $D_a = D_1 + D_2$, defining the joint distribution of design plus procurement, may be obtained from the probability tree in the normal way. For example, $D_1 = 5$ and $D_2 = 3$ defining $D_a = 5 + 3 = 8$, involves a probability $P(D_a) = 0.2 \times 0.2 = 0.04$. However, the common-interval form allows the probability tree of Table 2.2 to be collapsed in the process of computing $P(D_a)$ values, as illustrated by Table 2.3. Each possible combination of D_1 and D_2 values is considered, the joint probabilities producing the computation entries, and entries associated with the same D value are summed. In Markovian process

Table 2.2 Design and procurement probability tree

Design D_1	$P(D_1)$	Procurement D_2	$P(D_2)$	$D_a = D_1 + D_2$ D_a	$P(D_a)$
5	0.2	3	0.2	8	0.04
		4	0.1	9	0.02
		5	0.7	10	0.14
6	0.6	3	0.2	9	0.10
		4	0.1	10	0.05
		5	0.7	11	0.35
7	0.3	3	0.2	10	0.06
		4	0.1	11	0.03
		5	0.7	12	0.21

Table 2.3 Design plus procurement tabulation

D_a	Computation			$P(D_a)$
8	0.2×0.2			0.04
9	$0.2 \times 0.1 +$	$0.5 \times 0.2 +$		0.12
10	$0.2 \times 0.7 +$	$0.5 \times 0.1 +$	0.3×0.2	0.25
11		$0.5 \times 0.7 +$	0.3×0.1	0.38
12			0.3×0.7	0.21

(Chapman, Cooper and Page, 1987) terms, if D_1 and D_2 do not need to be remembered individually, only their sum need be remembered, D_a.

If D_i values are associated with integers, the procedure of Table 2.3 provides precise results. If the classmark interpretation is used, Table 2.3 involves some computation error. Most of this error can be avoided by appropriate within-class distribution assumptions and the use of numerical integration techniques (Cooper and Chapman, 1987). Whether or not such approaches are adopted, precision is a rapidly increasing function of the number of classes, and a suitable level of precision can be obtained, depending upon the importance of precision in relation to computer time costs.

The common-interval version of the CIM treatment of independent probability distribution addition involves a computational procedure which is not widely used, and a brief comparison with other procedures may be helpful.

First, skewed and multimodal distributions present no difficulties, as illustrated by $P(D_2)$. This is not the case for a simple mean-variance approach (for example, see Chapman, Cooper and Page, 1987), or for more sophisticated higher-moment approaches (for example, see Kottas and Lau, 1982). However, some of the simplicity of mean-variance approaches is lost. A risk-engineering approach should preserve the use of a mean-variance procedure in appropriate circumstances.

Second, Monte Carlo simulation approaches, often used for this kind of analysis (Van Slyke, 1963), would involve much greater computation costs for the same level of precision. However, Monte Carlo approaches can deal in a simple general manner with very large networks, which is not the case for CIM approaches. CIM operations include a 'greatest' operation to deal with activities terminating at a common node, but when very large complex networks require consideration, a risk-engineering approach may have to integrate Monte Carlo and CIM procedures, and other complex causal relationships can give rise to a similar need for simulation.

Third, functional integration (for example, see Chapter 25 of *Management for Engineers*, Chapman, Cooper and Page, 1987) involves restrictive distribution shape assumptions not required by the procedure of Table 2.3. However, some of the generality of the results provided by the functional integration approach are lost. A risk-engineering approach should use functional integration in appropriate circumstances.

Fourth, numerical integration could be very similar to generalized CIM versions of Table 2.3 in practice. However, the simple conceptual framework of Table 2.3 is useful, and it facilitates generalizations which compound the comparative advantages of a CIM approach as the complexities of the following sections are considered, without introducing any new disadvantages.

Finally, other approaches with some characteristics of the CIM approach have been discussed (for example see Driscoll, 1980; Kaplan and Garrick 1981), but such approaches do not treat computation error as an explicit and controllable part of the computation procedure.

ADDITION OF DEPENDENT DISTRIBUTIONS

Consideration of the dependence of delivery on the supplier might lead to the definition of the conditional probabilities of Table 2.4. The format of Table 2.1 is a simplification of that of Table 2.4, given independence. Table 2.4 can be put in the tree form of Table 2.2, and that tree can be reduced as indicated in Table 2.5, defining $P(D_b)$, $D_b = D_2 + D_3$.

This addition procedure, with the second distribution dependent upon the first, involves the same computational effort as the independent case. Only the effort associated with specification of $P(D_3)$ is increased, requiring $P(D_3/D_2)$. However, specification effort is important. If the dependence is simple and well understood, unlike that of $P(D_3/D_2)$, which involves a marked change in the distribution shape as D_2 changes, simpler procedures can be used in practice,

Table 2.4 Delivery distribution, conditional on procurement

Procurement D_2	Delivery D_3	$P(D_3)$
2	2	0.8
	4	0.2
4	3	0.7
	4	0.1
	5	0.1
	6	0.1
5	4	0.3
	5	0.4
	6	0.3

Table 2.5 Procurement plus delivery

D_b	Computation			$P(D_b)$
6	0.2×0.8			0.16
7	$0.2 \times 0.2 +$	0.1×0.7		0.11
8		0.1×0.1		0.01
9		$0.1 \times 0.1 +$	0.7×0.3	0.22
10		$0.1 \times 0.1 +$	0.7×0.4	0.29
11			0.7×0.3	0.21

involving percentage dependence analogous to a coefficient of correlation (Cooper and Chapman, 1987).

Having obtained $D_b = D_2 + D_3$ as described above, $D_c = D_1 + D_b = D_1 + D_2 + D_3$ could be obtained using the independent addition procedure of the last section. However, CIM software could allow the computation of D_c via $D_a + D_3$, by preserving a 'memory' of D_2 when computing $D_a = D_1 + D_2$, so $P(D_a/D_2)$ can be used with the $P(D_3/D_2)$. More generally, CIM software could allow the specification of $P(D_3)$ to be conditional upon D_1 or D_a in addition to or instead of the D_2 dependence of Table 2.4. That is, a sequence of distributions can be combined such that any distribution is dependent upon any previous distribution or partial sum of previous distributions, provided the number of 'memory dimensions' this requires at any stage does not exceed the capabilities of the computer being used.

Whichever approach is taken to computing $P(D_c)$, in the common-interval framework of this chapter the result will be the same, with D_c values of 11, 12, ... 18, these eight D_c and $P(D_c)$ values summarizing the underlying three-level probability tree with $3 \times 3 \times 3 = 27$ end-points. A memory of associated D_1,

D_2, D_3, D_a, or D_b values would not be necessary unless a subsequent activity needs to be specified as conditional upon one or more of these possible memory dimensions.

MARKOVIAN PROCESSES THROUGH TIME

An inventory of uncoated pipe for the pipe-coating activity would be assured once delivery began by a delivery rate very much faster than the coating rate. This would allow coating to overlap delivery without concern for uncoated pipe stock-out. Similarly, a coating rate faster than the pipelaying rate might allow overlapping of the coating and laying activities, but uncertainty associated with pipelaying and all prior activities and the high cost of laying equipment might suggest planning to start laying at a date providing a high probability of more than 70 km of coated pipe in stock.

To model the time-dependent nature of coated-pipe inventory, assuming single-shift working with no overtime, Table 2.6 might be used to define the rate of coating, R km per month, and $P(R)$.

This transition distribution might be assumed to be independent of time, and it might be associated with state distributions defining the stock of coated pipe at the end of each month, S_t km, $t = 0, 1, 2, \ldots$ The end of month 0 defines the start of month 1 initial conditions, assuming coating starts at the beginning of month $t = 1$. Ignoring prior activities for the moment, initial conditions might be assumed to be $P(S_0) = 1$ for $S_0 = 0$, an initial stock of zero. Then the Markov process of Table 2.7 can be developed, using successive applications of the procedure of Table 2.3 (addition of independent distributions), adding $P(R)$ to $P(S_0)$ to get $P(S_1)$, adding $P(R)$ to $P(S_1)$ to get $P(S_2)$, and so on. $1 - CP(S_t)$ are the probabilities of more than S_t.

The distributions defined by Table 2.7 for $t = 0$ and 1 indicate no chance of more than 70 km of coated pipe; the $t = 2$ distribution indicates a 0.39 probability of more than 70 km; the $t = 3$ distribution indicates a probability of 1 of more than 70 km. Jointly, these probabilities define the probability distribution for S_t greater than 70 in terms of t, $P(D_4/70$ km required).

In a similar way, if 220 km of pipe was the total required, distributions for $t = 6, \ldots 8$ would provide a probability distribution for the completion of

Table 2.6 Coating rate

R	$P(R)$
30	0.2
35	0.5
40	0.3

Table 2.7 Stock of coated pipe at end of months 1, 2, 3, ...

t	S_t	Computation			$P(S_t)$	$CP(S_t)$	$1 - CP(S_t)$
0	0				1	1	0
1	30	0.2×1			0.2	0.2	0.8
	35		0.5×1		0.5	0.7	0.3
	40			0.3×1	0.3	1.0	0
2	60	0.2×0.2			0.04	0.04	0.96
	65	$0.2 \times 0.5 +$	0.5×0.2		0.20	0.24	0.76
	70	$0.2 \times 0.3 +$	$0.5 \times 0.5 +$	0.3×0.2	0.37	0.61	0.39
	75		$0.5 \times 0.3 +$	0.3×0.3	0.09	1.00	0
3	90	0.2×0.4			0.008	0.008	0.992
	95	$0.2 \times 0.20 +$	0.5×0.4		0.060	0.068	0.932
	100	$0.2 \times 0.37 +$	$0.5 \times 0.20 +$	0.3×0.04	0.186	0.254	0.746
	105	$0.2 \times 0.30 +$	$0.5 \times 0.37 +$	0.3×0.20	0.305	0.559	0.441
	110	$0.2 \times 0.09 +$	$0.5 \times 0.30 +$	0.3×0.37	0.279	0.838	0.162
	115		$0.5 \times 0.09 +$	0.3×0.30	0.135	0.973	0.027
	120			0.3×0.09	0.027	1.000	0

coating, $P(D_4/220$ km required). However, to stop the computation process when the required amount of pipe is available, the unconditional D distribution of Table 2.6 should be generalized to the conditional distribution of Table 2.8. The result is a semi-Markov process with a state-dependent transition distribution. It will provide results identical to Table 2.7, maintaining results identical to that provided by the unconditional distribution of Table 2.6 until $t = 6$. For $t = 6, \ldots 8$, $S = 220$ will become an absorbing state, and when $P(S_t) = 1$ for $S_t = 220$ the computation process can terminate.

The $P(D_4/70$ km required) distribution obtained in this way could then be added to $P(D_c)$, to define $P(D_d)$, the probability of completing design, procurement, delivery and coating of more than 70 km of pipe. This distribution could then be used to set a planned start date for pipelaying. Alternatively, $P(D_d)$ could be defined by embedding $P(D_c)$ in the computation process of Table 2.7, via probabilistic specification of initial conditions. The former is simpler in the

Table 2.8 Conditional coating rate

S_t	R	$P(R)$
< 220	30	0.2
	35	0.5
	40	0.3
220	0	1

present case. However, the latter is useful if the probability that the coating yard will be available when required is not 1 for all t, or if decision rules related to the coating activity incorporated into the computation process of Table 2.7 must reflect an extended D_d, not just the pipe-coating operation.

Decision rules related to the coating activity can be incorporated into the computation process of Table 2.7, via further extension of the conditional distribution of Table 2.8. For example, Table 2.9 defines the transition distribution assuming the single-shift probabilities of Table 2.8 if time period n has not been reached or if time period n has been reached and at least m km of pipe have been coated. Double-shift probabilities are associated with time period n being reached and m km of pipe not yet coated. Computation using the conditional distribution of Table 2.9 involves successive computations as for Table 2.7, but the dependent addition procedure of Table 2.5 must be used instead of the independent addition procedure of Table 2.3, with R conditional upon t and S_t. Neither condition requires memory dimensions not preserved by the procedure of Table 2.7. It is simply a matter of selecting $P(R)$ from three possibilities depending upon readily available t and S_t values. $P(R)$ could be made conditional on previous R values if initial uncertainty about R would be partially resolved once coating started. This would require a memory of R.

Experiments with different values of n and m could be used to assess the associated alternative decision rules. Other decision rules could also be tested, related to initial R values, for example. Specifying all possible decision rules in advance is clearly not practical. However, observing results without embedded decision rules initially, attacking the obvious problem areas first, and then refining, will allow the development of reasonable and rational decision rules. Further refinement could follow after the duration for pipelaying has been assessed.

Even if the programme avoided overlapping coating and pipelaying, obtaining $P(D_4)$ in this way is easier for the project team. The coating rate and

Table 2.9 Coating rate with second-shift option

t		S_t	R	$P(R)$
$<n$			30	0.2
or			35	0.5
$>n$	and	$>m$	40	0.3
$>n$	and	$<m$	60	0.1
			65	0.2
			70	0.3
			75	0.2
			80	0.2
$>n$	and	220	0	1

associated decisions are necessarily the basis for duration assessments. Even if the coating rate and associated decision rules are not dependent upon D_c, estimating the conditional distributions of Table 2.8 or 2.9 is much easier than direct estimation of the associated $P(D_4)$. Any duration based upon an amount of work to be done and a rate of progress may be modelled in this way, and although the semi-Markovian framework is more complex than that of Tables 2.3 and 2.5, it is often easier to use. The notion that more complex models may be easier to use is an important one, and it may extend to the approach of the next section in some circumstances.

SOURCES OF UNCERTAINTY AND ASSOCIATED RESPONSES

Direct specification of conditional transition distributions for a semi-Markovian process representation of pipelaying would be difficult because weather impacts on the transition distributions are date dependent, pipe-buckle effects are weather dependent in a related but different and rather complex manner, and other factors such as barge productivity rates and reliability also need consideration. However, attempting direct estimation of pipelaying duration would be still more difficult, considering all these factors plus barge and pipe availability influencing the starting date. To make the task tractable, it may be necessary to probe the uncertainty structure of $P(D_5)$ even more deeply than the treatment of $P(D_4)$ just discussed.

The basis of activity duration uncertainty is a set of sources of uncertainty: specific reasons for deviations from the target plan, such as weather, buckles, and so on, as noted above. Also important in the determination of activity durations is a set of responses to faults or events associated with the sources of uncertainty. Some of these responses may be specific to a particular source of risk. For example, if a pipe buckle occurs, repairing it is a specific response. Other responses may be general in the sense that they relate to a number of sources of risk. For example, a second lay barge in a second season might be used to overcome a first-season delay related to a range of possible difficulties. The effect of appropriate specific and general responses must be examined in an appropriate context, specific responses requiring separate treatment of each source of risk.

To begin, the effects of weather variations on a 1.6 m barge might be considered in terms of the number of lay-days available in a month, L, and associated $P(L)$. Weather records and simulation studies could be used to assess wave heights, but decision rules associated with lay-barge procedures must entail subjective input. A simplified representation of such assessment might provide the date-dependent $P_t(L)$ of Table 2.10.

Table 2.10 Lay-days available each month

L	March	April	May	June	July etc.
0	0.3	0.2	0.1		
5	0.4	0.3	0.2	0.1	
10	0.2	0.3	0.3	0.1	
15	0.1	0.2	0.2	0.2	0.1
20			0.1	0.3	0.2
25			0.1	0.2	0.4
30				0.1	0.3

Assuming a lay rate of 3 km per day, the L scale of Table 2.10 could be multiplied by 3 and relabelled R, pipelaying rate, transforming the $P_t(L)$ to $P_t(R)$. To consider the effects of weather in isolation, given a 3 km per day lay rate and a specified start date, this transformed version of Table 2.10 can be used in the framework of Tables 2.7 and 2.8. Transition probabilities are a function of time, but no new memory requirements are involved. If the 1.6 m barge is inadequate, this analysis provides a clear case for a barge with a larger maximum wave height or a greater expected lay rate.

To extend this analysis to buckles, the probability of a buckle in each month, $P_t(B)$, might be specified as indicated in Table 2.11. Buckles are weather dependent, given laying is attempted, and the extent to which laying is attempted is also weather dependent. The chances of a buckle in April may be more likely than the chances of one in March, as indicated in Table 2.11, because more laying is likely to be attempted in April. However, the chances of a buckle may drop off again in May, despite the likely further increase in laying, because of the improved weather conditions, with this trend continued through June and July.

Buckle repair might be assumed, and associated with lay-days, equivalent to a loss of kilometres of pipe laid. Uncertainty about when the buckle might occur and how many lay-days will be required might be considered jointly, to define a distribution of lost kilometres of pipe laid given a buckle such as that of Table 2.12.

The $P(-R)$ given a buckle of Table 2.12 might be combined with the $P(B)$ of Table 2.11 and the $P(R)$ version of Table 2.10 to provide a $P(R)$ transition

Table 2.11 Probability of a pipe buckle each month

B	March	April	May	June	July etc.
Buckle	0.05	0.07	0.05	0.03	0.01
No buckle	0.95	0.93	0.95	0.97	0.99

Table 2.12 Buckle repair

$-R$	$P(-R)$
65	0.1
70	0.2
75	0.3
80	0.3
85	0.1

distribution incorporating both weather and buckle effects, and this transition distribution used in the framework of Table 2.7. Nothing new is involved from a computational point of view. If buckles are an important potential problem, this analysis will provide a clear case for examining other responses, or the procedures which underlie Tables 2.11 and 2.12, or the effect of a more capable barge.

Other sources of risk can then be added, one at a time, and the accumulated effect considered. For example, different lay rates which persist can be modelled in successive runs, as can different start dates.

Secondary risks and associated responses associated with primary risk responses may also be added, if appropriate. For example, if buckle occurs and repair is attempted, a 'pig' is sent through the pipeline to clear it before raising the end. If the pig sticks, a secondary risk is realized. Secondary risk responses include raising the hydrostatic pressure to pop the pig through, which involves a tertiary risk of bursting the pipe, and so on. Even in an offshore pipeline context there is a limit to the extent to which the pursuit of such decision trees is useful. However, they are inherent in the nature of the task even for very simple activities.

Having modelled each specific response of interest in the context of its associated source of risk, general responses can be considered in relation to uncertainty net of specific responses.

Some risk sources and responses may be best treated in probabilistic terms as described above, but others may be best considered via sensitivity analysis. For example, if the ability to begin construction in year n or year $n + 1$ depends upon obtaining government approval, probabilities might be estimated, but most project managers would prefer two separate analyses based on the two possible start dates.

Not all sources of risk will require quantitative treatment. Most will require attention and concern, but many can be treated as conditions associated with quantitative risk analysis. For example, laying an offshore pipeline may involve crossing several existing pipelines. This involves a considerable risk of damage to the other pipelines from lay-barge anchors. If the damage occurs, the implications include a major time delay because of the need to divert equipment on-site to repairing the other line. However, most project managers would not wish to see associated probabilities embedded in a normal planning risk analysis. They prefer estimates which are conditional upon damage to another line not occurring. Identification of such potentially costly conditions is important. Probability estimates which do not identify such conditions are impossible to interpret with precision. It can be safely assumed that any finite expected duration estimate does not incorporate very remote risks which invalidate all plans such as those resulting in the immediate end of civilization as we know it, but there is a wide range of other conditions which may or may not apply. Often when experts disagree about probabilities of events occurring, the underlying reason is that they have different implicit assumptions about associated conditions.

METHODOLOGY

Effective and efficient use of models as complex as the pipelaying example requires a methodology or series of steps designed to capitalize on the characteristics of both the kind of problem and the range of available models. Table 2.13 provides an outline of a method used for timetable risk analysis of this kind.

Table 2.13 A method for time schedule (programme) risk analysis

Phase	Step
Scope	Activity identification Primary risk identification Primary response identification Secondary risk identification Secondary response identification
Structure	Minor and major risk identification Specific and general reponse identification Simple and complex decision rule identification Risk/response diagramming
Parameter	Desired parameter identification Scenario identification and probability identification
Manipulation and risk computation Interpretation	Risk efficiency decision-rule assessment Risk balance decision-rule assessment Budget contingency sum assessment

The first (scope) phase defines the aspects of interest, in terms of activities, sources of risk and responses. In addition to the use of precedence and bar chart representations of the activities, extensive structured verbal documentation of what is involved in activities, risk and responses is required, as illustrated by Tables 2.14–2.16.

The next (structure) phase provides further structure to this information, summarized in the final step to the risk/response diagram format of Figure 2.1, three pages in this format being required for this activity in the actual study. Circles represent risk sources, the boxes underneath primary risk circles represent ordered responses to mitigate the effects of realizing a risk. Preventive responses are indicated by notes above the risk. The 'yard not available' and 'mobilization problems' risks of Figure 2.1 are mutually exclusive, but all others are additive or multiplicative in effect. General mitigating responses are collected together under a 'net delay' risk circle at the extreme right of the last of the sequence of diagrams, not shown in Figure 2.1. Links in from other activities and links out to other activities may also appear on these diagrams.

The third (parameter) phase involves estimation of probabilities when such probabilities are deemed useful. At least half the effort involved in most studies is

Table 2.14   Activity list for an offshore project

Number	Title/Details

8	FABRICATION, ERECTION AND TESTS
	This activity covers fabrication of the platform structure including offsite fabrication of nodes, erection of the structure, installation of all associated equipment (cathodic protection flooding, grouting, internal leg inspection, strain gauges, environmental monitoring and 'J' tubes/risers), painting of the structure, inspection of the welds and any resulting repair and testing of all equipment prior to float and tow-out.
	    The award of the fabrication contract is planned for the beginning of November 1986. The sub-contract(s) for rolling jackets, tubulars, rolling and fabricating node/piles and assembly of the structure should be in accordance with the procedures summarized in Activity No. 5 details list.
	    Fabrication of the jacket assembly has a planned duration of 29 months available and should be complete by the end of March 1989. The principal keydate associated with this activity is 1 April 1989 planned float-out in preparation for the tow to site.

Prepared by	date

Table 2.15 Risk list for an offshore project

Number	Title/Description and notes	Cross ref.
8.0	FABRICATION, ERECTION AND TESTS	
8.1	YARD AVAILABILITY: Contracted yard may not be available at the required fabrication start date (e.g. due to modifications necessary to accommodate the platform or to work on a previous contract).	6
8.2	MOBILIZATION: Yard may have been idle for some time leading to equipment and manpower mobilization problems. NB 8.1 and 8.2 *are mutually exclusive*	6
8.3	PRODUCTIVITY: Contractors's ability to proceed at the expected rate to the required specification (speed and effectiveness of work and minor interruptions).	6
8.4	INDUSTRIAL DISPUTES: Significant interruptions not covered under productivity (8.3).	6
8.5	EQUIPMENT BREAKDOWNS: Significant breakdowns of any equipment not covered under productivity (8.3) (e.g. main yard crane(s)).	6
8.6	CONSTRUCTION TECHNOLOGY: Significant practical problems not covered under productivity (8.3) in following fabrication procedures.	6, 4
8.7	CONSTRUCTION DAMAGE: Significant damage, other than under productivity (8.3), caused during construction/erection/testing of the structure.	4, 6
8.8	FIRE, EXPLOSION OR OTHER DAMAGE.	6
8.9	WEATHER: Significant departures from expected weather patterns, not covered under productivity (8.3) (e.g. high winds affecting operations involving cranes).	6
8.10	DESIGN MODIFICATIONS: Significant late changes in design.	7.11
8.11	MATERIAL SUPPLY: Any major setback in delivery dates not covered under productivity (8.3, minor interruptions).	5.6
Prepared by		date

prior to this step, and this effort is essential as a basis for estimation and interpretation of the probabilities.

The final (manipulation and interpretation) phase provides a portrait of the relative role of each risk within an activity (Figure 2.2) and the relative contribution of each activity to total project risk (Figure 2.3).

At intermediate stages in these four phases feedback begins. This continues

Table 2.16   Risk/response list for offshore project

Number	Title/Description and notes	Secondary risk	Class
8.0	FABRICATION, ERECTION AND TESTS		
8.1	YARD AVAILABILITY:		
8.1.1	MOBILIZE: Mobilize as much equipment/ personnel as possible (preferred is likely to be short).	No	S1
8.1.2	ALTERNATIVE YARD: Search for an alternative yard if delay is likely to be very long—this will depend on activities in offshore structure fabrications yards. NB The costs involved in implementing the above and/or the delays could be (partially) recovered from the contractor if appropriate contractual clauses are incorporated.	Yes	S2
8.1.3	ACCEPT DELAY: In awaiting availability of contracted yard.	No	G
8.2	MOBILIZATION:		
8.2.1	IDLE YARD: If a yard is idle, it is possible that preliminary work can be commenced before the scheduled date— ability to do this will depend on material availability. A more gradual build-up effort may be possible.	Yes	S1
8.2.2	CLIENT SUPERVISION: A client represent- ative on site from start to supervise/ oversee supervision of mobilization.	No	S1
8.2.3	ACCEPT DELAY: Accept the delay in starting work; the delay (if short) could be absorbed in any planned 'float' or the base plan may require rescheduling (if long delay).	No	G
Prepared by			date

until everyone is satisfied with the problem description, structuring, probabilities, decision rules, and their schedule implications.

When the project team is satisfied with the schedule risk analysis, associated cost risk is considered. For example, activity duration distributions are combined with unit of resource per unit time distributions, and probabilistic treatment of exchange rates and inflation rates are used if appropriate. The relative impact of each source of cost risk is portrayed in the format of Figures 2.2. Only when management is satisfied that they have an understandable and

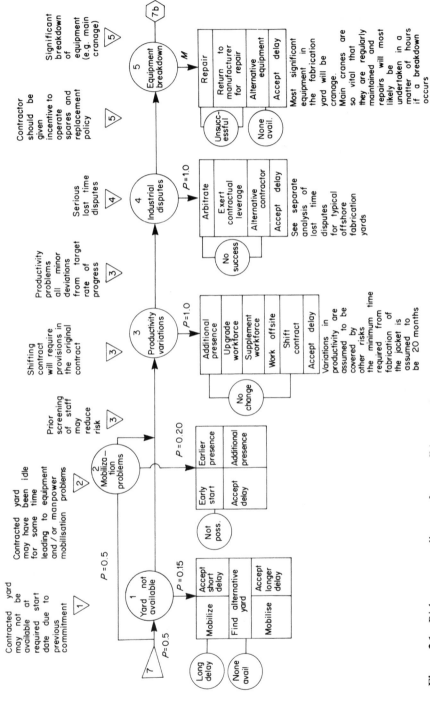

Figure 2.1 Risk–response diagram for an offshore project

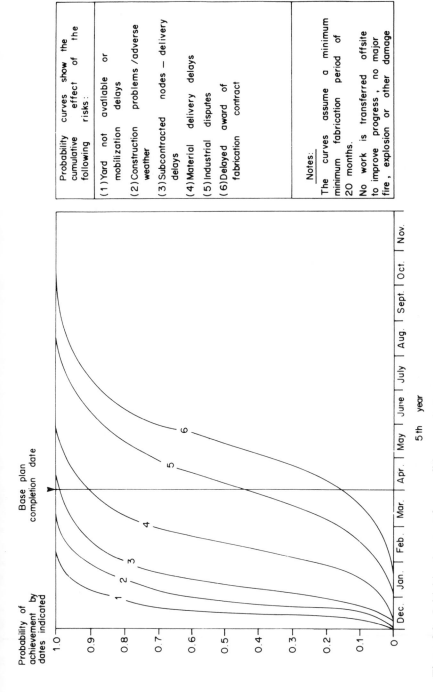

Figure 2.2 Initial level output for an offshore project

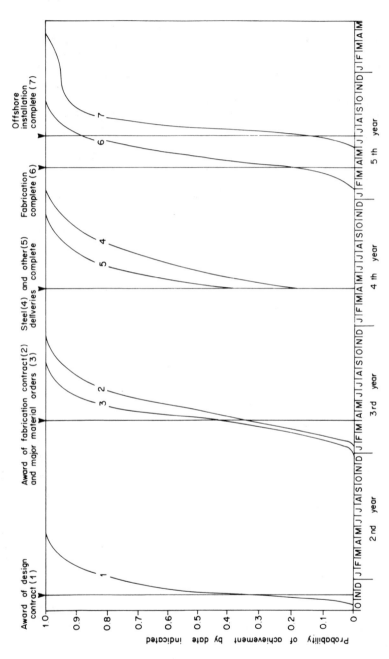

Figure 2.3 Intermediate level of output for an offshore project

justifiable case for all major decisions inherent in this overall result are the associated plans (including contingency plans) and budgets released. A more detailed treatment of this method is provided elsewhere (Chapman, 1979), based upon the quite extensive guideline manual developed for the first studies. Other risk-engineering contexts require a similar pattern of structuring, but some structural differences, and often very different terminology. For example, in a reliability analysis, sources of risk become reasons for failures or faults, responses become repair procedures, and a probabilistic assessment of the extent to which production or availability is reduced must be assessed (Cooper and Chapman, 1987).

COMPUTER SOFTWARE

The first applications of the risk-engineering approach in a project planning context in 1977 involved models like the pipelaying example, with detailed consideration of sources of risk, responses, secondary risks associated with responses, secondary responses to those risks, and so on. Pocket calculators were used to avoid preconditioning the model structure by computer software limitations. However, even with simple model structure, computer software to perform the computations is clearly desirable.

In 1978 common interval software was developed, with nine versions incorporating a range of extensions over the period 1978–82 (Clark and Chapman, 1987). Significant modifications were made to deal with some projects (Chapman, Cooper and Cammaert, 1984; Chapman et al., 1985) but a range of other projects have employed existing software. A new generation of controlled interval and memory software has been developed, and a microcomputer version. No single software system will cope with all possible application areas and styles of analysis. However, the new generations of software under consideration will be quite general. For current information, please contact the author.

Other commercially available computer software for risk analysis falls into two main groups. One contains general simulation languages and packages based on Monte Carlo procedures, which could in principle be used to do everything discussed earlier. In the author's view, such packages would benefit from incorporating a CIM capability. The other group contains specific model or technique based software, like the GERT package by Pritsker and Associates, Monte Carlo based PERT packages, and Monte Carlo based spreadsheets like those provided by @RISK. Only certain special cases might benefit from incorporating a CIM capability, like Monte Carlo based PERT packages.

There is a very natural tendency to approach formal risk management procedures by first acquiring computer software, then tailoring the procedures adopted to the software capability. In the author's view this is understandable but undesirable: it is important first to design appropriate models and methods and then select suitable software, given the analysis required by those models and methods.

RISK MANAGEMENT METHOD DESIGN

Method design involves choosing or developing an appropriate model/method/ software combination for a particular kind of risk management in a particular context. The time and money available to perform the analysis, and the expected future use, are obviously important considerations, as well as the immediate task. Method design is a process which is necessarily dependent upon experience and intuition.

A very detailed treatment of sources of risk and responses has important benefits. It also involves considerable expenditure in terms of staff effort and information requirements. However, a method for project planning can be designed to make use of simpler models, following a fairly obvious sequence of simplifications, discussed in detail elsewhere by Chapman et al. (1983).

In other contexts the transformations required of the methods to coincide with revised model structures can be more significant. Some have proven remarkably easy to deal with (Chapman, Cooper and Cammaert, 1984). Others have required considerable effort (Chapman et al., 1985).

OTHER CONSIDERATIONS

Risk Analysis and Specialist Expertise

Risk management models, methods and software provide valuable tools for project planning and design, but obtaining the right answer still depends upon specialist expertise. Judgements must be made, in some cases based upon hard data, in others based on sound conventional guidelines. In other cases creative innovation and well-schooled intuition based upon a wide range of relevant experience must be used. Expertise involving an effective and efficient blend of all these aspects is not made less important by adopting general risk management methods: it is simply made use of more effectively.

Risk management can involve many forms of expertise. Economics, finance, environmental issues, contractual issues, etc., are clearly involved in most major projects. What is not always appreciated is that they may directly impact on the way the design and planning are done, and they should be properly considered in a timely manner. A risk engineering approach helps to provide this integration.

Risk Engineering Study Team Management

Risk engineering study team management requires special consideration. Like the model/method/software aspects of risk analysis method design, it must be adapted to the circumstances. For example, one company uses an in-house risk analysis group in an internal audit role most of the time. Analysts examine a project plan and cost estimates in detail over a period of six to eight weeks. Their work then provides useful immediate feedback to the project staff, but they report to the project manager and the head of the planning and costing function group. Other companies have used large teams over several months to perform a complete analysis, externally to the project team, and to make recommendations based upon fundamental judgements which go beyond the risk analysis itself. Other studies have involved only two or three professionals over an elapsed time of just a few weeks. Very different kinds and styles of management are clearly necessary for such diverse operations.

CONCLUSION

Successful risk management requires

- a flexible and general set of verbal, graphical and mathematical models, supported by appropriate computer software;
- a family of related methods, designed to suit the models, which link the models and the circumstances in which they are to be used;
- a wide range of relevant expertise and specialist skills;
- the experience and leadership to design and integrate models, methods, and software for specific risk management tasks, to organize and manage risk analysis study teams, and to execute successfully analyses for projects.

It is arguable that the emphasis of this chapter on models and computation is excessive. In practice it is method and method design issues which dominate, related computer software issues being very important. However, to understand method and method design, models and their computational implications must be understood in detail. This view and the obvious constraints on available time and space are responsible for the balance of material here.

It is arguable that the CIM and risk-engineering approaches are not central to project risk management as it is generally conceived. Some would see a single model like PERT (Chapman, Cooper and Page, 1987), barely mentioned here, as the only approach to project risk management. Others have quite different views of the subject (Lichtenberg, 1983). However, the author hopes these quite disparate views will be better understood if the reader wishes to pursue them as a consequence of the insights provided by this chapter. It would not have been possible to do justice to more than one or two in this chapter, and the author freely admits his bias. A summary of the benefits provided by the risk-engineering approach is provided below, some being direct, some being spinoffs. Other approaches should be assessed in relation to these benefits, bearing in mind relative costs.

- A better perception is developed of the nature of the risks faced, their effects on the project, and their interactions. Understanding is enhanced.
- Better contingency plans are developed, including preemptive responses which reduce or mitigate the effect of risks. Expected cost is reduced, and an appropriate balance between expected cost and risk exposure is achieved, usually with a reduced risk exposure.
- Feedback into the design phase and base planning stages is developed as part of the search for risk efficiency and risk/expected cost balance. Feed forward into the construction and operation of the project is developed as part of the search for risk efficiency and risk/expected cost balance. This builds continuity.
- Opportunities are recognized and responded to as well as threats, as part of the search for risk efficiency and risk/expected cost balance. This makes the process more interesting.
- Creative and lateral thinking to capitalize on opportunities and avoid threats is encouraged. This makes the process more fun.
- The integration of planning and costing in estimating and control is improved. This builds cooperation.
- Members of the project team develop an understanding of likely problems and responses in their own area, and problems in other areas which will impact on them. Team work is developed.
- Attention is focused on specific problem areas, and further analysis is pursued until the project team is confident that it can handle all foreseeable events it ought to be able to handle, clearly identifying all events beyond the scope of the plan. This builds morale and responsibility.
- Project management is provided with a means of signalling trends to its board or client without redefining objectives. This avoids crises.
- Knowledge and judgements are formalized and documented, making similar projects at later dates much easier to deal with, even if the personnel involved are not available. Corporate knowledge is captured.
- External technical, environmental and political influences are specifically considered in direct relation to internal technical and political issues, and appropriate strategies to deal with these complex interactions are developed. This provides a balanced view of the total project.
- Probability distributions are provided for completion date and cost esti-mates, but this may be a less important aspect of the exercise. The approach is an enhanced and enriched planning process, intended to provide a basis

for developing a risk-efficient and cost-effective approach which is robust and credible. It is based upon a need for insight, creativity, balanced judgements and technical skills in a thoughtfully managed manner.

As noted earlier, and discussed elsewhere (Chapman *et al.*, 1983), these benefits involve costs, and an approach at the level of detail of the pipelaying activity as discussed earlier is not always suitable. However, project risk management, tailored with care to an appropriate application area, can often provide a very useful subset of these benefits at a cost which makes it good value for money.

REFERENCES

Chapman, C.B. (1979). Large engineering project risk analysis, *IEEE Transactions of Engineering Management*, **EM-76**, 78–86.

Chapman, C.B. and Cooper, D.F. (1985). Risk analysis in G.K. Rand and R.W. Eglese (eds), *Further Development in Operational Research*, Pergamon, pp. 12–33.

Chapman, C.B., Cooper, D.F. and Cammaert, A.B. (1984). Model and situation specific OR methods: risk engineering reliability analysis of an LNG facility, *Journal of the Operational Research Society*, **35**(1), 27–35.

Chapman, C.B., Cooper, D.F. and Page, M.J. (1987). *Management for Engineers*, John Wiley and Sons.

Chapman, C.B., Phillips, E.D., Cooper, D.F. and Lightfoot, L. (1983). Selecting an approach to project time and cost planning, *International Journal of Project Management*, **3**(1), 19–26.

Chapman, C.B., Cooper, D.F., Debelius, C.A. and Pecora, A.G. (1985). Problem solving methodology design on the run, *Journal of the Operational Research Society*, **36**(9), 769–78.

Clark, P. and Chapman, C.B. (1987). The development of computer software for risk analysis: a decision support system development case study, *European Journal of Operational Research*, **29**(3), 252–61.

Cooper, D.F. and Chapman, C.B. (1987). *Risk Analysis for Large Projects: Models, Methods and Cases*, John Wiley and Sons.

Cooper, D.F. and Chapman, C.B. (1988). Risk analysis for large engineering projects in G. Gregory (ed.), *Decision Analysis*, Pitman, pp. 337–69.

Driscoll, M.F. (1980). Instructional uses of approximate convolutions and their graphs, *The American Statistics*, **34**, 150–4.

Kaplan, S. and Garrick, B.J. (1981). On the method of discrete probability distributions in risk and reliability calculations—applications to seismic risk assessment, *Risk Analysis*, **1**.

Kottas, J.F. and Lau, H.S. (1982). A four moments alternative to simulation for a class of stochastic management models, *Management Science*, **28**, 749–58.

Lichtenberg, S. (1983). Alternatives to conventional project management. *International Journal of Project Management*, **1**(2), 101–2.

Van Slyke, R.M. (1963). Monte Carlo methods and the PERT problem, *Operations Research*, **11**, 839–60.

Chapter 3

The Perception of Risk

Norman Jackson
Management Division
University of Newcastle upon Tyne

and

Pippa Carter
Department of Management Systems and Sciences
University of Hull

ABSTRACT

It is generally accepted that a lack of perception contributes to unexpected systemic failures and it is assumed that if more information were available then accidents would be avoided through rational action. In this chapter it is argued that the minimization of risk through increasingly rational behaviour is an unattainable goal. Since perception determines what is rational, we need to concentrate on perception rather than rationality. A systematic approach is proposed which offers some possibilities in this area.

INTRODUCTION

A major perspective in approaches to risk assessment has been centred on quantification in terms of probability. But this approach does little to explain the social/behavioural influences on risk. There have been major contributions

Risk: Analysis, Assessment and Management. Edited by J. Ansell and F. Wharton.
© 1992 John Wiley & Sons Ltd.

to this area of risk assessment in the work of Turner (1978) and of Douglas (1986), but the area is still clearly underdeveloped. Both Turner and Douglas offer useful frameworks in terms of a social–anthropological approach. Our own concern is at the epistemological level and in this chapter we attempt to assess the potential contribution of post-structuralist epistemological theory to understanding the social construction of risk assessment. In particular, on the basis of the maxim that the greatest levels of information are contained within those events which are least probable, we consider how this body of theory offers ways of expanding consideration of risk which legitimates inclusion of elements which enhance potential for information, as well as those which enhance meaning (cf. on the relationship between information, meaning and probability, e.g. Robbe-Grillet, 1977; Cooper, 1987).

Our interest is in the failure to perceive causal relationships which lead to system failure. The concept of system used here can be seen in an ordinary language or its more rigorous scientific sense, but it is used, generically, to refer to a set of interrelated activities which function for a specific purpose. These could be social or technical, but are most likely to be a combination of both. Such systems tend to be homeostatic in nature and are able to tolerate certain levels of disorder (uncertainty), but, ultimately, can only function satisfactorily within specific tolerances. Once the stability criteria are violated the system will fail in one way or another. Many system failures are not particularly significant and we tend to accept them as normal day-to-day events, even though we seek to minimize their occurrence—indeed, allowance for failure is usually built into the system and into our utilization of such systems. However, some failures do have catastrophic consequences, even though it is recognized, in retrospect, that they were preventable. Such cases also present the issues in the starkest possible ways, and thus we have taken our examples from disasters rather than from inconveniences.

Again, the concept of perception used here can also be seen in an ordinary language or a technical sense. The essential element of the term is the understanding that we do not simply register sense data which we gather from the world around us, but actively interpret such data. As an initial guide we take the following definition:

> *Perception* is the active psychological process in which stimuli are selected and organized into meaningful patterns.
>
> (Huczynski and Buchanan, 1991, p. 37)

This definition clearly does not embrace the most technical understandings of perception, but does emphasize that it is we who do the selecting and we who attribute meaning and will thus serve as an adequate starting point for the considerations of this paper.

PROBABILITY AND POSSIBILITY

Risk is a concept associated with the failure of a system, the likelihood of a system failure usually being understood in terms of probability. This rather elegantly parsimonious formulation, however, seductively obscures a highly complex set of phenomena. As Cooper (1987, p. 396) notes:

> ... probability is the expression of an assumed pre-existing order which rests on the idea of the expected and the certain, i.e. the recurrence of that which is already known ... [P]robability is a form of prediction or prior awareness which defends the system against the strange and the unknown; the system is therefore incapable of dealing with information that is non-probabilistic and unpremeditated.

Whilst, for the purposes of actuarial modelling, probability of system failure may be an appropriate concept, we would suggest that, for our purposes, system failure might more usefully be conceptualized in terms of the possibility of conditions arising in which failure might occur (cf. also Fuzzy Logic). In emphasizing possibility rather than probability we hope to shift the focus of consideration of risk. Probability expresses a tendency for a system failure to occur which applies equally in any population but, because it is the application of a ratio to what is essentially a binary condition, it must always be wrong in all actual cases. For example, 100 aircraft are about to embark on a flight and it has been computed that each plane has a 99% chance of arriving safely. But in practice each plane will either arrive safely or it will not, i.e. in any individual case such a ratio has no sensible meaning. If 99 aircraft arrive safely and 1 crashes, then for the 99 safe arrivals the prediction is overly pessimistic but for the one that crashed it is overly optimistic. For a passenger considering a flight in one of those aircraft the significant consideration is not the probability, but whether it *will* arrive safely. Whereas probability will deal with the likelihood of the occurrence of an event within a population, possibility focuses on particular events. For any given event, the probability of something occurring is the same, a priori, whether or not it actually occurs. The possibility of occurrence refers to actual occurrence.

If a system cannot fail (impossibility) the concept of risk is irrelevant. Where a system failure is utterly unpredictable, e.g. because of the absence of a technology which can predict failure, clearly there is little that can be done to minimize the propensity to risk. But in most cases of system failure such failure could and ought to have been predicted—our concern is with why the information which is available for such prediction is not used in the actual event. To give an example: suppose that the one aircraft of our 100 which crashes does so because not enough fuel is carried for the distance to be covered. A post-mortem on the event will identify why the aircraft crashed. But it would not be necessary for the event to occur for it to be predictable. Calculations of fuel consumption for distance to be covered before the aircraft set off would be feasible, and would, equally, indicate the inevitable outcome of not carrying enough fuel. (This may sound like a simplistic example, but it does have parallels in real events—is it conceivable that the outcome of sailing a ship with the bow doors open could not have been predicted in advance?) As potential passengers our concern will be, not the probability that the aircraft sets off without enough fuel, but the possibility that it can do so—i.e. not how likely it is, but the potential for it to happen. Once a system contains the possibility of its own failure, it becomes a matter of time and luck as to whether failure actually occurs. Our concern, then, is not with systems which do not, or cannot, fail in practice (even though there may be a probability that they will fail), but with those which either have failed or will fail because of a specifiable set of system conditions. In other words, we are concerned with those events where information exists to show the circumstances under which the system could and would fail, but where either the information is not used or the occurrence of those conditions is not recognized at the moment when failure is induced. The question we would try to address is, given that the information exists, why is it that it is either not recognized or not considered in the decision-making process? Most system failures originate in a prior failure to anticipate that failure will occur. They originate in failures of the perception of risk.

DECISION MAKING AND RATIONALITY

For the purposes of our discussion we assume that decisions are goal oriented and that the goal in respect of risk assessment is to avoid system failure. Informed judgement is used to assess how this goal may be achieved and, with the information available, the optimal solution is chosen, given the parameters of the decision-making process. This is a basic description of a rational process of decision making. Whilst Simon's (1976) concept of bounded rationality in decision making recognizes that perfectly rational decision making is not feasible, it is still the case that satisficing decisions are seen as rationally derived: though Simon's concept can be seen as a radical questioning of the assumption of perfect rationality, it does not deny that the process is, given its limitations, still characterizable as rational.

Before the probability of a failure—its risk—can be assessed and legislated for, its possibility of occurrence must be recognized. Once such possibility has been recognized, there are well-established techniques for quantifying the risk. By possibility we mean that a set of conditions which can cause system failure is perceived to exist. Thus, in order for system failure to be avoided, the causes of such failure must be known and understood. Furthermore, risk of system failure can only be limited at the level of cause. Of course, risk of consequence of system failure can be limited at the level of effect, but this is not as desirable as that the failure should not occur. In terms of our previously noted concerns therefore, the issue must lie with unperceived causality.

The traditional response to system failure—i.e. to unperceived causality—has been to use negative feedback from a system failure, which has occurred either in reality or by simulation, to prevent future recurrences in like situations. The application of rational thought allows us to use the information we have got to prevent recurrence, through modification of our understanding to enhance system reliability. However, not only can it be used to control similar situations but also it can be extrapolated to dissimilar situations which embody significant analogous characteristics (for a classic exposition of this process in relation to the Board of Trade enquiries into railway accidents, see Rolt, 1978).

The perception of similarity in the dissimilar is the classic definition of metaphor, which, we will argue later, is itself a fundamental characteristic of human thought processes. Thus this ability to recognize analogy in apparently dissimilar cases both extends and enhances rational thought by allowing comparison of cause/effect relationships in related conditions. Given that all system failures are in some respect unique, the application of negative feedback is almost always essentially metaphorical, but the more that the boundaries of metaphorical understanding can be successfully extended, the more utility negative feedback will possess.

The rational approach to assessment of risk and prevention of system failure assumes that all actual or simulated system failures provide an accumulated understanding of causality which is then used to prevent similar occurrences. Once all possible failures have occurred and been understood, therefore, all future failure can be avoided—the assumption implies that we are moving inexorably, if somewhat asymptotically, towards zero failure due to our increasing stock of knowledge.

However, in real life it seems to be stretching credibility to accept this assumption. Accidents continue to happen even though the causality is already known. For example, from the earliest development of railways a high risk factor has been that a train will run into the back of a preceding train, and a common cause of this event has been drivers over-running signals. Such accidents still happen despite some 150 years of development of technology and system control aimed at their prevention. Ironically, such attempts at prevention of this type of accident have depended fundamentally on the expectation of mechanistic behaviour on the part of the driver (i.e. that the driver will consistently respond correctly to signals), and thus the knowledge that people do not behave mechanistically ought to have been built into any model for such preventions, but this has not generally been the case in the United Kingdom (though there is now some evidence of change in this).

Yet we generally expect that railway accidents should not occur. There is a paradox involved here: the knowledge that the system is fallible is repressed by the necessary assumption that it is infallible (perception of probability of risk is infinitely deferred). This assumption of infallibility is necessary in so far as, if the system is to function, a belief in its fallibility would require a strict adherence to those rules which had been developed in order to make the system function safely, but, as has been demonstrated on a number of occasions when employees have adopted a practice of working to rule, under those conditions chaos rapidly ensues. Indeed, the expression 'working to rule' has come to signify a form of strike without withdrawal of labour and has become synonymous with the inducement of chaos. Thus, underlying the first paradox there is another paradox: the rules in any system which have been formulated, on the basis of perceived causality, precisely in order to prevent system failure can, when strictly adhered to, be the cause of sub-optimal operability of the system—in other words, can lead, to a greater or lesser extent, to system failure. Clearly, this situation has drastic implications for the viability of the rational model of decision-making processes. Equally clearly, where a system is deemed infallible despite the knowledge that it is fallible, however practical the reasons for so doing, there must be repercussions on the ability to perceive risk.

ATTENUATION

As Turner (1978, p. 163) says, it is a

> question of how a situation could come about in which reasonable men [sic], attempting to behave rationally, could still be in error.

We have suggested elsewhere (Jackson and Carter, 1984) that this can be seen in terms of faulty attenuation of variety. This argument derives from recognition of the problem that the world consists of too much information (variety) for humans as information processors to be able to make sense of, making it necessary for a decision to be made (though not necessarily consciously) as to which information should be retained and which can be discarded. The rubric for such selections is goal oriented, where the goal is, normatively, one of system viability, whatever level of system might be involved. In other words, we cannot survive in an unmediated world of pure information, it is essential that this cognitive process of attenuation of variety functions. Variety attenuation gives us a model of the system with which we can cope. Nonetheless, simply because the process is goal oriented does not guarantee that it is always correct information for system viability that is retained, and incorrect information that is discarded. Indeed, it is just as likely that, in the process, key pieces of information are discarded, and irrelevant ones retained. This is due to the nature of the attenuation process, which is conducted within a guiding framework (meta-theory) which consists of a set of beliefs about the nature of the world. We have characterized these beliefs as myth in that they are deemed adequate for viability but are not, in any absolute sense, true—as Ashby (1970) has noted, the truth is the whole system, not any model of it. Thus the models of the system, whichever system may be in question, with which we work are fundamentally ideological, i.e. non-epistemological in that they derive from opinion rather than fact (see Case 1: RMS *Titanic*).

Case 1:   RMS *Titanic*

On 14 April 1912 the White Star liner RMS *Titanic*, in the hours of darkness whilst in the vicinity of a known ice field, sailed at speed into an iceberg. The ship, which was on her maiden voyage, sank in approximately 2 hours 40 minutes and out of a total of 2201 passengers and crew only 712 were saved. The ship carried lifeboats for only 1176 people, but this exceeded the Board of Trade requirements (980 places) for a vessel of that size. The *Titanic* was believed by many to be unsinkable, although the designers did not assume that this was the case. However, as the Builders' Representative, who was also the Designer, and the captain both perished in the disaster, one can assume that key actors in the design and operation of the *Titanic* were not expecting it to sink. Within 20 minutes of the collision, the designer came to the conclusion that it was inevitable that the *Titanic* would sink quite rapidly. Certainly, during the construction of the *Titanic*, a plan was devised to equip it with lifeboat capacity for all passengers and crew, but this did not materialize in the final design, the number actually fitted being less than necessary but more than required.

The relevance of this case is in the way the system was modelled. If a systematic understanding of saving life in the event of a ship sinking is modelled on the basis of what is required by the regulating authority, then the *Titanic* was a safe ship. If, on the other hand, it is understood in terms of providing an adequate means of escape and survival until rescued, then the *Titanic* was not a safe ship. Clearly, experience confirmed the latter model as the more correct—corresponding more closely to reality—though equally clearly it was not necessary to demonstrate the consequences of a ship sinking with inadequate lifeboat space before the problem could be understood (*Wreck Commissioner's Report—1912*, 1990; Eaton and Haas, 1987; Hutchings, 1987).

Certain things were done to avoid repetition of the *Titanic* disaster. The specific outcomes of the inquiry included provision of more lifeboats, ice patrols and 24 hour radio watch, and the move to a more southerly, ice free

_____ *cont.* __

_____ cont. _____

route. However, even this has not prevented ships from travelling at speed in obviously dangerous conditions (see Turner (1978) on the collision between the MV *Redthorn* and the MV *Efpha* in 1971).
(NB   In this case and in the subsequent cases other causal relationships are involved—the points identified are only for illustration.)

Clearly, from a rationalist point of view this is problematic. The rational solution is to identify such non-epistemological attenuation and replace it with attenuation based on scientific knowledge. This project is precisely analogous to the approach to prevention of system failure and risk assessment which uses negative feedback from a failure to prevent reccurrence. Yet it is the utterly fundamental and ubiquitous process of attenuation itself which casts doubt on the potential of this project to make negative feedback effective in eliminating risk. This ability also depends on how the problem which caused system failure is defined, which is also influenced by processes of attenuation and the associated non-epistemological factors. In the case of the sinking of the *Titanic*, the first objective was satisfied in the replacing of the non-epistemological 'fact' that the *Titanic* was unsinkable (cf., e.g. Lord, 1976) with the scientific fact that all ships could sink. This progression was particularly important in bringing about a reassessment of perceived risk which enabled action to be taken to limit effects of this particular type of system failure, e.g. *inter alia*, after the sinking of the *Titanic* all ships had to carry sufficient lifeboats to hold their full complement. However, in the case of limitation of cause the results have been rather different. For the sake of argument, we can suggest two vastly different conceptualizations of the cause of system failure: did the *Titanic* sink because it hit an iceberg at speed, or because it violated the physical 'law' that two objects cannot occupy the same space at the same time? If the former is perceived as prime cause then negative feedback can be said to have been remarkably effective in preventing similar occurrences. However, it has not prevented other ships sinking which also violated the *spatial* conditions. In terms of the latter specification of perceived cause, operating at the level of principle, and which enables extension by analogy to myriad other causes of ships sinking, it may have been less effective, perhaps demonstrating the limitations on the potential of negative feedback to operate efficiently. But, even given a means of rationally defining cause which might overcome the tendencies of attenuation, it could still be argued that the project of replacing non-epistemological influences with scientific knowledge is Utopian, though this should by no means constitute a reason not to pursue it. In the case of the *Herald of Free Enterprise*, we must presume that no one involved knowingly set sail with the bow doors open—it was believed that they were closed. Had that belief been replaced by scientific knowledge—that the doors were open, or closed—the accident would not have occurred. But it did. If even such readily verifiable knowledge is not used, despite all the information available about why ships may sink, what hope for the far more complex knowledge that must more usually be necessary to prevent system failure?

THE RISK OF PERCEPTION

We have argued so far that the assessment of the risk of a system failure needs to be rooted in understanding of discrete events, rather than in terms of long-run probability; that risk can only be anticipated through perception of causality; that perception is not objective or even predominantly rational in the formal sense, but is influenced by non-epistemological factors which do not have to be true but merely to be believed to be true; that this is an inescapable process; that the assessment of risk and prevention of system failure should be rooted in the substitution of non-epistemological influences by scientific knowledge about it; and that there is a fundamental contradiction in the way in which we believe in rational solutions but, since we ourselves are not rational, this amounts to a belief in rational systems whose components are themselves irrational.

Contemporary theorizing in the field of epistemology, particularly post-structuralist thinking (see, e.g. Norris, 1985; Sturrock, 1979), has questioned the very possibility of non-ideologically influenced thought. The argument is put forward that the world consists of relatively unstructured data which are organized into meaningful patterns, not as the result of any inherent logic within the data, but as the result of the mental processes of the observer. In other words, structure, intelligibility and meaning are products of the mind, not of the data. There is not necessarily any immediate external validation of whether or not the believed structure is correct, i.e. has a reasonable approximation to reality, but potentially such validation is usually possible—though, unfortunately, it is often only demonstrated as a result of system failure. The alternative to invalidity being demonstrated by system failure is the possibility that it might somehow be demonstrated before the fact, in which case that particular potential risk might be eliminated. However, it must be noted that, given that such demonstration is non-experiential, it would be necessary to create a belief in the changed structure of the data—it would constitute a change in belief systems, not an accretion of scientific knowledge. A notable case in point can be seen in the processes which led to the Challenger space shuttle disaster, where information was presented which predicted the disaster if it was not taken into account. This information failed to convince the managers of the project—they did not relinquish their prior beliefs (see Case 2: Challenger Space Shuttle). This case also provides some interesting examples of problems of group dynamics, such as conformity and groupthink, which can also have profound effects on attachment to belief and thus on the perception of risk (Boisjoly and Curtis, 1990).

Case 2:   Challenger Space Shuttle

On 28 January 1986 the US space shuttle Challenger exploded 73 seconds after launching (Boisjoly and Curtis, 1990). This was due to failure of O-ring seals in one of the rocket booster joints. Nearly a year before this, engineers had become suspicious about the integrity of these joints as a result of leakage on previous flights. Investigations indicated that the seal was adversely affected by low ambient temperature. The seal was designed to operate in the temperature range 40–90°F. However, it appeared from the investigation that the lower threshold should be increased to 53°F. The day before the launch the engineering advice to the management team was that the launch should not proceed if the seal temperature was below 53°F. One of the engineers making this recommendation was considered to be the leading expert in the United States on O-ring joint seals. The overnight temperature prior to the launch was predicted to fall to 18°F. Nevertheless, the decision was to proceed with the launch.

The significance of this example is that the management team, when presented with new scientific evidence which contradicted their existing model of safe launch conditions, could not discard their old beliefs but clung to them and disregarded the new information. The reasons for this are complex and no doubt include such factors as the psychological commitment to the launch taking place as planned, given the enormous investment they had made in the project; pressure from other actors; aspects relating to the exercise of power, etc. But the crucial factor is that the evidence necessary to prevent the disaster was present but ignored.

Part of the underpinning of the post-structuralist argument about epistemology is focused on the centrality of the psycho-social function of language. Language is the foundation stone of cognition, and thus we cannot understand the world except through the mediation of language. Thought itself is structured in the same form as language. The world consists of cognized data sets (signifiers) which we relate to some meaning (their signifieds), but we do so in an essentially arbitrary manner. Thus we may perceive a signifier which we would call a tree—this signifier has no meaning independent of the concept of a tree, i.e. a linguistic formulation. Yet there is no necessary relationship between the word tree (sound, marks on the page, etc.) and the material object 'tree'. A simple demonstration of the argument can be given by noting that, in French, an almost totally different group of sounds, marks on the page, etc., signify precisely the same object. The arbitrariness of the relationship between signifier and signified is further compounded by the fact that, in English at least, the concept 'tree' refers to several distinct classes of object, e.g. a large plant, a model of decision making, a device to be put into shoes, a representation of one's ancestry, a constructional framework of wood, etc. Therefore, we decide on the signification of any particular signifier by reference to its perceived context.

This necessarily brief portrayal of the argument focuses on the 'building blocks' of language, but, in practice, the world is presented to us as a complex mass of signifiers which we have to 'read' as a 'text'. Because of the inherent ambiguity of language this text is open to a number of interpretations, some of which are more 'correct' than others, Yet, because, at least at the level of cognition, correctness is a function of the mind, not of the data, we again lack external validation of truth. Thus, when assessing the potential for system failure, reading of the data set will suggest either no-risk or risk—the task for the 'reader' is to try to ensure that when the data seems to signify no-risk that is indeed the case.

This formulation of human cognition and the acquisition of knowledge highlights very clearly the enormous difficulty in assessing whether, and if so to what extent, risk is present in any particular set of conditions. Obviously, it would be a considerable advantage to be able to specify the nature of the relationship between data and meaning, between signifier and signified. One way of understanding their connection is in terms of metaphor. We have already suggested that, by extending our appreciation of 'the similar in the dissimilar', the predictive value of negative feedback can be enhanced through recognition of the potential for a particular cause to have the same effect in different but analogous situations (see Case 3: Hixon Railway Crossing Accident). On the basis of the arguments about the role of language in cognition, and the characterization of the arbitrary relationship between signifier and signified as metaphorical, we can now go further and argue that this extension of the rational process of risk assessment is not merely desirable, but is essential. Thus, suppose that the data set under consideration is a ship moving at speed into an ice field. In the case of the *Titanic*, at the time, this was perceived as no-risk, but events showed that it was in fact a situation of very high risk. If a metaphorical approach is added to this negative feedback, it might reasonably be reformulated, as we have previously suggested, at the level of principal as a problem of two objects moving relative to one another and trying to occupy the same space at the same time. Thus the question to be asked might be, in what other data sets, which might not contain icebergs, or even ships, but which do contain two such objects, might the same effect be produced?

Case 3:   Hixon Railway Crossing Accident

In January 1968 a 45 metres long slow-moving road transporter carrying a heavy load was struck by an express passenger train, resulting in the deaths of 11 people (Turner, 1978). The transporter was traversing an automatic half barrier level crossing at the time. With this type of crossing a 24 second

_____ *cont.* __

___ *cont.* ___

warning was given of the approach of a train. However, the transporter moved at less than 1 metre per second and thus required more than 50 seconds to complete its crossing.

Some time previously another vehicle from the same company grounded on another level crossing in front of an approaching train (Turner, 1978, pp. 60, 66, 71, 72). The hauliers expressed their concerns about the safety of the new style of crossing. The railway company's position was that hauliers must must ensure vehicles did not become immobile on level crossings: system failure would be averted if everybody did the 'right thing'. However, the haulier did not learn from the previous event because the lorry then involved was a small one rather than a large one. This is an example of failing to use negative feedback in a metaphorical sense—similarities in the dissimilar were not perceived. Equally, the railway company was aware of the problem of heavy loads, but did not think to work out the time it took a 45 metre vehicle to traverse the crossing.

(This case is extracted from Turner (1978), who gives an extended analysis of the socio-psychological factors involved.)

In the approach to analysis called deconstruction (see, e.g. Norris, 1985), post-structuralism offers a rigorous framework for data analysis which, rather than regarding the arbitrary nature of the relationship between data and meaning as problematic, actively builds upon it to expand potential interpretations. Conventional rationalistic approaches to 'reading the text', i.e. to data interpretation, assume that there is an authoritative interpretation, that there is one correct interpretation. Deconstruction, by emphasizing the multiplicity of signifieds derivable from any signifier, denies the possibility of any authoritative interpretation but generates any number of feasible readings, none of which can, a priori, claim authority. In the event of system failure it is particularly clearly demonstrable that the authoritative interpretation of data has been shown to be wrong but, because of the emphasis on its authority, there is no alternative to its acceptance until it is proved to be wrong. A deconstructive approach to interpretation of data, etc., would provide, at least, a safety net of competing interpretations, all of which are subject to a test of plausibility and which can therefore be legitimated. Whether an interpretation is feasible, therefore, becomes a matter of empirical testing, rather than an assumption built into the interpretation process. In such an approach, authority derives from explanatory power, not from conformity to some preconception about how such issues should be addressed.

CONCLUSION

Risk is a human problem. Preventable system failure inevitably stems from human action, when the people involved in the design, construction and operation of a system fail to perceive some set of conditions which might arise and cause the system to fail. Systems which have a high degree of uncertainty/ unreliability attached to them are not much use for human purposes. Given human ingenuity in designing relatively fail-free systems, it is reasonable to say that, for most of the time, most systems operate correctly—although people operating a system tend to understand the risk of system failure as a problem, the general expectation is that, on a day-to-day basis, systems will tend not to fail rather than to fail. Not only do most systems operate successfully most of the time, but even where we actively accept the possibility of failure (most cases), we tend to believe that such failure will not involve us—Douglas's (1986, 23ff.) notion of subjective immunity. Thus, although the possibility of failure is acknowledged, the assumption is that the system will not fail in the short term, but only at some indeterminate point in the future. This assumption is underwritten by the approach to risk assessment rooted in probability, which focuses on interpretation of risk in terms of some definition of 'the long run'. In other words, the probabilization of risk results in its perceived deferral.

However, as we have argued, actual system failure is a binary concept: particular systems either fail or they do not. Consequently, our interest has been in the actuality of failure, especially where the system conditions for failure are knowable in advance. Whereas probabilistic interests in risk reasonably centre around trying to reduce probability of system failure, this does not help to resolve the associated issues of actual system failure which, though less frequent, will still occur. We have further argued that preventing specific system failure requires the perception of system conditions which will cause failure. While learning from previous examples of system failure undoubtedly contributes to enhancing system security, its utility is circumscribed by the epistemological conditions of cognition. Thus, because of our intrinsic limitations as information processors, we have to filter out a proportion of the available information which is perceived as irrelevant, using only that which is perceived as relevant for decision-making purposes. But there is no mechanism which ensures that retained information is that which is actually relevant. We have described this in terms of non-epistemological influences on perception. Furthermore, because of the general uniqueness of individual failures, the utility of negative feedback approaches is limited by our ability to extrapolate from the specific to the general, from the similar to the dissimilar. This essentially metaphorical understanding, which creates the link between sets of data and their potential meanings, is characteristic of understanding in general where, through the processes of signification, we attribute certain meanings to particular signifiers, such attribution being inescapably arbitrary. The arbitrary reading of data sets allows the possibility of assessing sets of information in terms of absence of risk when, in practice, risk is present. This is the failure to perceive causality and is what allows preventable system failure to occur.

Given that perception is influenced by non-epistemological factors and that this is an irreducible condition, it seems that the prospects for the systematic elimination of risk are exceedingly poor. But there may be ways to ameliorate this depressing scenario. Whereas conventional monist understandings of systems where system failures have occurred have clearly failed to include potentially relevant formulations of explanation by virtue of their lack of authority, deconstructionist approaches deny the authority of a single interpretation and thereby permit any reasonable interpretation to be included. This expansive pluralist approach gives a better chance that all relevant information will be discovered and, given that such claims of relevance can be judged and tested in terms of explanatory power, the possibility of identifying causes of system failure should be considerably enhanced.

REFERENCES

Ashby, W.R. (1970). Analysis of the system to be modelled, in R.M. Stodgill (ed.), *The Process of Model-Building in the Behavioral Sciences*, Ohio State University Press, Columbus, Ohio.
Boisjoly, R.P. and Curtis, E.F. (1990). Roger Boisjoly and the Challenger disaster: a case study in management practice, corporate loyalty and business ethics, in W.M. Hoffman and J.M. Moore (eds), *Business Ethics*, 2nd edn, McGraw-Hill, New York.
Cooper, R. (1987), Information, communication and organization: a post structural revision, *Journal of Mind and Behavior*, **8**(3), 395–416.
Douglas, M. (1986). *Risk Acceptability According to the Social Sciences*, RKP, London.
Eaton, J.P. and Haas, C.A. (1987). *Titanic: Destination Disaster*, Patrick Stephens, Wellingborough, Northants.
Huczynski, A.A. and Buchanan, D.A. (1991). *Organizational Behaviour*, Prentice-Hall, Hemel Hempstead.
Hutchings, D.F. (1987). *RMS Titanic—75 Years of Legend*, Kingfisher, Southampton.
Jackson, N. and Carter, P. (1984). The attenuating function of myth in human understanding, *Human Relations*, **37**(7), 515–33.
Lord, W. (1976). *A Night to Remember*, Penguin, Harmondsworth.
Norris, C. (1985). *The Contest of Faculties*, Methuen, London.
Robbe-Grillet, A. (1977) Order and disorder in film and fiction, (trans. B. Morrisette), *Critical Enquiry*, Autumn, 1–20.
Rolt, L.T.C. (1978). *Red For Danger*, Pan, London.
Simon, H.A. (1976). *Administrative Behaviour*, 3rd edn, Free Press, NY.
Sturrock, J. (ed.) (1979). *Structuralism and Since*, Oxford University Press, Oxford.
Turner, B.A. (1978). *Man-Made Disasters*, Wykeham Publications, London.
Wreck Commissioner's Report (1990). *Report on the loss of 'The Titanic' (SS) (1912)*, Alan Sutton Publishing, Stroud.

Chapter 4

Financial Risk Management Models

L.C. Thomas
Department of Business Studies
University of Edinburgh

ABSTRACT

Financial institutions have become very sophisticated and scientific in their analysis, assessment and management of their financial risks. This chapter outlines some of the areas of commercial financial risk such as portfolio analysis, insurance and option pricing. It will then discuss the techniques for analysing and management of risk in the area of credit control.

INTRODUCTION

Financial risks are some of the most obvious risks that individuals recognize that they are taking, be it gambling on a 'sure thing' on the 2.15 at Wetherby, buying insurance policies to cover life, home and car, or deciding on which type of house mortage policy to choose. These latter examples involve commercial organizations, whose business it is to assess, manage and profit from these risks. This chapter will sample briefly some of the areas of financial risk management which have developed into significant commercial operations for these banking and finance companies before concentrating on one particular area—the extension of credit to individuals—and looking in slightly more depth at the statistical techniques and mathematical model used in that area.

Risk: Analysis, Assessment and Management. Edited by J. Ansell and F. Wharton.
© 1992 John Wiley & Sons Ltd.

The first section below refers to three areas of financial risk management—insurance, portfolio analysis and option pricing—which are huge commercial businesses. The literature, models and techniques in each area are legion and all this chapter can do is outline an application and refer the reader to introductory texts. A fourth area—credit scoring—is introduced in the following section. Credit scoring is the name given to the statistically based techniques used by commercial lenders—banks, credit card companies, mail-order firms, finance houses—to determine to whom to extend credit. Thus the objective is to assess the financial risk associated with each applicant for credit, and hence aid the decision on whether credit should be extended. The next section looks at the subsequent decision of when an individual has been accepted and further information is available on his borrowing and repayment pattern. How this information can be used to determine a limit on the amount of credit the individual may borrow. The statistically based techniques used in the initial decision of whether to extend credit can also be used here, but so may ones based on Markov chain models of repayment patterns. These last two sections are based heavily on papers by Thomas (1988) and Boyle et al. (1992) which look more closely at these areas of credit and behavioural scoring.

EXAMPLES OF FINANCIAL RISK

Many of the finance, banking and insurance industries of the world are concerned to some extent or other with financial risk—its estimation, and its management. In this section we touch on three areas—insurance, portfolio analysis and options.

Insurance

The idea of paying a premium P, in order to protect oneself against a potential loss L if something or someone is stolen, broken or no longer able to function, underlies all facets of insurance—life, home, car, pension, health. This is a standard decision problem represented by the decision table (Table 4.1). If p is the belief that the item will be damaged and $u(.)$ is the individual's utility function, based on variations around his existing wealth, one would take out

Table 4.1 State of nature

	Item safe	Item damaged
No insurance	0	$-L$
Insurance	$-P$	$-P$

insurance if,

$$u(-P) > pu(-L)$$

The problems for those offering insurance policies, are more complex—which policies to offer, what premiums to charge, and whether to accept all of the clients who apply.

Consider the following very simplified example. The firm offers to pay 1 unit if an event with probability p occurs. Since the expected payout per contract is p, the premium P must be at least p. Suppose it can sell $n(y)$ contracts if the premium is y and the cost of servicing n contracts is $c_1 + c_2 n$. Then to expect to break even,

$$P = p + c_2 + c_1/n(P)$$

To survive, however, the firm must set the premium higher than this to allow for uncertainty and profit—but how much higher? One model says let $u(.)$ be the firm's utility on capital, assuming its existing capital is S. Let $F(z)$ be the probability distribution function that an insurance contract pays out z ($z = 0$ or 1), and let $P(x)$ be the corresponding distribution function over the sum of n contracts. Suppose the number of contracts sold, n, is a function both of the premium P and the advertising spend a, then the firm's objective of maximizing utility becomes

$$\underset{a,P}{\text{Max}} \int_0^n u(S + n(P, a)P - a - c_2 n(P, a) - c_1 - x) \, dF^n(x) \qquad (4.1)$$

Realistic problems are much more complex. So is the whole question of how should the firm minimize its financial risk by reinsuring the risks with other insurers. Borch (1974) and Hammond (1968) give many more examples of the types of models used in their introduction to the subject.

Portfolio Analysis

The old adage of 'not putting all your eggs in one basket' is particularly relevant when the 'eggs' are a pension fund's or an individual's wealth. In such cases, one wants to try and minimize the financial risk of losing a substantial amount, while ensuring a satisfactory return by choosing a diversified portfolio of investments and securities. This is the objective of pension fund managers, unit and investment trusts, and broking houses who advise corporate and individual clients. The scientific approach to such risk management was started by Markowitz (1952), and though there have been substantial developments since then both in the theory and in the number of different types of financial instruments one can invest in, Markowitz's approach remains relevant.

The assumptions underlying the Markowitz model are as follows:

- Investors want to maximize the expected utility of their portfolio of securities over a single period. A logarithm utility function means this criterion makes sense over multi-period problems.
- The expected return and variance of each security over the period is known as is the covariance between the securities. (The standard index model assumes that the returns on a security are significantly correlated with the movements in the whole market, and uses this to reduce the number of variables required to describe the covariance between securities.)
- A portfolio consisting of a combination of securities can be described completely from the investor's viewpoint by the mean and variance of its expected returns. The investor's utility function depends only on these and is risk averse. Thus the problem becomes given a set of securities $i = 1, 2, \ldots, n$ where the ith security has an expected return of r_i, a variance of return of $\sigma_i{}^2$ and the covariance of the return of the ith security with the return of the jth security is $\sigma_{i,j}{}^2$, find the optimal portfolio where a portfolio is determined by its weights $x_1, x_2, \ldots, x_n$ with

$$x_i = \frac{\text{value of funds invest in security } i}{\text{total value of funds invested in portfolio}}$$

Then the expected return on the portfolio is

$$R_p = \sum_i x_i r_i$$

while the variance of the expected returns on the portfolio is

$$V_p = \sum x_i{}^2 \sigma_i{}^2 + \sum_i \sum_j x_i x_j \sigma_{i,j}{}^2$$

where

$$\sum_i x_i = 1.$$

Most investors' utility functions, u, are functions of R and V, i.e. $u(R, V)$, and these functions are monotonic increasing in R and decreasing in V. Since it is usually impossible to get more detail on an investor's utility function, one then finds the Pareto optimal portfolios, i.e. those which are not dominated by other portfolios. (Portfolio 1 with mean R_1 and variance V_1 dominates portfolio 2, with mean R_2 and variance V_2 if $R_1 \geq R_2$, $V_1 \leq V_2$ and at least one inequality is strict.) Pareto optimal portfolios are those that minimize $-\beta R_p + V_p$ for some $\beta > 0$, and thus finding Pareto optimal portfolios reduces to solving the following quadratic programming problems as β varies.

Minimize

$$-\beta \sum_i x_i r_i + \sum_i \sum_{i=j} x_i x_j \sigma_{i,j}{}^2 + \sum x_i{}^2 \sigma_i{}^2$$

subject to

$$\sum_i x_i = 1$$

$$x_i \geq 0 \qquad i = 1, 2, \ldots, n.$$

Further details can be found in the introductory books by Allen (1983), or Lorie and Hamilton (1973).

Options

Since 1973 it has been possible to buy the option of buying or selling shares at a fixed price at some time in the future. These options can themselves be traded and are ways of dealing with the financial risk involved in the fluctuations in the share price over time. They have proved so popular that the trade in options on a share is often greater than the trade on the share itself. There are four main types of options—European puts, European calls, American puts and American calls. A call gives the purchaser the right to buy the share; a put the right to sell the share. A European option can only be exercised at its maturity date, while an American option can be exercised any time up to its maturity date. In all cases one of the interesting questions is how much one is willing to pay to take part in this financial gamble.

Consider the problem of pricing an American call option which gives one the right to buy the stock at a price K up to a time T if the risk-free interest rate is r. If at present time t, the stock price is S_t, the price value of the option depends on the models assumed for the stochastic process which describes the change in the share price, S_t, over time. Black and Scholes (1973) assumed that S_t is log normally distributed with

$$E(\log S_t) = S_0 e^{(r - \sigma^2/2)t}, \; \text{Var } [\log(S_t)] = \sigma^2 t$$

and arrived at the famous formula for the value of an option namely

$$S_t N(h) - K e^{-r(T-t)} N(h - \sigma\sqrt{(T-t)}) \qquad (4.2)$$

where

$$h = \log (S_0/K e^{-r(T-t)}/(\sigma\sqrt{(T-t)}) + \tfrac{1}{2}\sigma\sqrt{(T-t)}$$

$$\text{and } N(h) = \int_{-\infty}^{h} (2\pi)^{-1/2} e^{-x^2/2} \, dx$$

Cox, Ross and Rubinstein (1979) developed an option pricing algorithm assuming the stock price followed a multiplicative binomial process, where if S_t is the price at period t, and S_{t+1} is the price at period $t + 1$

$$S_{t+1} = S_t e^u \text{ with probability } q$$

$$S_t e^{-v} \text{ with probability } 1 - q$$

For further details on options see the texts by Rubenstein and Cox (1984) or Jarrow and Rudd (1983).

CREDIT SCORING

Consumer credit is one of the major growth areas of modern retailing. Over the past 50 years the average yearly growth in consumer credit is close to 10%. In 1988 there was over £3 billion of new consumer credit extended each month and the outstanding debt was running around £36 billion.

There are two types of credit-granting decisions made by retailers, credit card companies, mail-order firms, and finance houses, which involve them in financial risks:

(1) whether to grant credit initially to an applicant;
(2) whether to extend further credit to an existing creditor.

The difference between the two is that in the second case one usually has extra information available—the repayment and order history of the creditor.

In order to make the decision on whether to extend credit to a new applicant, the company has available to it the information supplied by the applicant on the application form, a possible referral to a credit reference agency, the application form and credit histories of previous clients and possibly the application forms of those refused credit. The company can then use one of the following methodologies to assist in this decision:

- judgmental evaluation;
- expert systems;
- recursive partitioning algorithms;
- mathematical programming;
- logistic regression;
- discriminant analysis.

The latter four systems lead to a credit score for each applicant which if it is greater than a certain value implies 'accept this applicant', and if below, 'reject the applicant'. Some systems will have a middle range of scores which suggest that the company should seek further information. In the last three systems in the list, the score is obtained by summing the scores of the various characteristics on the application form. Typical examples might be as shown in Table 4.2.

The statistical methods—discriminant analysis, logistic regression, recursive partitioning algorithms—all use a sample of the previous clients as a data set. The credit granter determines which of their credit histories are acceptable to him and which are unacceptable, i.e. the data set is split into the 'goods' and the

Table 4.2   Credit scores

Title		Length at present address	
Mr	28	Less than 6 months	17
Mrs	40	6 months to 2 years	0
Ms	42	2 years to 5 years	20
Others	0	More than 5 years	32

'bads'. The criterion used to determine goods and bads is vital to the decision. Until recently this was always to equate defaulting on the loan as 'bad', and this led to systems that minimized the default rate at given levels of acceptances. Recently companies have started to consider profit as a measure of 'goodness'. This is harder to measure than defaulting and could lead to credit card companies refusing applicants because they were too good and would always pay off all their outstanding balance.

The use of statistical techniques to aid the initial credit granting decision was first tried in the 1930s (see Durand, 1941 for one example). It was not until the US Congress passed the Equal Credit Opportunity Act in 1974 and its amendments of 1976 that statistical 'credit scoring' became established as the standard methodology for the initial credit granting decision. The Act proscribed many characteristics from being used in judging whether or not to advance credit, unless they were used as predictive characteristics in statistically sound and empirically derived systems. This together with the advent of sufficient computing power to enable the requisite databases to be held, gave these initial scoring systems a considerable boost. Comparisons of the advantages and disadvantages of statistical scoring systems and judgemental ones are given by Capon (1982) and Chandler and Coffman (1979).

In this chapter we outline the ideas underlying discriminant analysis—the most widely used of the statistical methodologies. For a comparison of its results with those of recursive partitioning see Boyle *et al.* (1990) and the references therein. Breiman *et al.* (1984) give a detailed description of recursive partitioning. Wiginton (1980) outlines logistic regression while Srinivasan and Kim (1987b) compare these statistical methods and outline the mathematical programming approach.

Discriminant Analysis

Discriminant analysis considers the credit-granting problem as one of dividing the initial information set (in effect the observations) into two exclusive and exhaustive regions I_g and I_b so that if the information vector x of a client falls into I_g, credit is extended and if into I_b it is refused. Let the cost of misclassifying a client, who is really 'good' as 'bad' be L (L for lost profit) and that of classifying a client who is really 'bad' as 'good' be D (D for debt that will have to be written off). If, a priori, the probabilities of goods and bads in the population applying for credit are p_g and p_b then the expected loss is:

$$p_g L \int_{I_b} f(x|P_g) \, dx + p_b D \int_{I_g} f(x|P_b) \, dx \tag{4.3}$$

where $f(x|P_g)[f(x|P_b)]$ is the density function over the initial information set for the population of 'goods' (P_g) ['bads' (P_b)]. The objective is to determine I_b and I_g which minimize equation (4.3). Despite Eisenbeis's (1978) reservations it is often assumed that $L = D = 1$ so that equation (4.4) becomes the expected rate of misclassification. In that case the solution is to define

$$I_g = \{x | p_g f(x|P_g) > p_b f(x|P_b) \tag{4.4}$$

If the two populations have multivariate Normal information distributions so that $f(x|P_g)$ is multivariate Normal with mean μ_g and covariance matrix Σ, and $f(x|P_b)$ is multivariate Normal with mean μ_b and covariance matrix Σ, the rule (4.4) becomes the Fisher linear discriminant function, where one classifies x in I_g if:

$$x\Sigma^{-1}(\mu_g - \mu_b) > \log(p_b/p_g) + \tfrac{1}{2}(\mu_g + \mu_b)\Sigma^{-1}(\mu_g - \mu_b) \tag{4.5}$$

This is a linear scoring rule in that one extends credit to a client if the weighted linear sum of the initial information responses—the left-hand side of equation (4.5)—exceeds some value—the right-hand side of equation (4.5).

In practice, the means and covariance are not known and so μ and Σ are replaced by the usual sample estimators x_g, x_b and S. There is then no assurance that this sample linear discriminant function will minimize the expected rate of misclassification, but it has proved satisfactory in practice when the populations have multivariate Normal (information) distributions. It has also proved fairly satisfactory in other situations—see the survey by Choi (1986). This is because Fisher actually developed this discriminant function in another way. If one looks at two univariate Normal populations with means μ_g and μ_b respectively and a common variance σ^2 it is clear that an observation x would be classified in I_g if it is nearer to μ_g than μ_b. The risk of misclassifying then is clearly related to $(\mu_g - \mu_b)/\sigma$ since when this is large there is little overlap between the two populations. So Fisher felt that when dealing with two multivariate populations of information vectors, one should look for a linear combination of the information data so that for this linear combination the distance $(\mu_g - \mu_b)/\sigma$ is maximized. In other words he looked for a vector a of constants which maximizes.

$$\frac{\{\text{Mean } (ax) \text{ for } x \text{ in popn } P_1 - \text{Mean } (ax) \text{ for } x \text{ in popn } P_2\}}{\text{Standard deviation of } ax} \tag{4.6}$$

This turned out to be the left-hand side of equation (4.5) and so this discriminant function maximizes the ratio of between group dispersions to that of within group dispersions. This property may well make the discriminant function more robust to changes in distributions.

One of the major difficulties in applying this methodology to credit scoring system is that many of the characteristics in the initial application form are qualitative not quantitative—e.g. postcode, employment category, residential status—and so they correspond to discrete rather than continuous variables. One can deal with this in several ways:

(1) Introduce binary variables, i.e. (0, 1) variables for each possible outcome of each discrete variable. Thus if residential status is classified into N categories, one introduces $N - 1$ binary variables where the first might be 1 if owner occupier; 0 otherwise; and the second might be 1 if living with parents; 0 otherwise. These are then dealt with like the continuous variables in the discriminant analysis, but will lead to a large number of variables, which are clearly non-normal.

(2) A second approach is the location model (see Krzanowski, 1975) which constructs a different linear discriminant function over the continuous variables for each possible combination of the values of the discrete variables. Thus for postcodes beginning EH and residential status, owner occupier, there would be a linear discriminant function over age and income with a different one for other combinations of postcodes and residential status.

(3) Translate the qualitative variable into a quantitative one. If the qualitative variable has m values, let g_i be the number from the population of 'goods' who take the ith value and b_i be the number from the 'bad' population who take the ith value, where if $G = g_1 + g_2 + \cdots + g_m$, $B = b_1 + b_2 + \cdots + b_m$ then G is the total number of goods in the sample population and B the total number of bads. Then one could translate the ith value of the variable into a quantitative one depending on g_i, b_i, G and B. Possible choices would be $g_i/(b_i)$, $g_i/(g_i + b_i)$, $(g_i \ B)/(b_i \ G)$, $\log\{(g_iB)/b_iG\}$ or $\log\{g_i/(g_i + b_i)\}$ which are all related to estimates of probability odds or log probability odds of the goods and bads taking the ith value of the variable.

For some variables, like postcodes, there are a large number of values the variable can take, so it is worth aggregating values together, to ensure that the aggregate values appear sufficiently often in the sample set to make the results statistically robust.

It is often the case that credit risk appears not to be monotone in the continuous variables such as age, income, or years at present address. Figure 4.1 shows the age results when grouped in blocks of years.

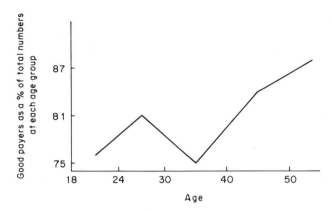

Figure 4.1 Relationship of credit risk with age

One problem in building a credit scoring system based on discriminant analysis is to determine which of the variables obtained from the initial information should be included in the discriminant function. Since high degrees of collinearity between the variables, so that the variables have a nearly linear relationship, lead to unstable coefficients, it is better to omit highly correlated variables. Similarly variables that add little or nothing to the discrimination of the scoring system can be dropped.

Another problem is that the sample used to build the system is biased because it consists only of people who were accepted previously by the company. Thus the good/bad status of those applicants who were refused is not known. Various techniques, some based on cluster analysis, are used to try and infer information about the creditworthiness of these refused applicants in order to get an unbiased sample, but in reality one is just guessing what they would have done if they had been given credit. Eisenbeis (1978) gives a systematic account of the problems that arise in using discriminant analysis for credit scoring.

BEHAVIOURAL SCORING

The development of statistical and model based systems to assist with the second problem of extending credit to existing customers has been much slower, and it is really only in the last few years that such systems have been implemented. Before that companies involved in the consumer credit business had developed systems to determine credit limits for existing customers but they were ad hoc ones built on past experience rather than statistical techniques or models of payment behaviour.

We will describe three types of systems that incorporate the knowledge of the creditor's repayment history into the credit extension decision:

(1) *Performance or behavioural scoring systems* These use the same multivariate statistical methods as are used in the initial credit granting decision. The difference is that the characteristics that are scored include ones describing the repayment and ordering history of the creditor over a suitably defined performance period.

(2) *Orthodox Markov chain models* These methods build models of the repayment behaviour of the creditors in terms of the 'state' of the creditors' accounts. They use the records of a sample of other creditors to estimate the chance of moving from one state to another—the Markov chain—and hence to calculate the chance of the client defaulting.

(3) *Adaptive Markov chain models* These again build models of the repayment behaviour of clients in order to determine who are the most likely to repay if further credit is extended. The main difference compared with the methods in (2) is that the parameters of the repayment model for a particular client are automatically updated using his repayment behaviour and so eventually depend only on his payment characteristics.

Behavioural Scoring

In behavioural scoring, a sample of agents is taken and their initial characteristics and performance history obtained. A particular instant in time is taken as the observation point and a length of time, say 12 months preceding the observation point, is taken as the performance period.

```
       PAST BEHAVIOUR ------------- FUTURE BEHAVIOUR
     | PERFORMANCE PERIOD       |    OUTCOME PERIOD      |
                                +
                           OBSERVATION
                              POINT
```

The creditors' payment and order history in this performance period is noted. Creditors are then classified according to their credit position at the end of an outcome period which follows the observation point—say six months later. Crudely an account is classified as good or bad at that point.

Multivariate statistical techniques like discriminant analysis or regression are then applied to determine which are the factors in the initial application and in the payment history on the performance period which best discriminate between the good and the bad accounts. These are then weighted to construct a scoring rule. Typical performance characteristics that are considered would be average balance, whether there was a payment in the last billing period, and the number of times payment has been delinquent.

Such behavioural scoring systems have the same advantages over judgemental ones as occur in the initial decision case. Gentry (1974) and Chandler and Coffman (1979) discuss these in some detail. They include the fact that validation is possible, that decisions will be consistent, and that there is some form of management control. There are some disadvantages, though, of behavioural scoring systems that do not occur in the initial scoring case. Accounts may change character over time and it could well be 18 months from the start of the performance period to the end of the outcome period. Also the credit history in the performance period is affected by the credit controls in operation then and so the connections made between these and satisfactory performance may not apply under the new controls based on the scoring system. The extension of credit decision is not the yes/no one of granting initial credit but must relate to the extra amount requested. It is not clear how one should relate a creditor's performance score to the credit limit he is given.

Orthodox Markov Chain Models (Credit Risk Monitoring)

The idea of building a model of the repayment behaviour of a creditor, as opposed to the black box approach of performance scoring, was first suggested by Cyert, Davidson and Thompson (1962). Various modifications of the idea have subsequently been suggested by Cyert and Thompson (1968), Liebman (1972), and Frydman, Kallberg and Kao (1985).

The idea is to identify different states that the creditor's accounts can be in and to estimate the chance of a payment next billing period for accounts in each of these states. The states depend mainly on information concerning the current position and past position of the account, but can also depend on the initial application information. Thus current balance, number of periods overdue and number of follow-up letters in past year would be typical factors in describing a state. The object is to identify states which are homogeneous in the chance of a payment next period.

To find these states, one suggestion is to use the recursive partitioning algorithm (1984) on a sample of accounts. This method which was mentioned in the previous section, as a way of aiding the initial credit decision, divides the sample in two using the characteristic that gives the biggest difference in either the probability of payment next period or of chance of account going bad in a specified period. Each of the two subgroups is then split in a similar way and the process repeated until one has a number of subgroups each defined by certain characteristics and each fairly homogeneous in the criterion one has split on, i.e. chance of account going bad or chance of payment next period.

The chance of repayment next period is estimated from the sample for each of these groups, or alternatively the chance of 'ageing', i.e. non-payment, is calculated. This is then used to calculate the chance of an account moving from one state at one period to another one at the next, under each possible credit policy. In some cases where the state of the account is given by the number of periods overdue this is easy to do. In other cases it is more complicated.

One then has to choose the decision criterion under which the credit extension is made. Again the two obvious criteria are:

- to minimize the amount of bad debt subject to reaching a sales revenue target;
- to maximize profit over a given time horizon.

In both cases one needs to use the sample of credit histories either to estimate the sales level at each state or to estimate the profit under each credit level in each state. Finally, one uses dynamic programming techniques to find the optimal credit limit in each state. In the profit criterion case, this can be done by solving the optimality equations which connect $v(n, s)$—the maximum profit over n more periods if currently the account is in state s—and the optimal credit policy is followed. A typical such equation would be

$$v(n, s) = \max_L \left\{ r(s, L) + \sum_s p(s, \hat{s}, L)v(n - 1, \hat{s}) \right\} \tag{4.7}$$

where $r(s, L)$ is the profit in state s and $p(s, \hat{s}, L)$ is the probability of moving from state s to state $\hat{s}$ between one billing period and the next given that the credit limit is L.

An advantage of this approach is that it results in a credit limit being given to each of the states an account can be in. Thus it does differentiate between the creditworthy and the 'very creditworthy'. Also, since there is a model of repayment behaviour, this can be used to estimate cash flows and projected bad debt in the future. The system is also consistent and is open to validation checks.

One of the problems with the model is that the states are chosen to be homogeneous in probability of payment or bad debt rate but not in the probabilities of which state they go to next. However, these are the very parameters which are then calculated. Also it is necessary to make regular recalculations of the states since the economic situation of the creditors constantly changes. Operating versions of this system tend to use the maximize profit criterion but this means one has to estimate the level of profit in each state under each credit limit—a difficult exercise!

Adaptive Markov Chain Models (Dynamic Order Vetting)

The major philosophical difference between this approach and the previous one is that although it again seeks to build a model of a creditor's payment pattern, the parameters of the model for an individual creditor depend in the long run only on that creditor's payment history. The parameters of the model are automatically updated in the light of a payment or a non-payment by the creditor each period. These models are based on a Bayesian rather than an orthodox statistical approach to the problem. Bierman and Hausman (1970) were the first to discuss the possibility of such a system in the one billing period repayment problem. Dirickx and Wakeman (1976) dropped the requirement that one non-payment meant an immediate writing off of the debt, and modifications of the model are still being proposed (Srinivasan and Kim, 1987a). Bunn (1981) pointed out that a more empirical Bayesian approach of combining the payment history of a creditor with information about the payment histories of creditors with similar initial characteristics might also be appropriate.

The idea of the system is that the payment and order database for each agent has value fields attached which enable estimates of future payments to be made. These values are automatically updated at each payment (and are implicitly updated at each non-payment). The values would include balance outstanding, number of periods since last payment, and ones that allow estimates of the chance of a payment next period and the expected value of the payment to be made. These probabilities and amounts of payment are then used to calculate the chance of defaulting if credit is extended and an order allowed. Alternatively one could calculate the expected profit one would expect with and without granting the extra credit.

In the minimizing bad debt criterion, the management then decides on the level of sales required and this then determines the cut-off level of the acceptable risk of bad debt. Since the risk of bad debt increases with outstanding balance this cut-off translates into a credit limit for each account.

To set the system up initially one has to give the parameters initial values. This can be done by using a decision tree approach on a sample, to subdivide the initial characteristics into states which are homogeneous in their payment behaviour. One then gives all accounts with these characteristics the same initial parameters which reflect this payment behaviour. Alternatively one could run the system for a period, before going live starting with the parameters set to some standard value initially. The values of the parameters at the end of this pre-operative period are then used as the initialization for the actual implementation. One would need to treat subsequent new accounts similarly.

It seems appropriate here to comment on the two different criteria suggested in both modelling approaches to the credit extension problem. Minimizing the bad debt for a given level of sales has several advantages over the maximization of profit one. Not only does it give the management considerable control over the process by adjusting the sales level they require but it avoids the problem of combining the two types of costs that is necessary in the profit approach. There are two errors that one can make in the credit granting decision: give credit to an account that subsequently defaults, and not give credit to one that would have proved creditworthy. The cost of the first error is clear, immediate and appears explicitly in the balance sheet; the cost of the second is almost invisible but could be substantial. In the mail-order context, not only is there the loss in profit on the order not accepted but also it is possible that it will mean the loss of future orders if the client decides to go to a rival firm. Examination of some profit related systems suggests that these costs are not fully taken into account and lead to systems that are more conservative and reject more requests for credit extension than do ones based on minimizing bad debt.

The main advantage of the adaptive Markov chain approach is that it gives a credit limit for each account that is automatically updated. Also since it is a model based approach it enables the management to get estimates of future cash flows and bad debt. It is consistent and validation is possible. Also there is no need to use a sample to initialize the parameters if one can run the system for a period before actually going 'live'.

A disadvantage of the system is that it can be quite volatile to new customers. It gives good customers high credit limits—perhaps more than the management would wish to give. Like the previous class of models it is quite sensitive to the billing period used. This should reflect the reality of inter-payment times. Finally, it is criterion specific. Thus, if the model is built so as to minimize bad debt and the definition of bad debt is non-payment for a specific period of time, the system will not be too harsh on creditors who are regular, but slow, payers.

CONCLUSIONS

This has by necessity been a very cursory glance at some of the areas of financial risk management. The aim has been to show the diversity of areas where financial risks have to be managed and the types of models and techniques used in them. The intriguing developments at present are how the techniques from one area are being found useful in other contexts. Thus as financial instruments get more and more complex, one needs to diversify both over instruments and over time, and so the ideas underlying portfolio theory and option pricing are needed together. Similarly the idea of scoring applicants is now used in the insurance industry to estimate more accurately the risk involved in underwriting the policy that applicants require.

Surely management of financial risk is one of the most exciting and challenging areas of mathematical modelling at present.

REFERENCES

Allen, D.E. (1983). *Finance*, Martin Robertson.

Bierman, H. and Hausman, W. (1970). The credit granting decision, *Management Science*, **16**, 519–32.

Black, F. and Scholes, M. (1973). The pricing of options and corporate liabilities, *J Political Economy*, 81, 637–54.

Borch, K.H. (1974). *Mathematical Theory of Insurance*, Lexington.

Boyle, M., Crook, J.N., Hamilton, R. and Thomas, L.C. (1992). Methods for credit scoring applied to slow payers, in J.N. Crook, D. Edelman and L.C. Thomas (eds), *Credit Scoring and Credit Control*, Oxford University Press, pp. 75–90.

Breiman, L., Friedman, J.H., Olshen, R.A. and Stone, C.J. (1984). *Classification and Regression Trees*, Wadsworth International.

Bunn, D.W. (1981). An empirical Bayes procedure for the credit granting decision, *Operations Research Letters*, 1, 10-12.

Capon, N. (1982). Credit scoring: a critical analysis, *Journal of Marketing*, 46, 82-91.

Chandler, G.G. and Coffman, J.Y. (1979). A comparative analysis of empirical vs. judgmental credit evaluation, *Journal of Retail Banking*, 1, 15-26.

Choi, S.G. (1986). Discrimination and classification: overview, *Comp & Maths with Appls*, 12A, 173-7.

Cox, J.C., Ross, S.A. and Rubinstein, M.E. (1979). Option pricing: a simplified approach, *Journal of Financial Economics*, 7, 229-63.

Cyert, R.M., Davidson, H.J. and Thompson, G.L. (1962). Estimation of allowance for doubtful accounts by Markov chains, *Management Science*, 8, 287-303.

Cyert, R.M. and Thompson, G.L. (1968). Selecting a portfolio of credit risks by Markov chains, *Journal of Business*, 1, 39-46.

Dirickx, Y.M.I. and Wakeman, L. (1976). An extension of the Bierman-Hausman model for credit granting, *Management Science*, 2, 1299-37.

Durand, D. (1941). Risk elements in consumer instalment financing, Financial Research Program, Study 8, National Bureau of Economic Research.

Eisenbeis, R.A. (1978). Problems in applying discriminant analysis in credit scoring models, *Journal of Banking and Finance*, 2, 205-19.

Frydman, H., Kallberg, J.G. and Kao, D.-L. (1985). Testing the adequacy of Markov chain and mover-stayer models as representations of credit behaviour, *Operations Research*, 33, 1203-14.

Gentry, J.W. (1974). Discriminate analysis in the credit extension decision, *Credit World*, November, 25-7.

Hammond, J.D. (1968). *Essays in the Theory of Risk and Insurance*, Scott Foresman.

Jarrow, R.A. and Rudd, A. (1983). *Option Pricing*, Irwin.

Krzanowski, W.J. (1975). Discrimination and classification using both binary and continuous variables, *Journal of the American Statistical Association*, 70, 782-90.

Liebman, L.H. (1972). A Markov decision model for selecting optimal credit control policies, *Management Science*, 18, 519-25.

Lorie, J. and Hamilton, M.T. (1973). *The Stock Market, Theory and Evidence*, Irwin.

Markowitz, H.M. (1952). Portfolio selection, *Journal of Finance*, 7, 77-91.

Rubenstein, M.E. and Cox, J.C. (1984). *Option Markets*, Prentice-Hall.

Srinivasan, V. and Kim, Y.H. (1987a), The Bierman-Hausman credit granting model: a note, *Management Science*, 33, 1361-2.

Srinivasan, V. and Kim, Y.H. (1987b). Credit granting: a comparative analysis of classification procedures, *Journal of Finance*, 92, 665-81.

Thomas, L.C. (1988). Behavioural scoring, *Working paper series* 88/32, Dept. of Business Studies, University of Edinburgh.

Wiginton, J.C. (1980). A note on the comparison of logit and discriminant models of consumer credit behaviour, *Journal of Financial Quantitative Analysis*, 15, 757-70.

Chapter 5

The Use of Risk Analysis Techniques in Capital Investment Appraisal

Simon S.M. Ho
The Chinese University of Hong Kong

and

Richard H. Pike
The University of Bradford

ABSTRACT

Why are those firms employing risk analysis methods very much in the minority? The empirical literature suggests that one reason for the lack of widespread acceptance of risk analysis methods by firms in assessing capital investment projects is that it is marred by some inherent and practical problems which still have to be resolved. The objective of this chapter is to examime UK managers' attitudes towards, and practices of, risk analysis, and the barriers that they encounter when introducing risk analysis. It reports the findings from a comprehensive survey of large UK firms on a wide range of issues related to the use and implementation of risk analysis in capital investment decisions. Some possible suggestions to bridge the gap between theory and management practice are discussed.

Risk: Analysis, Assessment and Management. Edited by J. Ansell and F. Wharton.
© 1992 John Wiley & Sons Ltd.

INTRODUCTION

The term 'risk' is often used to describe, characterize and rank new capital projects. Previous capital budgeting surveys indicate that actual practices of firms in handling risk have lagged well behind the theoretically prescribed probabilistic risk analysis (PRA) approach, despite the fact that there is a continuing trend towards greater formalization and sophistication of risk handling (see, e.g. Klammer and Walker, 1984; Pike, 1989). Furthermore, the existing and somewhat aged information on risk handling practices, mostly collected and reported as a part of broader-based surveys, inevitably provides only a limited view of risk analysis practices and its related problems. The purpose of this chapter is to report findings from a survey of large UK firms on a wide range of issues related to the use of risk analysis, particularly the perceived barriers to, and benefits from, such use.

INVESTMENT APPRAISAL CRITERIA AND RISK HANDLING APPROACHES

In order to put the risk analysis issues in context, this section briefly reviews the three most commonly used financial appraisal techniques and the two major risk handling approaches in capital budgeting analysis.

Financial Appraisal Techniques

Net present value

In most cases a project will require an immediate initial outlay and this will result in a series of future cash flows. The net present value (NPV) of a project is the sum of all future cash flows discounted at the required rate of return *minus* the present value of the cost of the investment. A positive NPV implies that the project yields more than the cost of capital and a negative one that it yields less. Other things being equal, all projects showing a positive NPV should be accepted.

Internal rate of return

An alternative approach to NPV is to calculate an investment's internal rate of return (IRR), sometimes called the yield. The IRR is the rate of return which equates the anticipated net cash flows with the initial outlay. A project is acceptable if its yield or IRR is greater than the required rate of return on the project. In the vast majority of cases the IRR method of appraising capital projects gives exactly the same accept/reject decision as NPV, although there can be differences when comparing mutually exclusive projects, in which case NPV is generally preferred.

Payback period

The payback period is the length of time required to repay the initial investment. The payback period is mainly used to test a manager's gut reaction to a project. It gives the manager a 'feel' as to the length of time cash is at risk. Payback period alone is usually inadequate to make a decision because it involves the subjective establishment of an acceptable payback period. It is often criticized as an appraisal method because it takes no account of big payoffs beyond the payback point. The payback period is very popular with managers, and when applied intelligently, combines well with the NPV method.

Risk Handling Approaches

Project risk usually denotes that the decision maker is uncertain as to the precise outcomes of a decision which involves the possibility of undesirable consequences or loss. Unlike 'pure' or 'non-speculative' risk usually discussed in the field of safety management (where there is usually no element of speculation or potential gain, i.e. the potential outcomes are loss or no loss), managers with entrepreneurial talent take certain 'strategic' or 'speculative' risks (where there are possibilities of gains as well as losses) in expectation of high returns. Unless otherwise specified, the term 'risk' in this chapter refers mainly to 'strategic risks'.

The integrative operational model for handling strategic risk developed by Ho (1990) suggests that all investment decisions in practice should go through a series of steps in a logical sequence. This requires first risk identification, then risk management and reduction, and lastly, risk evaluation—their subsequent incorporation in the final project decision process. After the measurement of risk at both project and portfolio level, a decision maker needs to judge whether some or all of the inherent pure risks can/should be avoided, reduced, tolerated or accepted. If the firm cannot tolerate some of the risks it would probably have to identify some methods to protect against unfavourable outcomes. If the project is still perceived as too risky (for example, in terms of maximum possible loss), it would be more likely to get rejected. Otherwise, the decision maker then has to make a risk–return tradeoff decision and decide to what extent the residual risks (largely probabilistic) can be accepted or compensated with a higher return. Finally, the manager must make an overall judgement about the project(s), and ultimately an accept/reject decision.

Except for some pure risk reduction methods such as diversification, acquiring insurance and vertical integration, approaches for handling strategic risk can generally be divided into two broad categories.

Simple risk adjustment (SRA)

Risk is handled by putting a more stringent requirement on financial evaluation (e.g. shortening required payback period or making more conservative cash flow estimates in the NPV or IRR model) or compensated with an intuitively determined risk premium (e.g. raising discount rate or required rate of return). This requires the analyst or decision maker to make a single best estimate of future cash flow variables, and provides a simple solution as to whether the project is or is not worth more than its cost. The major limitations of the two popular rule-of-thumb SRA methods to guard against risk can be summarized as below.

Reducing required payback period It implies (amongst other things) that risk is time related and shortening the required payback period for a project to be accepted reduces the risk. The disadvantages of payback are several. First, as mentioned earlier, focusing on near future cash flows, it ignores earnings of an investment entirely after the investment was recovered and thus does not measure the true return of an investment. Second, it fails to consider the time pattern over which funds were recovered. Third, it overemphasizes liquidity as a goal of the capital investment programme. To resolve these problems, the discounted payback period method and the use of probabilities of meeting required payback period have been suggested.

Increasing discount rate intuitively Clearly, the greater the risk, the higher will be the risk premium and discount rate in order to compensate for the added risk. There are, however, notable difficulties in applying this method. First, if risk does not increase constantly over time, using a single risk-adjusted discount rate is inappropriate. Second, setting the risk-adjusted discount rate arbitrarily without first conducting formal risk analysis or using a refined method such as the capital asset pricing model (CAPM) can cause other problems. Setting the discount rates too high may lead to missed opportunities for profit and growth. An understating of these rates may result in unprofitable investment and a fall in market value.

Overall, most SRA methods usually do not explicitly assess the risk involved and risk adjustment is sometimes made without real understanding of the inherent risk. Combining risk estimation, risk preference and risk adjustment may ignore and hide information which could be valuable in investment decisions. Also, it is possible that several SRA methods will be applied to the NPV calculation which could make the final outcomes difficult to interpret and 'ultra-conservative'. Despite their apparent ease of use, SRA methods could lead decision makers to accept decisions against their original intentions if the assumptions were not clearly understood. Nevertheless, even though not using these primarily as tools and while some firms show greater acceptance of the more sophisticated techniques, the SRA approach still offers useful supplementary tools and should not be dismissed.

Probabilistic risk analysis (PRA)

More commonly known as 'risk analysis' in the literature, this approach advocates formal measurement of investment risk before any risk adjustment is made, and the analysis itself does not incorporate the decision maker's risk preference. The approach usually involves estimating the uncertainty surrounding forecasts and then deriving probability distributions and other derived statistics for performance criteria (such as NPV and IRR). The added information gives managers better insight into the risk situation so that they can make a more effective risk/return tradeoff decision. Commonly prescribed PRA techniques include those described below.

Sensitivity analysis (SA)   This aims to identify the uncertainty factors which have a significant impact on a project's return. This technique usually involves a series of 'what-if' questions by giving a percentage change to each key assumption one at a time. It is viewed as a first step to screen those factors to be specified in probabilities in more sophisticated methods.

Probability analysis (PA)   This includes all probability-based analytical methods (decision trees, $E-V$ rule, etc.). It provides answers to questions such as what is the probability of making a given NPV or IRR? One simple example is to assign probability distributions of future period-by-period cash flows and produce a probability distribution of NPV/IRR.

Hertz-type risk simulation (RS)   This models a situation where a number of key variables which impinge on a project could vary simultaneously. A computer is usually employed to generate a series of possible returns for various combinations of values for these factors, and obtain a probability distribution achieved for the project's NPV/IRR.

More recently, the refined risk analysis approach incorporates both the risk simulation and some of the new capital asset pricing model (CAPM) concepts together in order to take account of the shareholders' preference. The CAPM measures the sensitivity of the investment's return to the changes in the return on market portfolio and it assumes only the undiversifiable risk requires a premium. As such the higher an investment's beta, the higher is its required discount rate.

It is suggested in the literature that the risk analysis approach has a valuable role to play in the process of corporate strategic planning through its input into such areas as: forecasting, firm risk positioning, environmental scanning, and managerial communication. Risk analysis enables the decision makers to examine, discuss, and eventually understand why one course of action might be more desirable than another. If applied properly, risk analysis techniques should foster managerial judgement rather than replace it in the decision-making process.

LITERATURE REVIEW ON IMPLEMENTATION ISSUES

Proponents of the PRA or 'risk analysis' approach argue that the increased quantitative information on the risks inherent in a project and the increased understanding of the precise nature of those risks lead to better decision outcomes and, ultimately, enhanced corporate performance (Hull, 1980; Hertz and Thomas, 1984). Despite the favourable attention in the prescriptive literature and a number of in-depth application case examples which attribute, in part, corporate success to the adoption of risk analysis for complex strategic projects (see, e.g. Coats and Chesser, 1982; Hertz and Thomas, 1983b; Hosseini, 1986; Karady, 1986), considerable disagreement exists in the business community as to the 'bottom-line' impact of using risk analysis. Many managers refuse to use risk analysis because there is little evidence that such use could improve corporate profitability (Hall, 1975). Until recently, the limited empirical research investigating the impact of capital budgeting sophistication on firms' performance has been mixed and inconclusive (Schall, Sundem and Geijsbeek, 1978; Pike, 1984; Haka, Gordon and Pinches, 1983). Ho and Pike (1989 and forthcoming), using an interrupted time-series experimental design, also found no evidence that the adoption of probabilistic risk analysis led to a significant change in relative capital expenditure and profitability within firms.

Another major reason for the lack of widespread acceptance of risk analysis is that it is marred by some inherent and implementation problems still to be resolved. For instance, Vandell and Stonich (1973) argue that the use of sophisticated evaluation techniques is based on erroneous assumptions that risk can and should be measured. In addition, these techniques tend to add rigidities and 'bureaucratic rituals' to the capital budgeting process that: (1) increase the resources necessary to process an attractive idea; (2) reduce the output of worthwhile investment ideas; and (3) decrease the ability of management to review the real merits of an investment proposal. They argue that most managers are suspicious of return calculations even when accompanied by measures of dispersion. In the first place, managers often disagree on what the distribution of probabilities should be, and second, there is a high probability of misuse of the information. Supporting this view, Hall (1975) also argues that managers should find ways of living with risks rather than analysing them. Similarly, Neuhauser and Viscione (1973) further added that these techniques emphasize the importance of data and often seem to downgrade managerial judgement in decision making.

One of the most significant and extensive studies of the implementation of risk analysis in business was carried out by Carter (1972) who focused on the experience of four American oil companies in using risk analysis with varying degrees of success. Carter found several persistent problems in risk analysis and his findings reveal that management's basic attitude towards risk analysis, the understanding of the approach, and the support and participation of all levels of management in the implementation process play an important part in its use and acceptance. Operational commitment, as opposed to staff curiosity, is the key to success.

More recently, in a survey of financial modelling users in the United Kingdom, McGregor (1983) found only about 10% of FCS-using firms surveyed used the risk analysis module in investment decisions. The major problems in building risk analysis models were the lack of sufficient data, the difficulties in obtaining probability estimates and understanding probability concepts, correlation assumptions between variables and across time, and the understanding of the output information.

Despite these studies, many standard prescriptions for implementing management science techniques and other planned organizational changes have been developed in the past two decades, which should help to alleviate some of those problems mentioned above (see, e.g. Lucas, 1975; Little, 1970; Ho, 1985). Others indicate the importance of top management support, manager participation and training, and the fit of the technique into the company's existing capital budgeting procedures as well as the managers' decision process. Cooper and Chapman (1987) further stress that successful risk analysis requires a flexible and easy-to-understand model, supported by sophisticated interactive decision support systems, a wide range of relevant expertise, and the experience and leadership to design and integrate models.

The many practical methods proposed for eliciting decision makers' subjective probabilities necessary for risk analysis (see, e.g. Moore and Thomas, 1975; Hull, 1980), together with the increasing use of those user-friendly microcomputer modelling packages (see, e.g. Higgins and Opdebeeck, 1984; Grinyer, 1983; McGregor, 1983), may well mean that some of the implementation problems mentioned above are far less applicable today. The risk analysis approach should, therefore, have experienced an increase in both recognition and use in recent years.

Of interest in this chapter is whether many of these implementation issues still concern UK managers, given the many technical and managerial developments in the 1980s. We also examine these managers' attitudes towards risk analysis, whether they use risk analysis for certain types of projects only, the difficulties and problems encountered, and the perceived impact and overall satisfaction of using risk analysis.

RISK ANALYSIS AND USER EXPERIENCES

For the current study, primary data were derived mainly through large-scale postal questionnaires and supplemented by interviews with 10 selected organizations. The pilot-tested questionnaires were distributed to named finance directors in the largest 350 companies in *The Times 1000* (1987), defined by sales turnover. After three mailings the whole process resulted in responses from 154 companies, 146 usable for this study (an actual response rate of 42.5%). Follow-up telephone and on-site interviews with selected respondents were carried out to seek further clarification on certain issues and obtain a more detailed picture of certain aspects of risk handling in the capital budgeting process. The industrial distribution of the sample firms presented in Table 5.1 suggests that the respondents were representative of the original sample.

Table 5.2 shows, on a six-point frequency scale (ranging from 'never' through 'sometimes' to 'very often'), the extent to which responding firms use each of the risk analysis techniques: sensitivity analysis, probability analysis, Hertz-type risk simulation, and capital asset pricing model (CAPM). These techniques are not mutually exclusive and many firms make use of a combination of methods. Respondents were also requested to list any other project risk analysis methods they employed. These included scenario modelling, earning per share (EPS) impact analysis, breakeven analysis, profitability index analysis, and several enhanced versions of sensitivity analysis.

Among the various analysis techniques listed, sensitivity analysis was found to be the most commonly used technique, with 85% using it—the majority on a regular basis. In its most basic form, sensitivity analysis requires little subjective probability estimating, and is therefore found by managers to be reliable and easy to use, particularly when supported by a computerized spreadsheet package. Such analysis entails varying input variables, one at a time, over their entire range to determine their relative effects on a project's predicted return. It provides decision makers with answers to a whole range of 'what-if' questions, and assists managers to screen and isolate the key variables requiring further evaluation.

Over one-half of the respondents (57%) use subjective probability estimates for key variables, with 30% of respondents using it regularly. Interviews with executives show that some use is made of decision trees for structuring the important factors in sequential decision problems, and analysing mutually exclusive options; but only occasionally are subjective probabilities assigned to the 'trees' for statistical analysis.

Other more advanced techniques, although highly developed in theory, are not in widespread use in the capital budgeting process. Table 5.2 clearly shows that Hertz-type risk simulation and CAPM are rarely used. In practice, as the interviews showed, the type of 'simulation' used by some firms is not necessarily

Table 5.1 Industrial breakdown of responding firms

1st digit SIC code	Industry	Sample number	%
1	Energy and oil	11	7.5
2	Mining and manufacture of metals, mineral and chemical products	25	17.1
3	Engineering and vehicles	41	28.1
4	Consumer and other manufacturing	33	22.6
5	Construction	9	6.2
6	Distribution and trade	15	10.3
7, 8	Public and business services	12	8.2
	TOTAL	146	100.0

Table 5.2 Use of risk analysis techniques (total number of responses: 142 firms)

Approach and technique	Extent of use (%)					
	Never 1	Rare 2	Little 3	Some 4	Often 5	Very often 6
1. Sensitivity analysis	15.2	11.0	10.3	23.4	17.9	22.1
2. Probability analysis	49.0	10.5	10.5	13.3	9.8	7.0
3. Risk simulation	78.0	8.5	5.0	5.7	2.8	0.0
4. Capital asset pricing model (Beta analysis)	73.6	10.0	1.4	9.3	3.6	2.1

the Hertz-type as described in existing literature (Hertz and Thomas, 1983a). These firms simply develop financial models consisting of all the key variables, with a subsequent 'simulation' of the performance measures, subject to changes in a few key assumptions. Such an approach does not necessitate the assignment of probability distributions for the key variables, as proposed in the Hertz approach. Probabilistic simulation and the CAPM technique are not new but their practical use is still in its infancy. In most firms visited, the production of a risk-return profile is still not a standard procedure in the evaluation of capital investment proposals. While many variations of risk analysis models are employed, one consistent requirement is that of flexibility in pursuing alternative analyses.

As a result of differences in project types approval levels (headquarters vs. divisions) and approval criteria, many companies are making use of multiple risk analysis methods. Over half of the sample firms use two or more formal techniques. The most popular combinations are sensitivity analysis and probability analysis (used by 20%), followed by all four techniques (used by 12%) and sensitivity analysis-probability analysis-risk simulation (used by 6%). The majority of companies using simulation also employ probability and sensitivity analysis in the decision-making process. For example, two firms visited for in-depth study used sensitivity analysis to identify key variables and subsequently used probability analysis of cash flows to find the best alternative. A simulation could then be conducted to build a risk profile and classify the project risk.

Respondents were also further asked to identify the three primary methods that they use to reduce risk during both project implementation and operation, given a choice of seven risk reduction methods commonly described in the literature. Table 5.3 shows that the three most popular risk reduction methods are 'maintaining tighter project control' (86%), 'diversifying the risk' (53%), and 'modifying policies and staffing within the company' (41%). Other risk reduction methods mentioned include conducting market research, phased approval/development, guaranteed supply agreement with customers, taskforce approach,

Table 5.3 Risk reduction and control (total number of responses: 143)

Risk reduction method	Percentage of total respondents
1. Maintain tighter control of project implementation	86.4
2. Diversify the risk (e.g. joint venture)	53.0
3. Modify policies and staffing of the company	40.9
4. Subcontract critical parts of project	31.0
5. Operate a contingency fund in the event of need	23.5
6. Secure market via vertical integration	15.9
7. Acquire commercial insurance coverage	8.3

obtaining 'expert' advice prior to implementation, and minimizing 'upfront' commitment.

To ensure that the respondents' perceptions are based on real experience, only organizations which used or planned to use probability analysis and/or risk simulation were included in the study of implementation problems below. In other words, 'PRA' or 'risk analysis' users in this study refer to those who formally and systematically determine the probabilistic distributions and its derived statistics of a project's performance.

CHANGE IN ROLE OF RISK ANALYSIS

Prior surveys (e.g. Pike, 1989) suggest that the use of risk analysis is growing, even if at a slow rate. To confirm this trend before examining other implementation issues, respondents were asked if the importance of risk analysis in their firms had changed over the last five years. They were then asked to estimate the changes over the next five years. The percentages of responses to the question are summarized in Table 5.4. A total of 41% of respondents stated that over the past five years risk analysis had become more important—less than 2% perceiving it to be less important over the same period. For the next five years, over half of the sample firms expect risk analysis to become more important, while no firm predicts it to become less important.

Interview discussions revealed that the greatest change is in the increased use of microcomputers for risk measurement. The interest of firms in greater use of risk analysis has been apparent, with additional emphasis on the use of probability concepts. If the observed trend continues (see Pike and Sharp, 1989), formal risk analysis may become as standard a technique for larger projects as discounted cash flow methods are today.

Table 5.4 Changes in the role of risk analysis

	More important	No change	Less important
1. Over the last five years risk analysis has been	41.4%	57.1%	1.4%
2. Over the next five years risk analysis will become	54.0%	46.0%	0.0%

CHARACTERISTICS OF PROJECTS USING RISK ANALYSIS

Sample firms claiming use of risk analysis techniques were asked whether they use the techniques for certain types of projects only, and if so, what are the specific reasons for their use. Among the 39 risk simulation users who replied, 35 reported that they use simulation for certain project decisions, while 4 use it for all investment decisions (see Table 5.5).

Analysis of these results suggests that the size of a project and its complexity of implementation are the most important factors in the choice of risk analysis technique. This indicates that the application of risk analysis is not primarily correlated with the type of project (i.e. replacement, obligatory, strategic, etc.) but rather the use is very much dependent on management's perception of risk within the specific project. Payback period and track record of the project sponsor appear to be of relatively little importance in the choice of techniques. Among the 'other reasons' mentioned were: high uncertainty of cash flow estimate, 'territory', past experience of similar projects, and required rate of return.

Clearly, while the risk analysis approach is widely advocated and can be applied on a 'blanket-basis', the study findings suggest that usage is very much situation dependent. The main criteria adopted being that of size and complexity.

PRIMARY USERS OF RISK ANALYSIS

This section aims to identify the personnel who actually use the risk analysis the most and to determine whether they are specialists or functional managers.

Table 5.5 Reasons for using risk simulation techniques

Reason	Percentage of total ($N = 39$)
1. Size of projects	73.7
2. Complexity of projects	73.7
3. New product development	47.4
4. New market	36.8
5. Payback period of project	26.3
6. Sponsor of projects	5.3

Table 5.6   Primary users of risk analysis

User level	Number of respondents	Percentage of total
Departmental managers	42	40.8
Budgeting/planning staff	34	33.0
Top executives/board	21	20.4
EDP/OR staff	1	1.0
Others	5	4.8
	103	100.0

Table 5.6 shows that the departmental/divisional managers involved in the project decision process use risk analysis most widely (41% of the total responses), followed by budgeting/corporate planning staff (33%) and top executives (20%). Only 1% of firms have electronic data processing/operations research (EDP/OR) staff as the primary users of risk analysis. Discussions with executives revealed that modelling for risk analysis is usually carried out by a project team under the general guidance of a steering committee composed of representatives from various interest groups. In many cases, there is a combination of financial analysts, accountants, and EDP personnel, who together build the model.

These results are indeed encouraging; they indicate that in over one-half of the companies using risk analysis, line managers rather than the EDP/OR specialists, are using the models. The use of risk analysis by top management was also impressive. There is much evidence in the literature that senior manager-user participation is important in the success of any computer systems development and its implementation.

ATTITUDES TOWARDS RISK ANALYSIS

One of the factors affecting the likelihood that managers will accept and beneficially employ risk analysis, is their underlying attitudes towards risk analysis (Hull, 1980). Such attitudes may well depend on their personal risk attitude and experiences of past investment decision outcomes. The survey examined such attitudes using a measurement of five items which pertain to the respondents' general attitudes towards several aspects of risk analysis. Respondents were asked to indicate how much they agreed or disagreed with each item ('1' = strongly agree, '6' = strongly disagree).

The average responses for each item and the overall attitudes are presented in Table 5.7. The respondents generally expressed a slightly favourable attitude regarding risk analysis (overall mean = 4.2). Focusing on responses with scores

Table 5.7 Attitudes towards formal risk analysis (total number of responses 141 firms)

	Strongly disagree				Strongly agree		
	1	2	3	4	5	6	
Attitude statement				%			Mean
1 Capital budgeting involves uncertainty	0.0	2.8	5.0	16.3	27.0	48.9	5.14
2 I am personally in favour of formal risk analysis	0.7	4.3	15.8	28.8	30.2	20.1	4.47
3 Managers prefer to make a range of estimates rather than a single-point estimate for an uncertainty factor	2.1	10.6	16.3	29.8	29.1	12.1	4.09
4 Project uncertainty requires formal risk analysis	0.7	9.9	29.1	27.1	25.5	7.1	3.89
5 Project uncertainty can be measured quantitatively	3.5	14.9	29.8	32.6	12.8	1.4	3.36
Overall mean:				4.179;	SD = 0.712		

of '5' or '6', it was found that while almost 76% of respondents agreed that capital budgeting involves uncertainty, only about 14% agreed that project uncertainty can be measured quantitatively and only 33% that project uncertainty requires formal risk analysis. Despite the lack of enthusiasm for risk measurement, over 40% of respondents agreed that managers prefer to make a range of estimates rather than a single-point estimate for an uncertainty factor.

The implication from both the survey and interview findings is that, for risk analysis to be effective, first, management should acknowledge that they are making a decision that involves uncertainty, and more importantly, should recognize that uncertainty requires some formal analysis. Second, management's understanding of the approach may greatly affect these attitudes. While it may not be necessary to have formal training programmes, at least managerial interaction and involvement during all phases of the risk analysis process appear to be important to ensure understanding and acceptance. Interview findings revealed that user acceptance can be enhanced when managers realize that the information provided conforms to their decision process and can be helpful to them in their decision responsibilities. Future studies may investigate the influence of other personal factors, such as age, personality, experience, and risk-taking attitude on a decision maker's attitude towards formal risk analysis.

It is important to recognize that these attitudes are not static and may change as social, technological, organizational and investment conditions change. As business competition becomes more intense, environmental changes become more difficult to forecast, and managers become more conversant with information technology, they may demand more risk analysis information. Some evidence of this has emerged from this study, particularly among those young business-school-trained managers who are directly involved in capital investment decisions.

DIFFICULTIES AND PROBLEMS IN USE OF RISK ANALYSIS

A number of barriers or problem areas were identified in the literature as well as in the preliminary stages of this study which would block the effective use of risk analysis in companies. These barriers occur both in the organization itself and in its management.

Respondents were asked the extent to which they have experienced each of the problems listed in Table 5.8 in the implementation and use of risk analysis in their companies. Again, a six-point scale ranging from 'not at all' to 'very much' was used. In general, seven out of the eleven problems listed can be considered as common, as at least half of the respondents rated these seven problems as 'some', 'much' or 'very much'. These are:

- Managers' understanding of techniques (69%)
- Obtaining input estimates (62%)
- Time involvements (60.8%)
- Cost-justification of techniques (57%)
- Human/organizational resistance (56%)
- Tradeoff between risk and return (56%)
- Understanding output of analysis (55%)

For the purpose of analysis, these problems can be divided into two types: inherent and implementation problems. Among the inherent problems, Table 5.8 indicates that the respondents perceived the problem of obtaining input estimates to be the most important . Over 31% of respondents reported they have had 'much' or 'very much' experience of this problem in their companies. For new strategic-type projects, project estimates are usually based on subjective judgement made by managers. Discussion with executives revealed that 3-point estimates are most popular, although 5-point estimates and normal distribution estimates are also used occasionally. Particular difficulties mentioned by the managers are the quantification of qualitative factors, measuring

Table 5.8 Barriers to implementation and use of risk analysis (total number of responses: 137 firms)

	Not at all 1	Rare 2	Little 3	Some 4	Much 5	Very much 6	Mean
			%				
Inherent problem encountered							
1 Obtaining input estimates	5.2	11.9	20.7	31.3	23.0	8.1	3.79
2 Time involvement	3.7	14.1	21.5	32.6	23.0	5.2	3.73
3 Understanding output of analysis	3.6	16.8	24.1	25.5	22.6	7.3	3.69
4 Tradeoff between risk and return	6.2	13.8	23.8	33.8	22.3	0.0	3.52
5 Managers cannot agree on estimates/judgement	5.2	22.2	29.6	31.9	10.4	0.7	3.22
6 Cost-justification of techniques	15.8	17.3	19.5	30.8	15.8	10.8	3.16
Implementation problem encountered							
7 Managers' understanding of techniques	2.2	14.6	13.9	35.0	23.4	10.9	3.96
8 Human/organizational resistance	3.7	16.2	23.5	35.3	14.7	6.6	3.61
9 Finding suitable methods	9.6	18.4	24.3	27.2	16.9	3.7	3.35
10 Lack of top management support	11.2	19.4	21.6	24.6	17.9	5.2	3.34
11 Lack of computing resources and assistance	25.6	23.3	25.6	17.3	5.3	3.0	2.62

interrelationships between variables, personal biases, and over-conservatism, etc.

Effective probabilistic risk analysis requires substantial amounts of internal as well as external data. Sample firms in this survey were also asked to indicate how often the various types of desired information for risk analysis and investment decisions was obtained from their formal information systems (see Ho and Pike, 1991). The results indicate that the project-specific data, such as estimates of cash flow, cost of capital, and economic life were seen to be quite adequate by the respondents. The vast majority of these data are collected either by updating previous forecasts or from internal historical record files. However, information on macroeconomics, competitors' behaviour and post-audit review was found to be far less adequate than other project-specific data. External future-information in many firms had to be collected through other unstructured, inconsistent and less reliable channels. It is believed that without a supportive information system, managers would find it very difficult to carry out any sophisticated or meaning risk analysis.

Interpreting and use of output information is another major problem; about 30% of respondents seeing it as 'much' or 'very much' a problem. Other comments regarding output include too much data to read, improper interpretation of output, and understanding limitations of the approach. As far as time and cost are concerned, some executives expressed that the costs are insignificant in terms of computer usage and other tangible costs. A more significant cost is incurred in assigning estimates in the form of personal judgement to be used in the analysis.

Regarding the implementation problems, Table 5.8 indicates the firms are most concerned with managers' knowledge of risk analysis, and least restricted by the problem of a lack of computing resources. Managers with little quantitative background would find the concepts of probability distribution, expected value and variance, difficult to use. Carter (1972) also found that inadequate knowledge could cause serious problems in both morale and operation. Although many executives appreciate the potential of risk analysis, they have to become more familiar with the technique before it can become a part of their capital budgeting system. It seems that knowledge of risk analysis has not reached many intended practising managers through the proper channels.

About 21% found 'managerial resistance' and 'lack of top management support' 'much' or 'very much' of a problem. Resistance problems are possibly due to a lack of communication between managers and the OR/budgeting specialists who implement risk analysis, in addition to the lack of manager-user involvement in the implementation process. Top management (including board directors) also play a vital role in risk analysis—they are the final authority for acceptance or rejection of new evaluation methods and investment proposals.

While the findings indicate that few companies suffer from lack of computing resources, many companies still only use deterministic models and very limited 'built-in' decision support functions of the financial modelling package (such as computing a project's NPV/IRR and conducting 'what-if' analyses). The study found that the probabilistic risk simulation module is used less frequently than most of the other functions, and indeed in over half of the companies is never used. Over 40% of user firms do not have access to external on-line databases, and only about 15% of respondents frequently use a database management system.

Summarizing these responses, while firms experience a number of barriers to the introduction and use of risk analysis, two main difficulties emerge: obtaining input estimates and understanding of the technique. This indicates only moderate progress in overcoming those persistent problems which have been recognized in the literature over the last two decades. However, these two problems seem increasingly solvable given the continuous improvement in information technology and our understanding of cognitive psychology. It should also be noted that the problems discussed above should be balanced by the benefits experienced, and other favourable responses by respondents, described in the next section.

PERCEIVED IMPACTS AND USER SATISFACTION OF RISK ANALYSIS

Probabilistic risk analysis can offer numerous benefits to managers and to the firm as a whole. For example, Hertz and Thomas (1983a) advocate that the use of risk analysis provides a systematic and logical approach to investment decision making, helps communication within the organization, allows managerial judgement to be presented in a meaningful way, and ultimately improves firm performance (e.g. Karady, 1986). However, criticisms of risk analysis, such as rendering proposals more difficult to accept, reducing managers' enthusiasm to generate investment ideas, and thus leading to lower capital expenditure, were also found in the literature (e.g. Vandell and Stonich, 1973; Hall, 1975). To examine such an important issue, nine specific items covering both tangible and intangible types of impacts were used in the questionnaire. It expands the concepts of risk analysis effectiveness to include 'process impacts' in addition to the commonly used 'outcome impacts'.

Table 5.9 reveals that the majority of respondents are reasonably happy with their use of risk analysis. The only two statements for which there was no reasonably clear consensus of concern were whether the use of risk analysis would improve (1) communication among the managers involved, and (2) ultimate project performance. In general, however, more managers agreed rather than disagreed with statements of a positive or favourable impact nature. With statements of a negative or unfavourable nature, more managers indicated

Table 5.9   Perceived impacts of risk analysis (total number of responses 114 firms)

Formal risk analysis	1 Strongly disagree	2	3	4	5 Strongly agree	6 (%)	Mean
Positive impacts							
1 Providing a useful insight into the project	0.7	2.8	10.6	29.1	38.3	18.4	4.57
2 Improves quality of investment decisions	0.7	0.7	12.4	35.0	38.0	13.1	4.48
3 Increases confidence in investment decisions	0.0	2.1	13.6	34.3	39.3	10.7	4.30
4 Improves efficiency of investment decisions	0.7	3.6	23.2	38.4	23.2	10.9	4.12
5 Enhances communication among managers	2.9	16.5	33.1	29.5	14.4	3.6	3.47
6 Improves ultimate project performance	5.8	17.5	29.2	30.7	11.7	5.1	3.40
Negative impacts							
7 Makes it more difficult to accept proposals	6.6	28.7	30.1	25.7	8.8	0.0	3.01
8 Reduces managers' enthusiasm to generate/sponsor projects	8.0	32.1	28.5	20.4	9.5	1.5	2.96
9 Leads to lower capital expenditure	9.8	30.1	29.3	20.3	9.8	0.8	2.93

disagreement than agreement. The majority of respondents agreed that risk analysis is particularly useful for providing an insight into the project decision (mean = 4.57), improving quality of investment decisions, and increasing confidence in investment decisions.

Overall, the survey findings show that the perceived impact of risk analysis on the investment decision process has been substantial, but its impact on the decision outcomes is less conclusive. Most respondents tend to agree that formal risk analysis has offered useful information to the decision maker in making his/her decision. In addition, even though the decision makers find risk analysis more difficult to use, it appears that the new information give rise to greater confidence in the final decision.

In order to assess the overall effectiveness of risk analysis, users were further asked to rate their overall satisfaction with the risk analysis techniques. Table 5.10 shows the summarized responses from managers. The majority of users are moderately pleased with their use of formal risk analysis (66.7% rated risk analysis in the top half of the scale). Users typically rated risk analysis better

Table 5.10   Satisfaction with using risk analysis

% Distribution								
1 I	2 I	3 I	4 I	5 I	6* I	Mean	Median	SD
0.0	8.1	25.3	47.5	18.2	1.0	3.79	4	0.872

* 1 = not satisfied; 6 = very satisfied.

than '3' (fairly satisfied) giving the approach an acceptable 3.79 average satisfaction rating. However, the results also show that many users are still ambivalent to risk analysis and there is much room for further improvement of the application.

The findings in this study suggest that, while various problems of risk analysis do exist, they do not negate the usefulness of risk analysis for many companies. In many decision situations, the qualitative benefits of using risk analysis were perceived to be substantial. This, in fact, supports Carter's (1972) observation that 'perhaps the greater benefits of risk analysis come from the preparation of the model, not from the results' (p. 78).

DISCUSSIONS AND CONCLUSIONS

This chapter has examined managers' preferences for handling risk within capital budgeting contexts, based on the authors' survey conducted in 146 larger-sized UK organizations. The main finding is that firms prefer relatively simple risk adjustment and sensitivity analysis. While risk analysis is more commonly employed on larger, more complex projects, there is still a sizeable gap between normative theory and observed practice. The major limitations most frequently found for the application of risk analysis are (1) obtaining input estimates and (2) managers' inadequate understanding of the risk analysis approach. However, the findings revealed that most managers view risk in capital investment decisions as important, and over half of the respondents expressed favourable attitudes regarding formal risk analysis. The major problem is that they simply do not possess the required knowledge to apply formal approaches, or are unable to find an approach which is systematic, easy to apply and cost effective.

Several lessons can also be drawn from the study. First, risk analysis should formalize managers' judgement about project uncertainty in a more precise way and also allow them to modify their judgement in the light of new information or 'second thoughts'. Second, regarding the problem of collecting probability estimates, further development and refinement of practical methods for eliciting the subjective probabilities necessary for risk analysis are required. With some prior discussion and training, we believe that such assessment can generally be obtained. As executives become more comfortable in dealing with outputs from these models, managers should be less concerned with the apparent over-emphasis on exactness and more concerned with the underlying assumptions. Misuse of risk analysis information can also be minimized as knowledge of the techniques increases.

More recently, the increasing widespread use of microcomputers in financial modelling packages has added to the potential, ease of use and efficiency of risk analysis in capital budgeting. Data are more readily available and can be analysed with more flexible statistical techniques and models in an interactive, end-user computing environment. This makes it easier to understand and use risk analysis in a more cost-effective manner, and with less dependence on traditional OR specialists. Gordon and Pinches (1984) and Srinivasan and Kim (1986) argue that a computer-based decision support system (DSS) environment provides the kind of conditions within which theoretically preferred risk analysis methods can become more effective.

The many implementation problems discussed earlier in this chapter, while being more procedural in nature, certainly require attention. For instance, more studies into the motivation for selecting particular types of risk models and information will be valuable. Other related research, which the authors believe to be worthy of further investigation, includes the extent to which (1) the methods of forecasting and (2) the presentation/manipulability of the models affect risk analysis effectiveness.

Overall, the study provides a timely review of risk analysis practice in capital budgeting in the United Kingdom, and the perceived barriers and benefits. Some possible suggestions to bridge the gap between theory and practice were discussed. These findings may help executives to re-evaluate and improve their own risk handling practice in the light of the revealed practices and problems of others. They also provide important research insights into several important aspects of risk management.

ACKNOWLEDGEMENT

This chapter is adapted, by permission of the editor, from 'Risk analysis in capital budgeting: barriers and benefits', published in *OMEGA*, **19**(4), 235–245 (1991).

REFERENCES

Carter, E.E. (1972). What are the risks in risk analysis? *Harvard Business Review*, July–August, 72–82.

Coats, P.K. and Chesser, D.C. (1982). Coping with business risk through probabilistic financial statements, *Simulation*, 111–21.

Cooper, D. and Chapman, C. (1987). *Risk Analysis for Large Projects: Model, Methods and Cases*, John Wiley & Sons.

Gordon, L.A. and Pinches, G.E. (1984). *Improving Capital Budgeting: A Decision Support System Approach*, Addison-Wesley, Reading, Mass.

Grinyer, P.H. (1983). Financial modelling for planning in the UK, *Long Range Planning*, October, 58-73.

Haka, S.F., Gordon, L.A. and Pinches, G.E. (1983). Sophisticated capital budgeting selection techniques and firm performance, *The Accounting Review*, October, 651-69.

Hall, W.K. (1975). Why risk analysis isn't working, *Long Range Planning*, **18**, December, 25-9.

Hertz, D.B. and Thomas H. (1983a). *Risk Analysis and its Applications*, John Wiley and Sons, NY.

Hertz, D.B. and Thomas, H. (1983b). Decisions and risk analysis in new product and facilities planning problems, *Sloan Management Review*, winter, 17-31.

Hertz, D.B. and Thomas, H. (1984). *Practical Risk Analysis*, John Wiley and Sons, NY.

Higgins, J.C. and Opdebeeck, E.J. (1984). The microcomputer as a tool in financial planning and control: some survey results, *Accounting and Business Research*, autumn, 333-40.

Ho, S.S.M. (1985). An integrated framework for participative system design: issues and implications, *Hong Kong Computer Journal*, **1**(2), February, 30-40.

Ho, S.S.M. (1990). An integrative operational framework for strategic risk analysis, in K. Borcherding, O.I. Larichv and D.M. Messick (eds), *Contemporary Issues in Decision Making*, Elsevier-North Holland, pp. 305-14.

Ho, S.S.M. and Pike, R.H. (1989). The impact of adopting risk analysis in capital budgeting on firm performance: a time-analysis analysis in *Proceedings of the International Symposium on Risk Management and Corporate Finance*, European Institute for Advanced Studies in Management, Brussels, Belgium.

Ho, S.S.M. and Pike, R.H. (1991). Information systems and decision supports for capital budgeting decisions, Working Paper, Faculty of Business Administration, The Chinese University of Hong Kong, 1991.

Ho, S.S.M. and Pike, R.H. (1992). Adoption of probabilistic risk analysis in capital budgeting and corporate investment, *Journal of Business Finance and Accounting*, **19**(3), 387-401.

Hosseini, J. (1986). Decision analysis and its application in the choice between two wildcat oil ventures, *Interfaces*, **16**(2), March-April, 75-85.

Hull, J.C. (1980). *The Evaluation of Risk in Business Investment*, Pergamon, London.

Karady, G. (1986). Risk analysis—a power planning tool for decision makers, *Today's Executive*, **9**(1), winter, 1-18.

Klammer T.P. and Walker, M.C. (1984). The continuing increase in the use of sophisticated capital budgeting techniques, *California Management Review*, fall, 137-51.

Little, J.D.C. (1970). Models and managers: the concepts of a decision calculus, *Management Science*, **16**(8), April, B466-85.

Lucas, H. (1975). *Why Information Systems Fail*, Columbia University Press, NY.

McGregor, J.M. (1983). What users think about computer models, *Long Range Planning*, **16**(5), 45-57.

Moore, P.G. and Thomas, H. (1975). Measuring uncertainty, *OMEGA*, **3**(6), 657-73.

Neuhauser, J.J. and Viscione, J.A. (1973). How managers feel about advanced capital budgeting methods, *Management Review*, November, 16-22.

Pike, R.H. (1984). Sophisticated capital budgeting systems and their corporate performance, *Managerial and Decision Economics*, **5**(21), 91-7.

Pike, R.H. (1989). Do sophisticated capital budgeting approaches improve investment decision making effectiveness? *The Engineering Economist*, winter.

Pike, R.H. and Sharp, J.A. (1989). Trends in the use of management science techniques in capital budgeting and prospects for future uptake, *Managerial and Decision Economics*.

Schall, D.L., Sundem, G.L. and Geijsbeek, W.R. (1978). Survey and analysis of capital budgeting methods, *Journal of Finance*, **XXXIII**(1) March, 281-6.

Srinivasan, V. and Kim, Y.H. (1986). A strategic capital budgeting decision support system, Working Paper, Northeastern University.

Vandell, R.F. and Stonich, R.D. (1973). Capital budgeting: theory or results? *Financial Executive*, August, 46-56.

Chapter 6

Industrial Risk: Safety by Design

G. M. Ballard
Director, Safety and Reliability Directorate (SRD)
UK AEA Technology

ABSTRACT

A number of well publicized accidents over the recent years have confirmed that our industrial activities involve significant risk for both the public and industrial staff. There exists, however, a well developed and well tried framework for identifying and minimizing potential hazards. In this chapter the concept of 'safety by design' and some critical issues arising in the design of industrial plant, including the reliability of engineering systems, the reliability of people and the management of risk are discussed.

INTRODUCTION

Seveso (1976), Bhopal (1984), Chernobyl (1986) and Piper Alpha (1988) were all major accidents which attracted extensive media coverage. The number of fatalities, and in some cases the environmental damage, were unacceptable. These accidents serve to remind us that safety in industrial operation cannot be taken for granted. Whilst it is inevitable that some accidents will occur, the frequency of occurrence can be reduced and consequences mitigated. All engineers and managers in industry need to appreciate the importance of proper approaches to safety and how to implement appropriate safety policy.

Following major accidents, it may appear that safety procedures and policies are determined by 'trial and error'. The faults from the past are eliminated in the

Risk: Analysis, Assessment and Management. Edited by J. Ansell and F. Wharton.
© 1992 John Wiley & Sons Ltd.

future. For many reasons this is not an acceptable way of proceeding. The public is rightly concerned that better procedures should be developed. Concern has given rise to legislation which requires increasingly a more structured approach to safety. The costs of plant failures are so high that they often dominate the consequences of any accident, even when high compensation to those killed or injured is taken into account.

Safety and environmental concerns therefore are added to the demands already placed on industry to be financially efficient and profitable. At times it may appear that to pursue these aims at the same time is impossible because of the conflicting requirements. In practice, since they are all imperatives for long-term survival, there can be no conflict and the task is to find the right balance. Good managers will generally have access to extensive 'technology' to help them with decisions on the business performance. They may be less familiar with the 'technology' available to integrate safety and environmental issues into the business operations. The techniques which have been developed to ensure the safety, reliability and environmental management are commonly grouped into risk analysis. These techniques have much to offer the business manager and there are strong similarities in principle to the management of financial risks. In this chapter an overview of risk analysis will be given.

As well as analysing existing risks there is a need to develop approaches which will eliminate or reduce risks from new plant operations. Such approaches are encompassed within the 'safety by design' concept. The three elements of 'safety by design' are, in order of effectiveness of defence, inherent safety, engineering safety and procedural safety. These will be explored in this chapter.

Procedural safety largely depends on the action of the company's staff at all levels. It has been recognized for some time that the role of the plant operative and maintenance personnel is particularly crucial to safety, either in reducing the likelihood of an accident or in minimizing its subsequent effects. There is a need therefore to take account of the operative during the design stage. This includes recognizing how human beings can 'fail'. Given its importance we will investigate this issue in somewhat more detail in the chapter.

THE NEED FOR ACTION

The recent Control of Industrial Major Accident Hazards (CIMAH) regulations, following the Seveso accident in Italy, illustrate the new requirements legislated for plant operators (see Table 6.1). The key element of these requirements is to be aware of the potential hazards and to determine the likely frequency and consequences of such hazards. The key requirement is that a plant manager must be able to demonstrate that he has acted responsibly in controlling the risk from his plant.

Table 6.1   The safety case

i.	Identify the nature and scale of the potential hazards.
ii.	Give a description of the arrangements for the safe operation of the plant.
iii.	Demonstrate that management appreciates the major hazards potential and considers the controls are adequte.
iv.	Provide information on the hazards and risks for offsite emergency plans.

Awareness of a potential hazard to both plant, employees and the public is central to devising a proper safety policy. Some hazards are reasonably obvious, though even then action must be taken. Too frequently, even with obviously hazardous substances such as flammable or explosive materials, accidents occur because of lack of adequate safety measures. In part, this sometimes stems from a lack of appreciation of the real magnitude of the potential consequences; the SRD slide library contains graphic examples of the havoc that can be caused from, for example, liquefied petroleum gas (LPG)/liquid natural gas (LNG) storage tanks which can travel large distances like rockets. The destruction at Flixborough following a cyclohexane explosion also amply demonstrates the potentially catastrophic forces which can be unleashed.

Apart from the obvious hazards there are more subtle hazards which designers and operatives need to be aware of: dust explosions within grain silos can be catastrophic; molten metals poured into liquid may explode; malfunctioning robots or robots which operate unexpectedly can cause considerable damage to life and limb.

The CIMAH regulations stress the need to study the consequences of the accidents. A liquefied petroleum gas (LPG) sphere may seem relatively harmless until engulfed in a fire which can lead to an enormous fireball as the result of a BLEVE (boiling liquid expanding vapour explosion). The Piper Alpha platform, a massive structure, was totally wrecked by heat and blast from a fire. The loss of life was also considerable. A larger death toll resulted from the Mexican oil and gas fire.

The above examples, and many more, demonstrate the potential risks on various scales that exist in many industrial plants. The realization of potential danger is important but there also needs to be appropriate action taken to reduce the potential and mitigate the consequences. This is the field of risk analysis.

RISK ANALYSIS TECHNOLOGY

Financial risk management involves identifying the potential gains and losses of activities, and taking action to minimize the potential 'downside'. A similar strategy can be developed for safety though the terminology may differ.

Criteria

Goals and objectives must be set. These business goals for safety and environmental impact should wherever possible be quantitative and measurable. They are analogous to turnover, cost and profit and in many cases have a very material effect on profits. The types of measures that have been used in the past include fatal accident rate (FAR), lost time accidents and major accident frequency. Having decided what is being managed, the next stage is to define the arrangement for management including personal responsibilities, monitoring and auditing. There is now considerable experience within a range of industries which provides the basis for 'good practice' guidelines for safety management. Under the auspices of the SRD a very helpful guide has recently been published.

Operations Analysis

As with financial management there is a need to consider the overall business or plant and not just particular projects or pieces of equipment. Decisions cannot be made in isolation without reference to potentially broader implications.

A systematic and structured framework of analysis can be provided. The stages are:

- Comprehensive identification of potential problems.
- Clear analysis of why the problem would occur.
- Quantitative statements concerning likelihood and consequences.
- Prioritization of areas for improvement.

Awareness of potential problems, safety hazards or environmental impacts, is the crucial first stage to be addressed at the design stage of any project. The very large cost of redesigning an operating plant because of the discovery of a hazard should provide sufficient incentive. Fortunately there are many identification techniques such as hazard and operability studies (HAZOP), failure modes and effect analysis (FMEA) and hazard checklist which can be used, working from design documents such as piping and instrumentation diagrams, operating instructions, etc. The output of such analyses is a list of events which might constitute a hazard to workers or the public. At this stage, no attempt is made to estimate frequency or consequences. The process is essentially a structured brainstorming session aimed in a different direction to the approach taken by designers. The designer is concerned with making a process work efficiently, the risk analyst is concerned with what may go wrong. As with any engineering discipline this requires knowledge and experience to do it effectively.

The next step is a more detailed analysis of the events which may lead to any of the hazards identified. In a typical logic tree development, a high level fault tree (see Figure 6.1) is constructed for major hazard categories. The fault tree uses the engineering design to systematically track back from the hazard to potential cause. The detail in the fault tree will depend greatly on the stage of the design process, but ultimately the aim is to link hazards directly to events involving component failures and human actions.

Even at this stage of the risk analysis, many design deficiencies, which might otherwise have been overlooked, will become obvious because of the systematic nature of the techniques. The analysis uncovers areas which were overlooked or misunderstood in the goal-orientated design activity. Once an issue is highlighted, the designer/operator will usually acknowledge the inadequacy and provide modification.

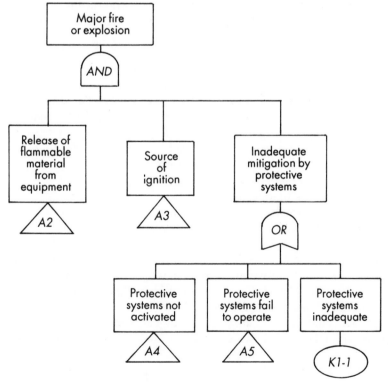

Figure 6.1 High level fault tree

Having established that a potential problem exists and having investigated how the problem may occur, further analysis is needed to decide on appropriate action. In many cases the action may be obvious and indisputable. In other cases there may be difficulties concerning the perceived magnitude of the consequences (financial, worker, public) or the likelihood of occurrence. Therefore, either aspect may now be investigated further. Sometimes more detailed calculation will show that while there are potentially serious consequences, in practice specific arrangements can be made which render the potential outcome of no significance.

More usually, there will need to be a careful investigation into the likely frequency of the hazard. Using the fault trees developed to understand the possible event sequence leading to the hazard, it is generally possible to obtain a quantitative estimate of the frequency/probability. Such calculations rely significantly on reliability data from engineering equipment, past records on the occurrence of incidents and data on human reliability. The availability of these data is often limited but generally a combination of actual data and sound engineering judgement can produce satisfactory estimates.

Analysis of either hazard consequence or frequency will often be sufficient to suggest a decision on action based on existing design criteria, but more generally there is a need to calculate 'risk'. In industry risk is generally defined as:

$$\text{Risk} = \text{Frequency} \times \text{Consequence}$$

This form provides a convenient measure of risk in that to be acceptable from the safety viewpoint, events which happen often must have a low consequence, or events involving serious consequences must be rare. Based on the above analyses a calculation is made of the risk from each accident scenario or the overall risk of any particular hazard. At this stage, there may need to be a judgement against a particular risk criterion or goal. More fruitfully, the risk analysis will provide information which shows:

- a relative ranking of different hazards;
- the relative importance of systems/equipment which contribute to hazards;
- the potential gains to be made by improving the reliability of the equipment.

This information gives a basis on which to decide what action is appropriate in individual cases, and, most importantly, highlights the priorities with which resources should be provided to address any individual improvement.

Risk analysis thus allows a design to be evaluated and provides a framework within which alternative modifications can be proposed and quantitatively compared. It is important, however, to appreciate the limitations of quantitative information. Frequently there will be uncertainty in such information concerning the physical processes, equipment reliability, human actions, etc. This uncertainty is *not* created by risk analysis but is a reflection of the state of our engineering knowledge. Risk analysis serves to highlight uncertainties so that their effect can be appreciated rather than hidden in superficially exact rules or judgements.

The most powerful tool at this stage for understanding the effect of uncertainties is sensitivity analysis. The risk assessment results can be examined to see how sensitive the results are to changes in individual assumptions or pieces of data. Thus, it may be that some data is uncertain but in practice the effect on the risk is insignificant: in this case, it may be shown that the results are very robust against uncertainty. In other cases, it may be that the uncertainty is insignificant providing the width of variation is limited to some specific extent; analysis may show that this extent of uncertainty is unlikely to be exceeded. It may be that the result is very sensitive to uncertainty in some parameters; in this case there is clearly a need to either reduce the uncertainty by data collection, experimentation, etc, or sometimes more effectively, remove the source of uncertainty by re-design of the plant.

'Safety by Design'

Quantification yields a ranking of risks involved with operation. It may indicate those potential hazards which require further action. The task is then to achieve a plant which is safe by design. There are generally three types of activity, presented in order of effectiveness as defensive measures:

(1)   Inherent safety.
(2)   Engineered safety.
(3)   Procedural safety.

Inherent safety

Inherent safety implies designing a plant that is safe because its characteristics either prevent a hazard or ensure that the hazard is minor. For example, where toxic or explosive chemicals are used as feedstock in the manufacture of some final product, it may be possible to use less toxic or non-toxic feedstock, although this may involve a cost penalty. In the case of intermediate chemicals which may be toxic, it may be possible to change the process to avoid producing the chemical. Alternatively, by substituting a process which creates and uses the toxic material as required, it may be possible to avoid the need for storage. Obviously explosives should be kept at the required separation distances. While inherent safety is clearly the most effective response to a potential hazard, it is often not possible to implement or too expensive. Clearly aircraft are inherently subject to the force of gravity and plants processing oil and gas inherently handle fire and explosion hazards.

Engineered safety

The next recourse is therefore to accept that major potential hazards exist but try to add engineering features to the plant which will prevent the accident occurring or mitigate the consequence of any accident that does occur. This is the most common aspect of 'safety by design', where plant is perceived to be dangerous. Oil tanks can be designed to contain spills and thus not let fire extend to other tanks. Water deluge systems can be added to LNG tanks or HF tanks. Protection and alarm systems or interlocks may be installed to prevent dangerous plant configurations. Engineering safety can be very effective but it does require reliable systems to ensure that protection really is available when needed.

Procedural safety

Finally, procedural safety, which is frequently the response to risks which were not or only poorly perceived at the design stage. Safety is then an afterthought — an add-on. This simply involves establishing rules and regulations (procedures) for operations so that although a hazard exists it is hopefully controlled by the people operating the plant. A typical example is the introduction of permits to work systems when plants enter abnormal states for maintenance and are then not protected by the normal safety instrumentation and control systems.

I have described three recognized responses to potential hazards. It is necessary though to use risk analysis techniques to ensure a comprehensive and appropriate response to hazards to satisfy CIMAH requirements.

PEOPLE AND SYSTEMS

Procedural engineering has been described above as a last line of defence and emphasizes the role of the human response in the control or avoidance of potential hazards. Since this approach is so common in industry to control safety it is worth discussing the issue in slightly more detail. The field of study is ergonomics. The problem is one of anticipating how human beings can 'fail'. Such failures are not usually deliberate since those who fail are often the first people at risk!

Firstly there is a need to understand how people make decisions (Figure 6.2). Ideally decisions should involve an extensive collection of information, analysis, planning and finally action. In practice, however, people do not generally go through the whole process, they take short cuts. The first short cut is the one we use most in our life, the instinctive reaction, a *cue* followed by *action*. This can be very effective provided the cues and actions are planned to minimize slips. The

Human error analysis

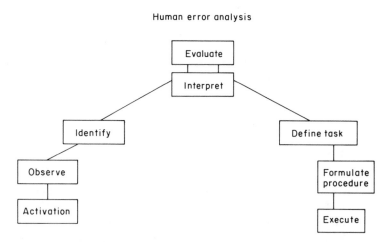

Figure 6.2 Decision-making framework

response is safest in situations which are frequently encountered, and therefore not very appropriate to the unique situation of an accident.

Instinctive responses can be replaced by written procedures when it is recognized that the action required is more complex, with too much to learn, or occurring more rarely. This can be effective provided people are well trained and can identify the right procedure to use. There are, however, real dangers that cues given in a hazardous situation are ambiguous, especially when learnt responses have been reinforced by experience, e.g. 'we've always had problems with that instrument' or 'we keep on getting spurious trips'. Another human response to a situation is an inherent wish to keep things easy and convenient. Complicated procedures will be simplified, perhaps inappropriately. If there is a need for a complex procedure then the reasons must be very apparent to the operator and adherence to the procedure should be monitored. The constant monitoring in the context of procedural safety will show management's commitment to the procedure. This will assist in reinforcement of the procedure among the operatives. This is particularly true where there are competing objectives which might encourage people to skip a procedure. Obviously engineered safety is more impartial in such cases.

One way good plant design can assist an operative is to ensure appropriate feedback. People have the ability to correct mistakes if they receive direct feedback from the plant. Such feedback is best when visual. The operative response should therefore be 'engineered' if possible. Other environmental aspects will affect the response the operative is going to make. Allowance should be made for stress and workload. Training plays a significant role in response as does the good design of instrumentation.

There is often most concern over the cognitive capability of operatives. Accidents often involve abnormal and sometimes complex situations which will lead to the least predictable response by the operative. The response will be influenced by a wide range of factors. Whilst aids to decision making are appropriate, feedback which flags errors and enables recovery is equally important. Despite the complexities involved, analysis is possible and has been successful in identifying potential/actual errors in human procedures.

DISCUSSION

Finally, while this chapter has concentrated on industrial safety issues, it is clear from the introduction to the chapter that financial, environmental and safety issues are not separate problems which can be considered in isolation. It is extremely important that new plants are designed to achieve a fully integrated approach. The good manager, whilst minimizing capital and operational costs, must also attempt to minimize the risk to the workforce and public and minimize the impact on the environment.

Such an integrated approach can only happen if all aspects are treated in a reasonable common framework which allows for evaluation, both qualitative and quantitative, of alternative designs. Risk analysis is close to providing a framework and will become an essential part of an engineer's tool kit, assisting in all stages of a project's life cycle from conceptual design to operational procedures.

Significant risks which have been identified can be tackled using one of the three 'safety by design' strategies outlined. From a number of points of view, including cost and effectiveness, the key message is that it is much easier to design for safety than to try and bolt on safety afterwards.

Chapter 7

Reliability: Industrial Risk Assessment

J. Ansell
University of Edinburgh

ABSTRACT

A great deal has been published concerning methods for assessing the reliability of plant and equipment. In this chapter the scope and limitations for different mathematical/statistical approaches are discussed. Although techniques have been developed as a basis for decision in making systems more reliable, the need for further development is discussed. The main problem is that the estimated probability of events is critically dependent on underlying assumptions which may not be valid.

INTRODUCTION

Most human activity has a risk associated with it whether the participant is conscious of it or not, be it driving a car, crossing a road, going to a fun fair or even tidying up. The great majority of risks are accepted without too much concern. Rarely do people attempt to evaluate the risks they are taking or even rank the risks. Often they have to be reminded by events or campaigns of the dangers which surround them. Public service advertisements warn about the dangers in the house, dangers to children crossing roads, dangers associated with drink and driving and the dangers of AIDS.

Risk: Analysis, Assessment and Management. Edited by J. Ansell and F. Wharton.
© 1992 John Wiley & Sons Ltd.

However, when it is proposed to build a chemical plant or site a nuclear power station the general public becomes concerned. There is a perceived need to examine the safety of the system being proposed. Whilst it seems to be accepted that risk cannot be eliminated completely, it is expected that wherever possible the risks should be reduced to a minimum level. The level of safety achieved obviously reflects the resources committed. In most cases a balance is struck between the societal risk and the economic cost. The societal risk takes into account the perceived cost to society if the risk is realized as well as the likelihood of realizing the risk. The risk of lightning hitting a person or building is relatively high in comparison to the chance of a chemical plant becoming critical, however the numbers of people at risk may be considerably higher in the event of a chemical plant failure.

Calculating societal risk is a complex process in which there is a need to assess the likelihood of the event and the numbers of individuals at risk. Both these figures are likely to be indicators of magnitude rather than accurate estimates. The level of precision reflects many aspects of our knowledge. The aim in calculating such figures is to assess the level of risk and whether it is acceptable rather than being unduly concerned with its accuracy in calculation. It is the ability to rank the risks which is being sought so that decisions can be made. Hence the objective in assessment is to develop yardsticks with which it is possible to gauge the risk in comparison to other events. It is important to stress that the development of such yardsticks is only of partial interest to reliability engineers. Their main concern is to achieve the best level of safety for a given level of resources allocation. This chapter, however, will concentrate on assessment though occasionally it will be necessary to comment on other facets of reliability engineering. The main emphasis in this chapter is on mathematical/ statistical modelling of risk, primarily of industrial risk.

Considerable progress has been made in the technology associated with risk assessment, yet there still appears a disparity between the predicted rate and the true rate of occurrence of both minor and major incidents. There are many underlying causes, some of which are intrinsic to the technology and others which are extrinsic to its use. Hence in examining the mathematical and statistical approaches it is necessary to consider their shortcomings. The critical approach taken, however, should not detract from the use of the models or the judgements which are based upon them. The models often provide the only guide to best practice and procedures. The endeavour is to improve understanding and hence general safety.

There is a large literature on reliability, however it is distributed over a number of disciplines, including engineering, psychology, mathematics and statistics. The more notable engineering texts are Green and Bourne (1970), O'Connor (1981) and Henley and Kumamoto (1981). On the mathematics of reliability there are a number of sound texts from the 1970s, for example Barlow and Proschan (1975). The statistical texts divide into general approaches to reliability and specific topics. Mann, Schafer and Singpurwalla (1974) produced a general statistical text for reliability analysis and more recently Crowder *et al.* (1991) have provided a wide review of statistical models for reliability. More recently interest in statistics has focused on analysis of lifetime data, and a number of both general and specific texts are available. For survival analysis there are texts by Lawless (1982) and Cox and Oakes (1980) of a general nature whereas Nelson (1982) provides a text orientated towards reliability. Ascher and Feingold (1984) have written a text specifically for repairable systems.

THE IDENTIFICATION OF RISK

A major problem in assessing the risk of a system is the recognition or identification of the complete range of possible risks to which the system is subject. As might be appreciated this is far from a simple problem, especially since our perception of danger is continually being increased, by past events and new technologies.

There is always the danger that the identification of risks will be seen as solving the problem. Such a view was sometimes taken in the early days of large plant construction. If a risk was identified then action was taken to eliminate it. This had an immediate appeal to the ingenuity of engineers and scientists. There are two obvious dangers in this approach: firstly, the notion that the systems can be built which are infallible; and, secondly, that the steps taken achieve their goals of eliminating the risk.

Since the costs of construction and costs associated with safety will always be higher further into a system's life cycle, consideration of risk (safety) should ideally start at the design stage. There is therefore the need for detailed examination of the design from a standpoint of likely hazards. This should be a distinctly separate activity from the process of design, since its goals are different from those of the design process.

Obviously no designer intends to build an unsafe or dangerous system, but awareness of all potential hazards cannot be guaranteed. Activity centred on detecting faults within a design may seem confrontational. There would be an implicit challenge to the knowledge, or theory which supports the knowledge, of the designer. It is therefore essential that the goal of improving the system's performance and safety is stressed during this exploration.

In the past, and especially in the contexts of inquiries, a false competition between designer and analyst has been established. Such approaches are rather naive since valuable information can be lost. The designers/engineers have to be fully involved with the safety analysis since they know the principles and practice on which the system was built. Also there is a false perception of independence. For designers and risk analysts tend to have the same backgrounds and therefore approach the systems with similar view. The same hazards will be recognized or missed, and, of course, similar solutions invoked.

It is now more widely accepted that safety analyses must involve those with the initial responsibility for the system design as well as those who operate it and, if possible, individuals not directly involved. It is essential that the team wherever possible should have a wide variety of backgrounds. The politics of such a group will play a part in its outcome. The political difficulties are not discussed here. The team brief should be to take a positive approach to safety with the aim of developing the safest system within the resources available. Fortunately most engineers/designers are increasingly aware of the fallibility of systems, and hence will have positive attitudes towards this approach.

The second major problem for risk analysts is that most systems which are considered are complex. This applies equally to pieces of equipment as to industrial plants. There is therefore a need to adopt methodologies which can render the system capable of analysis. This necessarily implies that not all risks a system might face will be discovered, but it is hoped that those most likely to occur or those with major consequences are. There are a number of possible approaches to identification. The main approaches are based on either top-down or bottom-up methodologies. A top-down approach will be to consider the dangers that a system might be holistically subject to and explore how they might arise, an example is the use of fault trees. A bottom-up approach takes a component/basic event and explores how it might cause the system to fail. Fault modes and effect analysis (FMEA) is an example of this approach.

Both approaches suffer from a narrowing of our vision of the system by either limiting the number of failure modes for a component or the types of risks considered. They both implicitly rely on the correctness of the technology or science on which the model is built. This is reinforced by cognate dissonance, only perceived possible risks can be guarded against. Often our own perception of the underpinning science lets us down when risks are not thought possible.

Fault tree analysis was pioneered by Fussell (see Fussell, 1976). It will produce a description of the relationship between the set of basic events and some specified top event, the event of interest. The top event would be the particular risk under study. Starting with this risk, the next stage would be to explore how the event could have arisen from contributing events. An example of a fault tree is given in Figure 7.1. The top event is the failure of an engine to start. This may arise from lack of fuel, failure of the starter motor, failure of the distributor or a flat battery. These are the contributing events. Each of the contributing events would then, in turn, be investigated as top events and hence cascade through the system until the basic events are reached. Returning to the example, a lack of fuel might be the next top event to be examined and this could arise because of failure of the fuel pump or empty fuel tank. These latter events could be considered to be basic events.

The events in the fault tree are connected by gates. The types of gates in

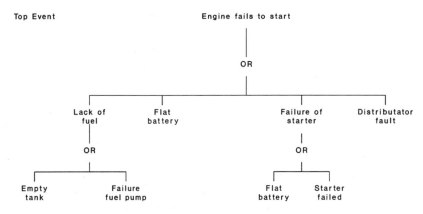

Figure 7.1 Fault tree for engine start failure

common practice are OR, AND, EXCLUSIVE OR, NOT and VOTING gates. The latter assumes that if there are n contributors to a gate then the outcome of each component is considered before a message is passed on the success or failure of the gate. An example would be 2/3 voting gate in safety system, it would only react if two of the three subsystems indicated action was necessary. For further details on fault trees see Fussell (1976).

A fault modes and effects analysis investigates for every component the consequences of all defined modes of failure. The investigation is usually carried out in isolation from the analysis of other components, since if combinations were considered the task would become intractable. The danger is that specific combinations of basic events or component failures which may cause system failure may be overlooked. The outcome of the study will usually be a report for each component giving details of failure modes, consequences and, where appropriate, action to be taken. Using the engine example above the process would start by identifying the basic components such as the fuel tank, fuel pump, battery, etc. For each of these components all possible failure modes then would be considered. An example might be that the tank was empty, punctured, overfull, etc. Each of these modes of failure would then be explored to see if it affected the system, in this case the engine starting. For further details see O'Connor (1981).

SYSTEMS DESCRIPTION

The identification stage forms the basis of a detailed document. In some studies the document may even have some initial values for basic events or component failure, though generally this is not the case. The next stage for the purpose of assessment is to produce a tractable model, usually a mathematical model. Whilst the model may be complex, the overall aim is to produce an 'adequate' description. The description should provide an overall assessment. It should also assist in the identification of the components or subsystems which significantly contribute to the risk. Again the aim would be to give relative rather than absolute measures of risk.

An adequate description might be described as a compromise between a detailed account which may be mathematically intractable and a simplification which will reduce the predictive power of the model. Often analysts attempt to circumvent such problems by modulization. This is an attempt to split the whole system into smaller units. This can in itself be dangerous since it may fail to take full account of the interaction and interplay between modules. However, it may be fruitful provided a holistic study is implemented as well.

Reducing the complexity can be achieved in a number of ways: it might be possible to reduce the number of failure modes for each component or subsystem; remove combinations of events which seem unlikely; or restrict the way faults are promulgated. Of these three options most analysts favour the second. The removal of unlikely combinations can be implemented in a number of ways. Typically either the number of 'independent' events allowed to occur is restricted or only events with a probability above a given threshold are considered. These two approaches are often applied to fault tree analysis and will be described in more detail later.

The method of obtaining the mathematical description will be described for a fault tree but could be amended for other methodologies. The fault tree is translated into a Boolean expression, starting with the basic events which are combined until the top event is reached. At each stage the gates are replaced by their mathematical equivalents. In Table 7.1 some illustrations are given.

To illustrate the approach consider the systems described in Figure 7.2 which is a fault tree of insufficient flow along a pipe. The reason for insufficient flow is either failure of pump and back-up pump or reverse flow due to values being inappropriately set. It is adapted from Johnston and Matthews (1983). The basic events are denoted by the circles each with a letter (a) to (e). Starting from (b) 'Pump B fails' this is combined with (c) 'Valve V fails to open' through an

Table 7.1 Fault tree translations

Fault tree gate	Mathematical expression
A AND B	ab
A OR B	$a + b - ab$
2 OUT OF 3	$ab + ac + bc - 2abc$
NOT A	$1 - a$

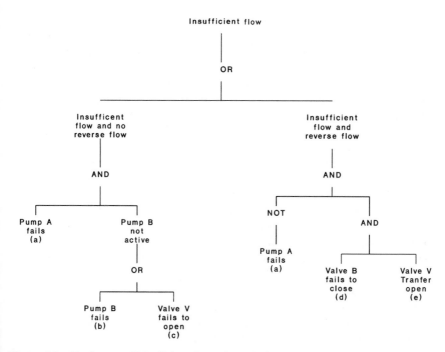

Figure 7.2 Fault tree of insufficient flow along a pipe

OR gate the Boolean expression is (*b*OR*c*), then this joint event is combined with (a) 'Pump A fails' through an AND gate so the Boolean expression is {*a*AND(*b*OR*c*)}. The process continues until the final Boolean expression is obtained, {*a*AND(*b*OR*c*)}OR{*ā*AND(*d*AND*e*)}. This expression can then be manipulated into the form {*a*AND*b*}OR{*a*AND*c*}OR{*ā*AND*e*AND*d*}. Without the NOT this Boolean expression is in Stone's representational form, in which combinations of events which occur together are joined with AND and these combinations are joined by ORs. Unfortunately the NOT ensures that this expression is not unique, see comments below.

The two examples used so far are very simple compared with the fault trees usually considered. Most fault trees have a large number of basic events describing possible states of components. Hence the process of obtaining the Boolean representation produces expressions which frequently are too large to manipulate. The size will reflect both the number of possible ways of failing as well as the complexity of some of the combinations which lead to failure. In the simple pipe example there are joint events with three contributing basic events. Therefore there is a need to reduce both the length of the expression as a whole and some of the more complex combinations. This is usually achieved by culling some of the combined events either by size or probabilistically. The culling is usually carried out during the process of combination to save computational time. Culling by size means removal of combinations in which the number of basic events is large. It is assumed that the probability of such a combination is likely to be small and therefore insignificant. The probability of the events is not taken into account. Probabilistic culling on the other hand uses the probability associated with each event. It culls a combination when the combined probability falls below some threshold. Culling by size can imply a lack of accuracy in our assessment of risk. Probabilistic culling suffers from the drawback of retaining information in the tree which slows the process of developing the expression, and in some cases it will not produce a Boolean expression within reasonable computer time.

In most cases the Boolean expression will be written as a list of subsets of the basic events. For example the pipe example would be presented as $\{ab\}$ $\{ac\}$ $\{\bar{a}de\}$. As illustrated these subsets may be overlapping with basic events occurring in more than one subset. The occurrence of every event in a subset will cause the top event to occur. Implicitly it is assumed that the basic events in a subset are joined by 'and' and the subsets by 'or', hence the expression will be equivalent to Stone's representation of a logical expression, as described above. The description produced could be used to calculate the overall likelihood of the top event if the probabilities of the basic events were known. Obviously it will be an approximation if culling has occurred, though hopefully it will be sufficiently accurate to enable the analyst to rank the risks. The expression can also be used to consider the relative importance of an event, and there are several ways of measuring this (see Barlow and Proschan, 1975; Xie and Shen, 1990).

The above approach has proved useful in many applications allowing analysts to achieve results which would have required too much manpower by other methods. The drawbacks to the approach are inherent to Stone's representation. A major problem is the lack of uniqueness of the representation. If a logical expression contains a negative then the representation is not unique, the expression for the pipe example may be written in a number of ways. It is possible, of course, to define a unique representation at this stage, sometimes this is achieved through consensus theory (see Johnston and Matthews, 1983), but then this would be subject to interpretation. Hence different analysts might produce different analyses. Associated with the lack of uniqueness there are other problems if a tree has 'feedback' loops, common within process production. If the outcome of one process feeds back to previous processes an algorithm may enter infinite loop. In these circumstances the description will obviously not be obtained.

The description, if it can be obtained, is then used as a predictor of the performance of the system. This means that the simplified form is then treated as a valid representation of the complete system. In some cases this is an adequate approximation to an order of magnitude. There are, however, a large number of cases where this is not the case, usually because some important factors have been overlooked or not accounted for. Often there is a lack of information on both the system's structure as well as the performance of the components of which it is comprised. There are often unperceived problems such as dependency of components or system. These lead the model to be either overoptimistic or overpessimistic.

Dependency among components is one of the major problems in reliability assessment of large plants. Components may be dependent if they are in the same environment, made of the same sub-components or affected by the same maintenance procedure. If the dependency is not recognized then the false assumption of independence will usually lead to overoptimistic estimates of a system's reliability. The concern was highlighted because of the apparent failure of safety systems based on redundancy to achieve their expected level of performance. Considerable attention has been devoted to this problem in both engineering (see Amendola, 1988; Ballard, 1989; Bourne *et al.*, 1981; Edwards, 1989) and statistical modelling (Ansell and Walls, 1990; Apostolakis and Moineni, 1987).

It is obvious that the validity of the model must be questioned. It should be stressed though that this does not mean one should throw out the model. It is possibly the best indicator of the system's performance to hand.

DATABASES

In the 50 years of development of reliability engineering a central theme has been the development of reliable information on which to base assessments. The database was seen as a device which could supply data of high quality. Hence it is not surprising to see that several large databases have been established. Whilst at the time of construction most of these databases were designed to state-of-the-art requirements they have not necessarily withstood the test of time.

A large percentage of the early databases unfortunately contained data of poor quality. The data from these if used inappropriately could be very misleading. Data were captured without being screened and their validity was therefore doubtful. The data were frequently taken from incident reports or maintenance records. These data were therefore a secondary source and have the disadvantage that the accuracy of the reporting may be limited for the purpose of future reliability studies since this was not the prime concern of the maintenance worker or the incident analyst. Valuable information such as the context the data arose from was often lost. This loss was increased by the inability of the databases to cope with qualitative data.

As an example of the types of problems that do arise suppose four components fail through some abnormal event, such as severe weather on a North Sea platform. The data could be recorded as four lifetimes or, even worse, as four independent lifetimes. The reason for failure may be recorded, but that it was abnormal might be omitted. Some databases do allow a commentary to be added to record but in a form that did not allow for automatic processing. Whilst useful for those with the time to search the database in detail it is unlikely to be used by most analysts. The data then would be added to the generic data set and the four values collected in extreme circumstances might be added to shore data which did not suffer such extreme conditions. Some databases were constructed in a way that one could obtain estimates for a whole group of items, which would not apply to any subgroups within the data. For example an estimate might be obtained for all the gas valves independent of size and usage but this would be useless for all practical purposes.

The above illustrates the need for care in the definition of the data on entry. There is also a need to consider how the user will employ the data. Where possible, the data must only be open to one interpretation. For example Newton (1991) using the same data shows how slight changes in the interpretation of the same data set there can be considerable changes in the outcome of the analysis. Hence the database should be constructed with some thought given to the purpose(s) it will serve. In the presentation of his paper, Newton gave an example which illustrated how the maintenance records can be particularly misleading. In the example every machine at overhaul was stripped down completely and reassembled from parts within the maintenance shop. Hence the machine serial number was the only stable part of any machine. The database reflected the performance of the serial number.

Another consideration is the level of recording since some databases contain derived values rather than the source data, e.g. they might contain the mean life rather than the original data. This means that one cannot check distribution properties of the data.

Too often in reliability it is assumed that data are exponential because there is no information to the contrary.

Obviously over time there has been considerable improvement in the collection of data and its quality (see Gibson, McIntyre and Witt, 1989; Moss, 1991). It is now often the practice to collect data directly relevant either from a site or in the case of future sites from sites with similar characteristics. There are also a greater number of databases for specific uses. The Safety and Reliability Directorate has invested considerable effort in producing the DEFEND database (see Gibson and Matthews, 1990). The DEFEND database has been constructed to aid with the study of dependency. However, until there is sufficient resource to collect primary data on a regular basis, much of the work of reliability engineers is going to be hampered. There will always be a slight impediment to reliability studies in that data are generally regarded as commercially sensitive.

A final comment must be made about the relevance of databases and the data they provide. Even if the data are recorded with due care and are clearly defined they may be irrelevant. The data will usually be used to project performance in the future. Although the context may have been correctly retained in the database the technological change in use or context may be such as to render the data irrelevant to such projection. There is also, particularly with electronic components, a need to ensure that the data collected apply generally to the population. O'Connor (1991) illustrates this by reference to electronic chips. If a chip has been manufactured with due care it will be robust, hence for simplicity one could assume only faulty chips fail. A good inspection programme should remove the faulty chips, hence recorded failures are mainly associated with only a small part of the population. Any analysis based on this would be misleading. The relevance of the data should therefore also be considered before being used in an analysis.

STATISTICAL ANALYSES OF DATA

Most statistical analyses of data within reliability engineering are routine and even often automatic. Many analyses for either components or systems yield a mean lifetime with or without a standard deviation. This single figure is used to predict future performance and, in the case of components, will be combined with other estimates to produce overall assessment of a system. There are obvious problems with such a blind approach some of which will be described below.

Statistical techniques are not often used to aid analysis and decision making in reliability. Even when used there is often a lack of methodology. Few statistical analyses start with a definition of the objective of the study. This often leads to inappropriate analysis. For example it is quite possible that calculating a mean lifetime may be irrelevant in achieving many objectives in a reliability. Once the objectives have been decided then the selection of the appropriate statistical approach may be relatively easy. The methodology will then depend on the type of approach selected.

A major pitfall in most reliability studies is the assumption that components have exponential lifetimes. This occurs throughout reliability studies in both theoretical and practical studies. Even if the exponential was an appropriate distribution for a particular context it would still be worth while checking if the data followed an exponential distribution. In the process of checking, other notable features within the data may come to light. Unfortunately in most analyses there is little checking of the data, and where checks are imposed often they are to eliminate wholly erroneous data such as negatively valued lifetimes. There are signs of a growing movement to improve the quality of data (see for example Moss, 1991).

Lack of quality in the data has led some reliability engineers to argue that the data do not warrant detailed examination and that on those grounds the assumption that the underlying distribution is exponential is reasonable. Whilst one may have doubts about the quality of the data, they still should be explored. Even poor quality data can yield useful information. Errors or misleading values contained in the data may be discovered by elementary analysis. Therefore if data are available they should be subject to a positive analysis.

An analysis should start with simple techniques including graphical methods to explore whether the data are likely to arise from an exponential distribution or not. Histograms (or stemleafs) can be very helpful in highlighting distinctive features. For example they may indicate possible outliers, points at variance with the rest of the data, mixed populations and whether the exponential distribution is a reasonable approximation. Basic statistical measures are helpful. The calculation of the dispersion index may indicate whether the data are under-dispersed or over-dispersed compared to exponential. These simple steps can be very informative and in some cases will avoid the need for more sophisticated analysis.

In reliability analysis plotting techniques have always been very popular. Historically Weibull plots have been used, or hazard plots, but more recently TTT plots have been introduced. A Weibull plot assumes the distribution of lifetimes has a Weibull distribution. The data are transformed accordingly and plotted (see Nelson, 1982), for specific detail. A straightline or nearly straightline plot may indicate a Weibull distribution. The plot will also provide the analyst with some view on how appropriate the Weibull model is. There are difficulties in interpreting such plots (see Walls and Bendell, 1985). The TTT plot or time on test plot was suggested by Epstein and Sobel (1953) but has been developed by Barlow (see Barlow and Campo, 1975). These plots have the advantage of being a distribution free technique. It will indicate whether a distribution has an increasing or decreasing failure rate. An increasing failure rate implies as the component gets older the component is more likely to fail, decreasing failure rate implies the component is less likely to fail as it ages. The techniques have been generalized. There are though drawbacks with its use especially if the data are highly censored (see Barlow, 1989). Lawless (1989) suggests that the information may be taken from a Weibull plot. These plotting techniques are extensively used and if used correctly can assist analysis. They provide an indication of the validity of the model in a way which can be readily interpreted.

There are a number of issues which are particular to reliability data analysis. For example components tend to be very reliable and hence in most studies the degree of censoring or truncation of data is high. Data sets with 80% or 90% censoring are common (see Bohoris and Aspinwall, 1989). A censored lifetime is a lifetime which has survived beyond the period of study. Therefore in the analysis one knows that the component lasted for a given period but not its actual lifetime which may be considerably longer. Empirical estimates of lifetime distributions exist for censored data. The best known is the Kaplan–Meier estimator (Kaplan and Meier, 1958). Several authors have explored the effect of applying statistical tests to censored data (see Bohoris and Aspinwall, 1989) for comments in a reliability context.

Management needs to know the cost of achieving target levels of reliability and several models for reliability growth have been developed. Growth models generally attempt to model the expected lifetimes of systems/components on the assumption that the system/component must be improved by technological changes. The most widely used growth model was proposed by Duane (1964). Crow (1982) provided a statistical underpinning for the Duane model describing it as a non-homogeneous Poisson process and pointing out various aspects of the model. A major concern is whether the changes do enhance a system's performance. In fact it can be shown that some growth may be expected even from a system where no changes to the system have taken place. The results were established by Jewell (1984) and are detailed in Ascher and Feingold (1984). The latter provides a good overview of growth models. Growth models are generally part of a wider product improvement plan which often results in product enhancement.

More recently there has been considerable interest in the effect factors or variables have on lifetimes. This has been partially sparked off by the technique suggested by Cox (1972, 1975), which is referred to as proportional hazard modelling (PHM) or Cox regression. The PHM relates the survival of components/systems to attributes of the system or its environment. The model is a regression model for survival times. There is a wide range of related models which could equally be employed—for example Weibull regression (see Smith, 1991), accelerated life testing (see Lawless, 1982), and for such models in a reliability setting see Newby (1987). PHM has the advantage that it is a distribution free method and can be shown to be very robust (Solomon, 1984, 1986). PHM has been used to explore the effect of design changes on system/ component performance (see Bendell, Weightman and Walker, 1991). The technique has also been used to estimate the underlying lifetime distribution (see Ansell and Ansell, 1987). The technique is usually regarded as exploratory, since the aim is to find features which can either be controlled or changed to improve the component/system's performance.

Apart from techniques which have been specifically developed for reliability analysis there are a number of techniques which have been applied to reliability data. These include techniques from multivariate analysis (Jerwood and Georgiakodis, 1987) and times-series analysis (Walls and Bendell, 1987). There is also a mounting literature on Bayesian statistical analysis of reliability data.

Given the range of tools that is available for statistical analysis of data there is unfortunately a strong tendency within the reliability literature to become fixated by a single technique. For example PHM, which is a powerful exploratory tool, has dominated the analysis of reliability data with covariates. Whilst the technique is fairly robust, it requires the data to comply with some specific assumptions for the estimates and analyses produced to be meaningful. There is a danger that such fashionable techniques are applied inappropriately. Engineers and managers obviously need guidance from statisticians when using sophisticated techniques to ensure that the data satisfy the underlying assumptions. For many statistical techniques used in reliability analysis there are fortunately diagnostic methods which will indicate whether the analysis was appropriate. Practitioners should generally be encouraged to use them.

It is worth reiterating that the relevance of the analysis should always feature in the analyst's mind. Too often sophisticated techniques are employed to answer the wrong question. A prime consideration must be the objective of the study not the techniques employed. A discussion of the objectives of reliability data analysis appeared in the discussion of Ansell and Phillips (1989) and was continued in Ansell and Phillips (1990).

SYSTEMS MODELLING

Based on the mathematical model developed and knowledge about the components' lifetimes it is possible to obtain an assessment of the system's reliability. It must be accepted that the steps already taken will have reduced the potential accuracy of the assessment. Given the reduction, it is arguable whether subsequent simplification will in fact reduce further the predictive power of the model. Hence authors have argued that it is not sensible to look for a high degree of sophistication in the model. The model parameterization should be simple and similarly the mathematics should not be overly complex. This argument has led to the use of the Markovian model.

In the Markovian model time to failure time and where appropriate time to repair for components are assumed to be exponentially distributed. This means that the component's failure does not depend on the length of its past lifetime. Thus, a generator is assumed to have the same chance of failure at the beginning of its life as, say, two years later. A number of arguments can be advanced to defend the assumption of exponential failure and repair times. The maintenance of equipment may be such that failure is a purely random event or it could be assumed that the component has reached a steady state of performance. Such assumptions are usually false, but as a first approximation may be worthy of exploration. Unfortunately it is not always possible to examine the assumption as the relevant information on components' lifetimes is often unavailable.

The model using the Markovian assumption becomes relatively simple. There is a considerable body of work on the properties of such models (see for example Cox and Miller, 1965; Beaumont, 1983). For specific use in reliability analysis see Billington and Allan (1983). There is a vast number of papers on specific Markovian models of failure and repair (see for example Fawzi and Hawkes, 1989). In Chapter 2 of this volume Chapman has already made use of exponential modelling for project planning. The mathematical details will not be explored in this chapter.

A frequent drawback to the assumption of the exponential distributions is that it keeps on being repeated. A system composed of components which have exponential failure distributions will not generally have an exponential failure distribution itself. Many analysts will blithely calculate the failure rate of a subsystem composed of components with exponential failure rates and when evaluating the whole system assume that the subsystem had an exponential failure distribution. This may be repeated several times. Hence the approximation rapidly becomes dubious.

At this stage it would be useful to explore the alternatives. These include using more appropriate distributions for failure. One may make allowance for failures dependent on time, hence the generator described earlier may be allowed to age and the Weibull distribution could be employed. Only in a few cases is it possible to produce explicit mathematical solutions to such problems. More usually the problem becomes too complex and approaches as described by Chapman in Chapter 2 might be considered. The alternative is to use simulation as a technique. In the context of reliability assessment, simulation often proves very expensive in computer time since it is often assumed that failure rates are measured in years whilst repair rates are measured in hours. This means that confidence in the methodology becomes doubtful. There are approaches which may prove fruitful such as careful design of simulation experiments or extrapolation from appropriately chosen models.

Whilst there is considerable criticism of Markovian assumptions, the alternatives attract an even poorer press among analysts. The lack of mathematical tractability or lack of confidence in the approach deters many from using non-Markovian models. Yet if there is departure from Markovian assumption this should be reflected in the modelling since ignoring it may equally invalidate the results. Statisticians and practitioners are attempting to resolve some of these difficulties.

DISCUSSION

The aims of this chapter are twofold—to give an account of mathematical/statistical approaches to industrial risk assessment and to discuss some of the current problems associated with it. By concentrating on the limitations, the whole validity of the approach may have been called into question. However there is a need to start with some model of the process even if it is faulty. The model will allow the process to be explored, it may even indicate its own inadequacies. The techniques generally provide useful insights into ways systems can be made more reliable. They also provide a method for comparison.

Therefore they should be judged on the basis of a very 'good' attempt rather than in absolute terms.

Most of the difficulties raised will be familiar to reliability engineers. The need is to produce methods which do not suffer from the drawback mentioned. As stated in the introduction it is only plausible to produce a relative ranking of the likelihood of events, rather than accurate assessments.

The reliability engineer should have sympathy with the food scientist who accepts the possibility for transfer from meat of bovine spongiform encephalopathy (BSE) to humans but feels it is unlikely. It is not possible for the food scientist to say it will never occur. Many honest engineers/scientists work in the field of reliability assessment with the intention of improving systems. They use the 'best' tools which are available where possible. The aim is to produce an objective assessment of the relative performance of a system. The main problem is that attached to the values they calculate are spurious concepts. Any figure produced would depend on the assumptions made. It is not the fault of the analyst that a new phenomenon arises which is not allowed for in the analysis. However, the analyst can be blamed if she/he has missed an event well established.

In other chapters there are alternative approaches to considering risk. Such approaches should be seen as complementary rather than as competitors. Accepting that there are risks involved with any human activity is the first step, trying to understand the nature of the risk is the second. Obtaining a mathematical description must be of assistance in gaining understanding. To paraphrase Lord Kelvin: to understand the risk you must be able to measure it.

REFERENCES

Amendola, A. (1988). Common cause failure analysis in reliability and risk assessment, in A. Amendola and A.S. De Bustamente (eds), *Reliability Engineering*, Kluwer Academic, London, pp. 221–56.

Ansell, R.O. and Ansell, J.I. (1987). Modelling the reliability of sodium sulphur cells, *Reliability Engineering*, **17**, 127–37.

Ansell, J.I. and Phillips, M.J. (1989). Practical problems in the statistical analysis of reliability data (with discussion), *Applied Statistics*, **38**(1898), 205–47.

Ansell, J.I. and Phillips, M.J. (1990). Strategies for reliability data analysis, in P. Comer (ed.), *11th Advances in Reliability Technical Symposium*, Elsevier, London, pp. 272–83.

Ansell, J.I. and Walls, L.A. (1990). Dependency modelling, in P. Comer (ed.), *11th Advances in Reliability Technical Symposium*, Elsevier, London, pp. 111–24.

Apostolakis, G. and Moineni, P. (1987). The foundations of models of dependence in probability safety assessment, *Reliability Engineering*, **18**, 177–95.

Ascher, H. and Feingold, H. (1984). *Repairable Systems Reliability*, Marcel Dekker, New York.

Ballard, G. (1989). Dependent failure analysis in PSA, *Proceedings of the IAEA International Conference on Nuclear Power Performance and Safety*, Vienna, pp. 119–33.

Barlow, R.E. (1989). In discussion of Ansell and Phillips (1989).

Barlow, R.E. and Campo, R.E. (1975). Total time on test processes and applications to failure data analysis, in R.E. Barlow, J.B. Fussell and N.D. Singpurwalla (eds), *Reliability and Fault Tree Analysis*, SIAM, Philadelphia, pp. 451-81.

Barlow, R.E. and Proschan, F. (1975). *Statistical Theory of Reliability and Life Testing*, Holt, Rinehart and Winston, New York.

Beaumont, G.P. (1983). *Introductory Applied Probability*, Ellis Horwood, London.

Bendell, A., Weightman, D.W. and Walker, E.V. (1991). Applying proportional hazards modelling in reliability, *Reliability Engineering and Safety Systems*, **34**, 35-53.

Billington, R. and Allan, R.N. (1983). *Reliability Evaluation of Engineering Systems: Concepts and Techniques*, Pitman Books. London.

Bohoris, G. and Aspinwall, E.M. (1989). Statistical comparison of reliability data sets, *Proceedings of Reliability '89*, Brighton, 3B/3/1-13.

Bourne, A.J., Edwards, G.T., Hunns, D.M., Poulter, D.R. and Watson, I.A. (1981). Defences against common-mode failures. A guide for designers and operators, *UKAEA SRD-R-196*.

Cox, D.R. (1972). Regression models and life tables, *Journal of the Royal Statistical Association*, B, **34**, 187-220.

Cox, D.R. (1975). Partial likelihoods, *Biometrika*, **62**, 269-76.

Cox, D.R. and Miller, H.D. (1965). *The Theory of Stochastic Processes*, Methuen, London.

Cox, D.R. and Oakes, D. (1980). *Analysis of Survival Data*, Chapman-Hall, London.

Crow, L.H. (1982). Confidence interval procedures for the Weibull process with applications to reliability growth, *Technometrics*, **24**, 251-6.

Crowder, M.J., Kimber, A., Smith, R.L. and Sweeting, T. (1991). *Statistical Analysis of Reliability Data*, Chapman Hall, London.

Duane, L.H. (1964). Learning curve approach to reliability monitoring, *IEEE Trans Aerospace*, Vol 2, 563-6.

Edwards, G.T. (1989). Dependent failure assessment principles, engineering structure and data requirements, *UKAEA Report No SRS/GR/83*.

Epstein, B. and Sobel, M. (1953). Life-testing, *Journal of the American Statistical Association*, **48**, 486-502.

Fawzi, B.B. and Hawkes, A.G. (1989). Availability of Markov systems with spares and repair facilities, *Proceedings of Reliability '89*, 2B/4/1-14.

Fussell, J.B. (1976). Fault tree analysis: concepts and techniques, *Generic Techniques in Systems Reliability Assessment*, NATO Advanced Institute Studies, Noordhoff-Leyden, pp. 133-62.

Gibson, I.K. and Matthews, R.H. (1990). Dependent failure analysis: DEFEND database, in P. Comer (ed.), *11th Advances in Reliability Technical Symposium*, Elsevier, London, pp. 139-48.

Gibson, I.K., McIntyre, P.J. and Witt, H.H. (1989). Aspects of a model to improve the reliability estimates of engineering components, *Proceedings of Reliability '89*, 4Aa/2/1-14.

Green, A.E. and Bourne, A.J. (1970). *Reliability Technology*, John Wiley & Sons, New York.

Henley, E.J. and Kumamoto, H. (1981). *Reliability Engineering and Risk Assessment*, Prentice-Hall.

Jerwood, D. and Georgiakodis, F. (1987). Application of multivariate techniques to monitor system reliability and detect common-mode failure, *Proceedings of Reliability '87*, Birmingham, 2B/5/1-10.

Jewell, W.S. (1984). A general framework for learning curve reliability growth models, *Operational Research*, **32**, 547-58.

Johnston, N.D. and Matthews, R.H. (1983). The use of not logic in fault tree analysis, *Proceedings of the 4th National Reliability Conference*, Birmingham, 5B/R/1-10.

Kaplan, E.L. and Meier, P. (1958). Non-parametric estimation from incomplete observations, *Journal of the American Statistical Association*, **43**, 457-81.

Lawless, J.F. (1982). *Statistical Models and Methods for Lifetime Data*, John Wiley & Sons, New York.

Lawless, J.F. (1989). In discussion of Ansell and Phillips (1989).

Mann, N.R., Schafer, R.E. and Singpurwalla, N.D. (1974). *Methods for Statistical Analysis of Reliability and Life Data*, John Wiley & Sons, New York.

Moss, T.R. (1991). Uncertainties in reliabilities statistics, *Reliability Engineering and Safety Systems*, **34**, 79-90.

Nelson, W. (1982). *Applied Life Data Analysis*, John Wiley & Sons, New York.

Newby, M. (1987). Accelerated failure models for reliability data analysis, *Proceedings of Reliability '87*, Birmingham, 2b/4/1-10.

Newton, D.W. (1991). Some pitfalls in reliability data analysis, *Reliability Engineering and Safety Systems*, **34**, 7-21.

O'Connor, P.D.T. (1981). *Practical Reliability Engineering*, Heyden, London.

O'Connor, P.D.T. (1991). Statistics in quality and reliability. Lessons from the past, and future opportunities, *Reliability Engineering and Safety Systems*, **34**, 23-31.

Smith, R.L. (1991). Weibull regression models for reliability analysis, *Reliability Engineering and Safety Systems*, **34**, 55-77.

Solomon, P.J. (1984). Effect of misspecification of regression models in the analysis of survival data, *Biometrika*, **71**, 291-8.

Solomon, P.J. (1986). Corrections, *Biometrika*, **73**, 245.

Walls, L.A. and Bendell, A. (1985). Human factor and sampling variation in graphical identification and estimation for Weibull distributions, *Reliability Engineering*, **13**, 133-56.

Walls, L.A. and Bendell, A. (1987). Times series method in reliability, *Reliability Engineering*, **18**, 239-56.

Xie, M. and Shen, K. (1990). Some aspects on component importance measures, in P. Comer (ed.), *11th Advances in Reliability Technical Symposium*, Elsevier, London, pp. 228-39.

Chapter 8

Some Recent English Transportation Accidents

Alec M. Lee
Formerly Professor of Management Sciences
University of Hull

ABSTRACT

Transportation in Britain has recently endured a startling variety of major accidents. These were in any specific sense quite unpredictable. In a generic sense and statistically they were not. The question posed is how these accidents might have been better managed if, indeed, there could have been a better way?

INTRODUCTION

It has been remarked that an accident or catastrophe that may be predicted will not occur, because prediction will lead to prevention. Unfortunately, accurate prediction of any specific accident is impossible. Any specific accident is the product of a chain of events, many of them unimaginable or foolish. Both the nuclear near-catastrophe at Three Mile Island (USA, 1978) and the actual nuclear catastrophe of Chernobyl (USSR, 1985) were of this type. Wagenaar has observed that: 'The forecasting of disasters can be done in a specific, general manner. We can predict how the frequency and size of disasters will increase and how the negative consequences will accumulate. But the purpose of such forecasts is prevention. If we do not predict how disasters are going to occur there is no way to prevent them.' 'Accidents will happen,' is a truism. With care

Risk: Analysis, Assessment and Management. Edited by J. Ansell and F. Wharton.
© 1992 John Wiley & Sons Ltd.

and discipline, however, the risk of accidents, where they take place and their seriousness may be controlled. It is prudent to take measures to limit their possible consequences and facilitate recovery from them afterwards. This is more difficult in the case of transportation accidents, because forecasting adds a further element of uncertainty to them. Where shall one take precautions, against what sort of accident that may happen and when? There are genuinely greater degrees of uncertainty than are met in providing planning responses to disasters of more static types: explosions at chemical plants, say, or fires at large hotels.

It is often popularly said of some catastrophes that 'it was waiting to happen'. It is also remarked that such and such an accident was 'looking for a place to happen'. The peculiar difficulty of uncertainty of place is appreciated when planning where to locate and how to secure emergency services. Speaking as a common traveller it appears that, fortuitously, the safest place for a railway accident to happen is just outside a railway station; for an air crash it is on or just off an airport; and for a marine disaster it is just inside, or outside a harbour. At least help should not be far away and communications good. So one might believe.

A great deal would depend in any case on the resources including skill, training and equipment of the available rescue and emergency services. A high morale, like that of crack troops in full training, would help. So would some clear, well-understood pattern of organization of all concerned: police, medical, nursing and ambulance staff, military personnel, and so on. In an emergency how well could they work as a team is vital.

Many, perhaps most, human institutions are primarily structured—their members instructed—so as to cope with life and its day-to-day tasks as routines. Now if any such institution is suddenly exposed to any shock or disaster, its normal, everyday structure and routines may prove wanting and fall into chaos. However, it is known from the history of war that the risks of such chaos can be reduced if two preparations have been made in peacetime:

(1) An alternative command structure suited to the needs of emergency situations has been planned, prepared and rehearsed, which will supervene in case of war when emergency comes.

(2) Staff have been assigned to, and rehearsed in the roles they will play in the emergency.

The organization and command structure ensuing must take precedence over all others in respect of the emergency or resources needed to deal with it. It must become an overlord. An excellent example of planning (not then quite completed) and need to activate an 'overlord' is provided by the case of the blowout at Ekofisk Bravo (Platform 24) in the Norwegian section of the North Sea in 1979. But there are others. Norway went further and eventually set up a national

Action Control (Overlord) Centre, which is held in reserve in a stand by state of readiness to this day. Similar action has been taken by other countries (e.g. Canada, France and several US states). Britain, however, has not done so despite these examples and much arguing of the case in the media, and notably in *The Guardian*.

The three fatal transport accidents discussed in this chapter, representing land, air and water, took place in England during the period from December 1988 to August 1989. They were not the only transport accidents that occurred then, but they were the worst in terms of fatalities; and, though each happened in a different mode of transport from the others, they all were in some measure the consequences of communications breakdowns of one sort or another. These accidents, coming as they did so close together, briefly revived public debate in Britain about the organization and delivery of emergency services to accidents in general and not only in the circumstances of major transport accidents. The Piper Alpha oil rig disaster of July 1988 in the North Sea oilfield was a greater disaster than any of them, with which it was more or less contemporaneous. And it showed, and shows up bleakly when compared to the earlier, Norwegian, Echo Bravo blowout; little seemed to have been learnt. But, despite all temptations to the contrary this chapter must be confined to transportation, Echo Bravo must therefore be omitted.

Kegworth did not in fact furnish the worst aviation disaster in Britain in 1988–89. The worst occurred just 18 days beforehand in late December 1988, when a Boeing 747 of Pan American World Airlines blew up and crashed over the village of Lockerbie in Scotland. This was, however, not an accident, but deliberate sabotage. The circumstances were of a special nature as was the 'search and recovery task'. So discussion of the Lockerbie accident has been set aside for later treatment. In addition, multiple collisions at Clapham Junction were not the only provoking railway accident of 1988–89. There were at least two others at Purley and Glasgow. But they were much smaller.

RAIL DISASTER AT CLAPHAM JUNCTION, 12 DECEMBER 1988

In November 1988, the Chief Inspector of Railways, Mr Robin Seymour, had publicly drawn attention to the increasing frequency of significant railway accidents due to technical malfunctions. In doing so he did no more than repeat the criticisms made in recent years by the Central Transport Consultative Committee (CTCC). In 1987 there had been 290 collisions of which 129 were due to 'staff error' including 24 of failure to read signals correctly, and two others by signalmen. Technical defects had caused a further 268 accidents of which 3 had concerned signalling equipment. In any event, British Rail had already made and was continuing to make investigations to find out 'why an increasing number of train drivers had passed signals "set" at danger and why drivers have problems coping with a new braking system'. Indeed BR in consultation with the unions was currently testing a modified braking system. There, matters stood in early December 1988. On the morning of Monday 12 December at 08.14, near Clapham Junction, one passenger train (the 06.30 Bournemouth-Waterloo), replacing the 06.10 Poole-Waterloo which had been cancelled due to a mishap the previous evening, ran into the back of another train (the 07.18 Basingstoke-Waterloo) which was standing there stationary. Seconds later an empty train from Waterloo crashed into the wreckage. The guard on this third train 'who perceived the further threat' managed to flag down and stop yet another train—the 4th train—and stop it just before it too crashed into the pile-up ahead. This was at 08.15.

The responses of the emergency services to the calls for help of which they

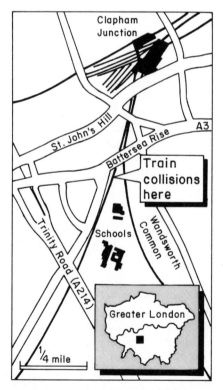

Figure 8.1 Map of rail disaster area, Clapham Junction 12 December 1988. (Copyright © 1990 *The Daily Telegraph* plc. Reproduced by permission)

received the first at 08.17 were very prompt. They began then with the first 28 ambulances, 3 fire engines and an emergency tender. These began to arrive at the scene of the disaster within 5 minutes. Uninjured passengers were already helping others to scramble up the embankment in search of safety. It was soon clear to these rescuers that more help was needed. A station officer from Battersea fire station who had arrived 'quickly radioed for five more fire engines, including three with ladders, another emergency reserve tender and a mobile surgical unit'. St George's and three other hospitals, earmarked in the disaster plan were alerted to prepare for an influx of casualties. By 08.35 the first ambulances had arrived there. At 08.38 a 'Major Incident' was declared.

The Daily Telegraph reported that 'As a disaster alert went out, hospitals put emergency plans into operation. Helicopters were used to ferry medical equipment and personnel to the scene. An urgent appeal was issued for blood supplies and the Blood Transfusion Service said that there had been an "overwhelming response". Queues built up outside blood donation centres in London.'

Back at the scene of the crashes, one experienced fire officer said, 'It was sheer bloody hell at the scene—the worst railway crash I have ever had to go to. My crews have performed an heroic job. Many of them refused to be relieved until the last person who was alive in the wreckage had been rescued.' Firemen had to hack away undergrowth from around the track before survivors could be pulled from the trains. Some shocked survivors walked to nearby Emanuel School, which was converted into a makeshift medical treatment centre. A temporary mortuary was set up at the 'Services Rendered' workingmen's club near the crash. Firefighters used heavy lifting jacks to try to prop up overturned carriages and a thermal image to search for bodies in the wreckage.

The disaster was a major test for St George's in Tooting, which was the nearest hospital. The accident and emergency department had been open for only a week, although the medical and nursing staff were trained people. Mr Roger Evans, Acute Unit General Manager, reported that '104 survivors were taken in and 30 of them were kept in for treatment'.

Within about 30 minutes of the crash a mobile emergency team had arrived from St Stephen's Hospital headed by a surgeon, Mr Booth, who later observed that he was 'very impressed by the way all emergency services were very efficient'. The worst practical difficulties encountered in his opinion were those associated with people trapped by large amounts of metal. Access to such patients was very difficult and the medical staff did rely heavily on the fire brigade to get to them. The former were thought to do a marvellous job. In fact the firemen had had to call up 12 extra vehicles with cutting equipment, which they would use to cut up the wrecked trains piece by piece, until no more bodies were inside. It was not until 12.40 that everyone agreed that all live casualties had been removed from the train. Dead bodies were known to be still trapped, so work continued to recover them until the arc-lights brought up by the fire services had been extinguished. By then it was evening, and it was thought that at least 36 people had been killed and 113 injured—32 so seriously that they had to be retained in hospital. But only 17 of the dead had been positively identified.

On the night of the catastrophe British Rail issued a public statement, which read as follows:

> Preliminary investigations indicate that the probable cause of today's tragic rail accident was a technical fault following preparatory work in connection with the Waterloo resignalling scheme. Further urgent investigations are being made to confirm this.
>
> Mr Maurice Holmes, British Rail's Director of Safety, will conduct the internal inquiry into the accident and the inquiry will take place on Wednesday, before a full inquiry in public already announced by the Government, at which all the facts will be made known.
>
> British Rail accepts full responsibility for the accident.

More than £32 million is being spent replacing the 50-year-old signalling system covering the area, where at 8.13 a.m. routine Monday journeys to work ended in death and injury.

No more telling postscript to his summary account of the disaster can be offered than the statement which appeared in *The Daily Telegraph*. It read as follows:

> The effect of the disaster on the victims would have been greater still had the accident happened eight days earlier—before a £2.25 million accident unit opened two miles from the crash.

The Unit at St George's Hospital, Tooting, one of the country's biggest, took 103 of the 120 injured. Nine underwent surgery with one other dying after admission. Doctors and nurses were fully prepared to receive accident victims within the 15 minutes' notice given by ambulance crews, as required by the emergency plan. Ambulance and fire services speed of response met target times laid down therein despite rush-hour congestions.

The prompt use of police helicopters, as previously planned and practised, for example in dropping four doctors at the scene of the accident, set the tone of smoothly mounted rescue and recovery operations.

At the peak of the operation 130 firemen were at the scene and 28 ambulances backed by 11 ambulance-coaches ferried the injured to five hospitals. Those not taken to St George's went to St Thomas's, Westminster, St Stephen's, Chelsea, or Queen Mary's, Roehampton. These were the pre-planned reception hospitals for such an accident as the Clapham Junction disaster. The advantages of utilizing several hospitals rather than one are that congestion of both traffic by road, and streams of casualties at a hospital is reduced. Furthermore, the concentration of visiting or worried relatives and friends is kept down, or dispersed and better controlled. As far as may be ascertained, practised decentralization was the principle underlying the whole response of the emergency services. They were, deservedly, much congratulated on their performance.

There were still questions to be asked and answered of British Rail's communications (signalling) systems development, perhaps. It was axiomatic in the airline industry in the 1950s and 1960s that it was necessary, even at small airports, to have at least two separate telephone networks. There would be access to the public switched network, of course, and additionally, a private network to which the members of the public had not the means of access—and with which they could not interfere in any way. Otherwise, at times of irregularity such as severe weather, fogs, traffic mishaps—and accidents—communication breakdowns or delays due to system overload might occur. Thus, operations might be put at greater risk. This experience is not uncommon in other spheres of activity. It occurred, for example, during the nuclear incident at Three Mile Island (1978). One may, of course, manage to muddle through, as reported by T. de Lisle of the Clapham Junction disaster:

> Basingstoke was the one place where both trains stopped, and all morning every telephone in the station was either in use or ringing. As soon as one worried wife, parent, child or colleague rang off, another got through.
> If the telephone was in the parcels office or the goods depot, that was better than nothing. 'They are so desperate to get some information', a spokesman said, 'that they are trying every number we have'.

By mid-morning, 400 people had come on the line and 400 people had been reassured. 'We have been able to comfort most of them by finding out what train they normally travel on', said Mr R. Davies, the station manager at Basingstoke. 'We have not actually come across anyone whose relations were on those trains, yet.'

Up the line at Farnborough, where the 07.18 from Basingstoke called at 07.39, they knew that they had. 'We already know that two of our train drivers are dead', said the station master. It has been the busiest Monday morning, they said, for a long time—and that was before the crash. Now, relatives who could not get through by telephone were coming in person, seeking news and reassurance, both at Clapham and Farnborough, perhaps, too, at Basingstoke. There was no provision of extra emergency telephones for any accident information service.

THE AIRCRASH AT KEGWORTH, 8 JANUARY 1989

On the night of Sunday, 8 January 1989, a Boeing 737 of British Midland Airways, carrying 126 people crashed into the side of the M1 motorway near Kegworth, Leicestershire. There were 44 deaths, all passengers. The crew members all survived though some, including the Captain, were seriously injured.

The aircraft had been flying from Heathrow to Belfast, when one engine failed. The Captain decided quite properly to make an emergency landing at the not too far distant East Midlands Airport. All appropriate measures for a single engine landing were taken and no unusual difficulty was anticipated. Then, it seemed that whilst the aircraft was still short of the runway, its second engine failed and it crashed. *The Daily Telegraph* reported the accident briefly on 9 January, but more extensively the next day, noting, *inter alia*, that:

> Local people and survivors of the crash praised the skill of Capt. Hurd in guiding the crippled aircraft clear of the village of Kegworth in his vain fight to reach East Midlands airport only 20 seconds flying time away.
> There was praise, too, for the airport fire brigade which reached the scene in minutes to put out a fire that threatened an explosion to the leaking fuel tanks in the jet's wings.

It is, of course, usual for airports to carry both firefighting equipment and personnel and to have emergency procedures in place with nearby brigades. There are commonly police on hand—at least at the larger airports. Similarly, there are medical personnel and at least some facilities on site, backed by outside more extensive facilities. Fortunately, East Midlands Airport in early January 1989 was in better circumstances still. *The Independent* of 10 January 1989 noted:

> Survivors from the crash were allocated to one of three emergency hospitals in Leicester, Derby and Nottingham, depending on the nature and severity of their injuries.

Derby Royal Infirmary (DRI) had been designated as the major accident hospital for the East Midlands, and its response was orchestrated under a series of procedures laid down in a 50 page document known as *Majax* or *Major Accidents Plan*. This plan had been devised by a committee chaired by Paul Pritty, consultant in the accident and emergency unit of the DRI. The procedures had been in place for 12 years, though periodically revised and updated. The latest draft had not yet been put to the test. The medical, nursing and ambulance staff were, of course, fully prepared in terms of the existing draft. There was to have been a presentation and discussion of *Majax* on the day following the crash, to consider whether to alter the plan in the light of new ideas and recent experience. So the plan was in the forefront of people's minds ready for a full reappraisal and revision in a week or so.

The emergency procedures, activated by the codeword *Majax*, work according to a system whereby each member of the hospital staff 'knows his or her duties and orders in advance, and acts under those orders, when the plan is activated'. On the whole, the plan in its existing form had worked smoothly on this occasion. Mr Pritty described the scenes inside the crashed 737 as survivors were carried to safety.

Some passengers at the bottom of the wreckage were buried under seats and other passengers and bodies of passengers for some considerable time. There had been no amputations at the scene, but one woman who was not freed until four or five hours after the crash, had extremely serious ankle injuries and might lose her foot.

The most seriously injured tended to be those who came out last, and there was a high proportion of lower limb and lower abdominal injuries. They were treated at the scene with pain-killers, sedatives and fluids, to replace blood lost through wounds.

Mr Pritty said that when he arrived at the scene, he had not expected to see so many survivors. He said '... wholehearted tribute to the firemen who had worked so magnificently in hazardous conditions to get people to safety'. In fact, there were several tales of fortitude and unselfish help for others on the part of passengers and passing motorists. But this behaviour is something one has come to expect and it is implicitly taken into account and allowed for in most emergency planning.

In one sense the victims of this accident were lucky. A landing on one engine only was expected. Firemen and ambulances, engineers, police cars, etc., would be standing on alert at the airport landing-strip in case of accident, and an accident did happen—but it was a nastier accident than could possibly have been fully prepared for. Still, some preparations were 'at the ready' close to the right place. There was no delay in starting rescue and recovery operations or in treating the injured.

Afterwards

The emergency services again received nothing but praise for their excellent preparations and procedures. With the causes of the accident we need not be concerned, as the whole thing is still a matter of inquiry. Since this chapter was delivered, however, the coroner's inquest has been held in May 1990, lasting for two days. There was much questioning directed at seeking the reasons why and how it came to pass that the right hand (good) engine of the aircraft was shut down when a landing was being initiated because the left engine was known to be disabled (by a fractured fan blade). The verdict of the Coroner's Court was 'Accidental Death'. There remains, still expected, the technical report of the Air Accident Investigation Board.

THAMES BOAT DISASTER, 20 AUGUST 1989

At about 01.46 hours on Sunday, 20 August 1989 a Thames pleasure cruiser the *Marchioness*, with reputedly 110 passengers and a crew of two aboard, collided with the much heavier sand dredger, *Bowbelle*. The *Marchioness* capsized and, within 3 minutes, it sank. Some passengers were swept overboard from the decks, others caught in the saloon bar managed to scramble or pump out, others were trapped inside. There was considerable confusion. Several, who fell into the river, were carried downstream and away from the site. There are two quotations from the press reports.

> Everyone was screaming and panicking, and we were thrown round the deck, crashing into each other. I remember being pushed into the water with legs and feet everywhere keeping me down. There was wood, and cans and debris of all kinds floating about as I finally came up. The exhaustion was terrible. I fought to try to keep myself afloat. I just did not have the energy, and more than once I thought I was going to die. I saw a bridge and swam towards it but was swept right by. The current was so strong.
>
> (Miss Louise Phillips, student, aged 19)

She was finally pulled to a life ring by two men and rescued by a police launch 15 minutes later.

Annette Russell 26, who runs a modelling agency, dived off the side as the *Marchioness* went down. 'It all happened terribly quickly. People were chatting and dancing to the music', she said. 'Then we were rammed from behind. There was no time to get hold of a life jacket. It was taken by the tide. It drew me under the boat and out the other side.' She was picked up there later and pulled out. There were many such cases and worse. These may suffice to convey the atmosphere of the incident.

Rescue operations began promptly. Another pleasure boat the *Hurlingham*, which was nearby, began picking survivors out of the water almost at once at 01.46. By 01.49 the Thames River Police had been notified via a police launch radio that the accident had occurred and where and what help was needed. By 01.53, however, 7 minutes after the collision, the London Ambulance Service had already received its first call. Thirteen ambulances were immediately dispatched to the scene. More continued to be sent during the night and were posted at all bridges from Westminster to Wapping. A Thames fireboat was in place presently and released 55 inflated life jackets into the river. All available boats were directed to the accident. There was a tumult of activity. In addition, the RAF Rescue Co-Ordination Centre at Culrose was promptly told of the emergency, and it dispatched a 'Sea-King' helicopter from Kent and a 'Wessex' from Cotishall, Norfolk. These helicopters were to prove invaluable in the search for survivors.

There was no shortage of rescue equipment, nor of competent personnel to conduct rescue operations—once they were mobilized, which it seems was as promptly as may be. Rescue and recovery work continued throughout the day and, at 17.09 the wreck of the *Marchioness* was hauled to the surface and 'the grim search for the remaining bodies began'.

There was not, indeed, any failure of readiness to respond to this incident properly on the part of any of the emergency services, civilian or military, the

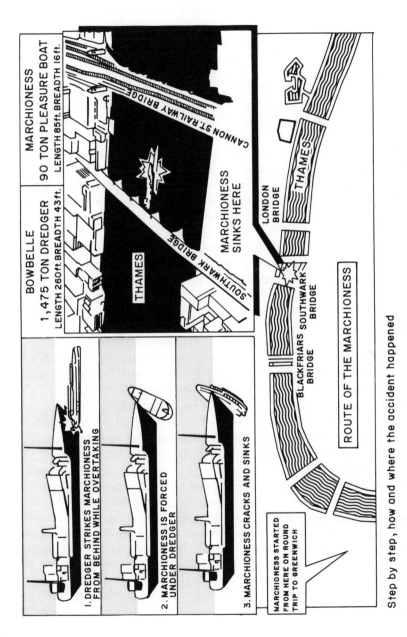

Figure 8.2 Details of the *Marshioness* disaster. (Copyright © 1989 the *Daily Mail*, London. Reproduced by permission.)

personnel of which came in for much praise and many thanks afterwards. It is clear that although no counter-emergency plan had been, or could be, rehearsed for a river accident of this specific type, there had been some effective pre-planning of a general sort. This is confirmed by a report of 21 August 1989 in the *Daily Mail*, which states: 'Scotland Yard had already been alerted by the river police. Immediately, it set in motion a long-standing river disaster plan agreed between itself, the military and the fire and ambulance services.' The beneficial effects of this prior activity were clear.

Prior planning and preparation of safety measures on board the *Marchioness* in several other respects were deficient. For some time after the sinking, no one knew for sure how many people had been aboard and, therefore, how many dead, injured and missing there were. This impeded the work of those searching for victims. This could have been avoided by the well-known device of boarding-cards or sailing-tickets. But nothing of that sort was done. There was no passenger list against which passengers could be checked off as they boarded. This easy-going attitude has long been commonplace—not only in Britain—for river and some other cruises. It is no longer the practice on British sea-going ferries since it created some difficulties when the *Herald of Free Enterprise* capsized off Zeebrugge. It is certainly not the practice with airlines. Eventually, the number of fatalities was confirmed as 51, the worst British transport accident of the year.

Afterwards

In March 1990, the report of Captain Marriott, Chief Inspector of the Marine Accident Investigation Bureau, was, in accordance with the usual, current, British official and political practice, leaked to the press. His report, according to *The Daily Telegraph* (20 March 1990), stated, *inter alia*, that the immediate cause of the tragedy was 'the failure of the look-outs on both vessels to see the danger'. This was elaborated presently to another statement: 'When the look-out on the *Bowbelle* finally spotted the danger and shouted a warning to the wheel-house it was not heard because of the noise of the disco.' It was 'clearly not satisfactory that this was the only means of internal communication between look-out and skipper at the time'. There were other factors. Some were managerial, but really nothing of great individual significance. The collision of the *Marchioness* and the *Bowbelle* seems to have been truly an accident. The captain of the *Marchioness*, Captain Stephen Faldo, was killed in the accident which, in terms of fatalities, was more serious than the accidents at Clapham Junction and Kegworth.

CONCLUSION

The three transport accidents discussed here have several features in common despite representing three different modes of travel: rail (land), aviation (air) and river-boat (water). It has not been the purpose of this short chapter to analyse the causes of the accidents themselves or to discuss ways of preventing their recurrence. Those are worthy technical matters, which it would take far more space to discuss than is available here. The aim has been merely to look at what forms the rescue and recovery (or emergency) services took and to gain some notion of their effectiveness. It may be said at once that in the opinion of the writer they performed well in all three cases. Every case required the use of several means of rescue and recovery, and several means had been provided for both in advance planning and on the day. Multiple ambulances, casualty wards and other hospital facilities were available, and so on. It has all been mentioned in the text. One is used to reading of muddles and inadequacies in the handling of many accidents as in some accounts of the Boeing 737 accident at Manchester Airport 1985. There was nothing like that at Kegworth in 1989. Despite the number of casualties, and the frightening experiences related by some survivors of this later crash, one can feel a certain degree of satisfaction of the conduct of all concerned—rescuers and rescued.

These three accidents involved emergency services, which had done some careful advance planning—it is mentioned in the press accounts of each accident, with praise. It proved its value.

To cope with transport accidents of the size and scope of those described above the staffing, management training, organization and equipment of the emergency services in Britain seem more than capable. Would they be sufficient for larger catastrophes? How about the King's Cross fire? That question may be discussed now. A fire in a metro (subway) stationed caused by a burning cigarette (or whatever) is not a transportation accident. If it were a result of the derailment of a train that was passing through, it might very likely qualify. The great explosion in the harbour of Halifax NS in 1917 was a transport accident, for it involved the collision of two ammunition ships. There would have been no transportation accident at Clapham Junction if none of the trains had been moving.

If some institutionalized overlord were to be created in Britain with managers and controllers based on a focus in, say, Bristol or two foci, one in Bristol and one in Stirling, say, it should be easier to manage the whole range of accidents or disasters in Britain with greater competence. This has been argued forcefully in *The Guardian* (15–16 June 1988) by Sandra Milne Henderson. Transportation accidents would be included. Whether or not they would be better handled than now is unclear. It is worth thinking about.

ACKNOWLEDGEMENTS AND REFERENCES

This chapter concerns three transport accidents which occurred between December 1988 and August 1989. The information upon which this chapter is based was derived from reports published at the time in the *Daily Mail, The Daily Telegraph* and *The Independent.*

This chapter was originally presented in the School of Management Seminar Series on 'Risk' at the University of Hull in March 1990 and was based on the available published material at that time.

In addition, thanks are due to the *Daily Mail,* and *The Daily Telegraph* for kind permission to reproduce diagrams of the *Marchioness/Bowbelle* disaster and the Clapham Junction disaster respectively.

Chapter 9

Science and Social Responsibility

Brian Wynne
Lancaster University

ABSTRACT

In the rapid escalation of environmental concern, various established norms and perceptions have been cast loose. In this context of multiplying uncertainties, scientific knowledge has been envisaged as the basis of authority for social decisions. This chapter analyses the role and limits of scientific knowledge as a basis for social authority in the field of environmental policy.

INTRODUCTION

One of the most important new goals of environmental and technology policies in the last decade has been the shift towards prevention. This hard-won change in attitudes is founded on implicit acceptance of the inherent limitations of the anticipatory knowledge on which decisions about environmental discharges are based. We can often only find out once it is too late, or at the very least awesomely expensive to clean up.

However, whilst the preventive paradigm is acknowledged in principle, its practice is extremely tenuous, not least because we cannot know definitively what is an adequate level of investment in technological or social change so as to prevent environmental harm. The preventive approach brings the need to refocus attention further upstream, from 'end-of-pipe' to decisions about industrial process design, about products, and about R&D strategies. Inevitably this means finding criteria to determine decisions affecting environmental loads,

---

Risk: Analysis, Assessment and Management. Edited by J. Ansell and F. Wharton.

at a point much further removed than conventional pollution control is from the point of immediate environmental discharge, thus from the point(s) of identification of environmental effects.

The usual technical approach to clean production poses the general question: how, and how far can we improve the efficiency of industrial processes in terms of resource use and waste outputs? The sub-text is, how far do we need to go in this direction, which is after all expensive and ill-defined? An even more difficult question is whether environmentally sustainable futures are feasible even if we assumed the most efficient systems of production to be universally in place tomorrow; might not growing consumption and production simply swallow up the advances provided by those imagined technical Utopias? How do we provide authoritative knowledge for defining even how far we need to enforce greater process efficiency (in both resource-use and waste-output dimensions), let alone to control production and consumption? And all this in the context of extreme global inequity which has to be reduced.

In this broad perspective the question of how one justifies where the balance is struck between costs, benefits and uncertainties becomes even more problematic than it has been for conventional 'end-of-pipe' approaches. The scientific burden of proof in environmental regulation has become a matter of intensifying conflict in recent years (Funtowicz and Ravetz, 1990). This has embodied two linked issues: first of all where to locate that burden on the spectrum from complete environmental protection to waiting for obvious damage? second what burden can the scientific knowledge actually sustain, or be expected to sustain anyway (Jasanoff, 1986)? One suspects that the answer to the first question has too often been set by unacknowledged weaknesses in the scientific knowledge-base for identifying environmental damage.

One particular regulatory principle which is associated with the preventive philosophy, and which gives it practical effect, is the Precautionary Principle (von Moltke, 1987; Jackson and Taylor, 1991). This was first developed in Germany as a means of justifying regulatory interventions to restrict marine pollution discharges in the absence of agreed proof of environmental harm. Despite being difficult to define in precise terms, it has been taken up in other environmental policy arenas, even including global climate change. The scope of the Precautionary Principle in terms of shifting the burden of proof onto the polluter is still not clearly defined in relation to the nature of scientific proof, and to the preventive philosophy. I will argue that the precautionary approach involves much more than simply shifting the threshold of proof to a different place in the same available body of knowledge. The different social premise which that shift implies, also opens up the possible reshaping of the natural categories and classifications on which that scientific knowledge is constructed.

Clearly, shifting the locus of environmental responsibility further upstream in the industrial commitment process opens up more room for uncertainty about eventual downstream environmental effects. However, the change is not only in scale. There are at least two fundamentally new kinds of uncertainty which are introduced, suggesting that established concepts of risk and uncertainty no longer serve us very well. These qualitative changes relate to the ways we think of decision making about environmental discharges and damage, and the way we think of the role and nature of scientific authority in relation to such decisions. Before discussing each of these, however, I would like to set the scene by reviewing in outline the evolution of environmental risk assessment as a framework for generating knowledge and authority for environmental decision-making problems.

RISK AND REDUCTIONISM

Risk assessment as a scientifically disciplined way of analysing risk and safety problems was originally developed for relatively very well-structured mechanical problems such as chemical or nuclear plants, aircraft and aerospace technologies (Otway, 1985). In such systems the technical processes and parameters are well defined, and the reliability of separate components is testable or amenable to actuarial in-service analysis. Indeed so controlled are the parameters of such systems that risk analysis did not develop after design and manufacture, to try to understand the built-in risks; it was an integral part of design, influencing criteria and choices in normative fashion, right through the whole process. (These systems have often shown themselves to be less well defined than analysts and designers thought, exhibiting surprising properties —such as exploding—which indicate that the system was less determined by controlling forces than the analysts recognized (Wynne, 1988). Nevertheless the point remains that relatively speaking this original cradle of risk analysis allowed its authors to build in assumptions of well-defined and deterministic processes.)

These intellectual and methodological origins of risk assessment are important to recall because its role has now grown far beyond these well-defined intensive risk systems, to badly structured extensive problems such as toxic wastes or pesticides, thence to environmental systems even on a global scale. For these latter kinds of problem the limitations of the available knowledge are potentially more serious because the system in question, not being a technological artefact, cannot be designed, manipulated and reduced to within the boundaries of existing analytical knowledge. In constructing analytic models of environmental systems, externally defined significant end-points, or pragmatic considerations such as what can actually be measured, frequently dictate the structure of the resulting knowledge. Many important parameters have to be charted at one or more removes, via observation of surrogate variables. In other situations variables are used which combine more than one parameter in complex form. Even something so apparently simple and precise as a single pH measure for a lake is strictly speaking such a composite variable, because we have to extrapolate and weight sample measurements which are always limited, into the mean value for that variable. These practices artificially reduce uncertainties and variations, for example by the ways in which averaging, standardization, and aggregation are performed. The fact that this is necessary and justified by the need to generate knowledge does not alter the point that it imposes man-made intellectual closure around entities which are more open-ended than the resulting models suggest. Yet these intellectual routines become so familiar to practitioners that their indirect and more provisional relationship to the ultimate parameters of interest is forgotten.

The very considerable amount of scientific work which has gone into the modelling of environmental risk systems over the last few decades cannot therefore be taken as reassurance that the main dimensions of environmental harm from human activities have been comprehended. To understand this requires not only intense and open examination of the scientific evidence and competing interpretations in an area of interest, but also an appreciation of the nature and inherent limitations in principle of that knowledge, however competently produced.

Some key distinctions can be seen by reference to Table 9.1.

Table 9.1 Sources of risk

RISK	Know the odds
UNCERTAINTY	Don't know the odds: may know the main parameters. May reduce uncertainty but increase ignorance
IGNORANCE	Don't know what we don't know. Ignorance increases with increased commitments based on given knowledge
INDETERMINACY	Causal chains or networks open

(1)   We can talk authentically about risk when the system of behaviour is basically well known, and the chances of different outcomes can be defined and quantified by structured analysis of mechanisms and probabilities.

(2)   If we know the system parameters, but do not have the odds nor any way of calculating them, we can talk of uncertainties—at least we know of their existence, and there are several sophisticated methods for estimating them and their effects upon outcomes. These uncertainties are explicitly included in analysis.

(3)   A far more difficult problem is ignorance, which by definition escapes recognition. This is not so much a characteristic of knowledge itself, as of

the linkages between knowledge and commitments based upon it—in effect, bets (technological, social, economic) on the completeness and validity of that knowledge. Since this is conceptually more elusive an example is justified:

In the aftermath of the Chernobyl nuclear accident, in May 1986 a radioactive cloud passed over Britain. Heavy thunderstorms rained out radiocaesium deposits over upland areas, and despite reassurances that there would be no lasting effects of the radioactive cloud, six weeks after the accident a sudden ban on hill sheep sales and slaughter was announced. Although this ban was expected to last only three weeks, because the radiocaesium was thought to be chemically immobilized in the soil once washed off vegetation, some hill farms in these areas of Cumbria and North Wales in particular, are still restricted several years later. The scientists made a spectacular mistake in predicting the behaviour of radiocaesium in the environment of interest. It was gradually learnt that the reason for this mistake was that the original prediction had been based upon the observed behaviour of caesium in alkaline clay soils, whereas those of the area in question were acid peaty soils. It was assumed by the scientists—wrongly as it turned out—that the previously observed behaviour also prevailed in the conditions which existed in the hill areas. Thus, contrary to the confident expectations of the scientists, the elevated levels of radiocaesium in the sheep from these upland areas did not fall, and restrictions had to be extended indefinitely, severely damaging the credibility of the scientists and institutions concerned. Eventually it was realized that the chemical immobilization which had been assumed, only took place in aluminosilicate clays, and that in the upland peaty acid soils caesium remains chemically mobile, hence available for root uptake and recycle via edible vegetation back into the food chain.

It is important to recognize that this highly public scientific mistake actually followed normal scientific practice. Scientists attempted to predict the behaviour of an agent (here radiocaesium) by extrapolating from its observed behaviour under certain conditions, making some assumptions about the new conditions. When the new observations did not fit with expected behaviour, the models underlying the predictions were re-examined. By these means certain previously unnoticed significant differences were identified, and the models were elaborated accordingly.

Had this whole process taken place in the seclusion of the professional community of research scientists, it would have been wholly unremarkable (unless some scientist or another had been too committed to a particular model, in which case a dispute might have erupted, or a reputation could have been tarnished). The point is that scientific knowledge proceeds by exogenizing some significant uncertainties, which thus become invisible to it;

as Kuhn (1962) noted, this is not a pathology of science but a necessary feature of structured investigation. The built-in ignorance of science towards its own limiting commitments and assumptions is a problem only when external commitments are built upon it as if such inherent limitations did not exist (Wynne, 1985)—as happened when scientists and government officials pronounced in June 1986 on the basis of then-sovereign models, that radiocaesium levels would come down within a few weeks.

The foregoing example underlines an important general point about scientific knowledge in public, and one not usually understood. The conventional view is that scientific knowledge and method enthusiastically embrace uncertainties and exhaustively pursue them. This is seriously misleading. It is more accurate to say that scientific knowledge gives prominence to a restricted agenda of defined uncertainties—ones that are tractable—leaving invisible a range of other uncertainties especially about the boundary conditions of applicability of the existing framework of knowledge to new situations.

Thus ignorance is endemic to scientific knowledge, which has to reduce the framework of knowledge to that which is amenable to its own parochial methods and models. This only becomes a problem when (as is usual) scientific knowledge is misunderstood and is institutionalized in policy making as if this condition did not pervade all competent scientific knowledge. Mature use of science in public policy would focus not on whether the science is 'good' or 'bad' as if that were a question with a universally true answer, but on the conditions under which it is valid, and whether those conditions prevail in the situation of interest.

(4) The important distinction between uncertainty and indeterminacy will be illustrated later, but here it is relevant simply to note that conventional risk assessment methods tend to treat all uncertainties as if they were due to incomplete definition, of an essentially determinate cause–effect system. In other words they suggest that the route to better control of risks is more intense scientific knowledge of that system, to narrow the supposed uncertainties and gain more precise definition of it. I will show that many risk systems embody genuine indeterminacies which are misrepresented by this approach; but I will develop the further argument that the scientific knowledge which we construct of risk and environmental systems is also pervaded by tacit social judgements which cover indeterminacies in that knowledge itself. The assumption that these conditions are universal natural truths renders indeterminate knowledge apparently determinate. Lack of recognition of this distorts public debate and understanding of the proper relationship between expert knowledge and public value-choices in constructing regulatory policies for sustainable environmental technolo-

gies. To appreciate the full extent of our human responsibilities as they shape the basis of policy options requires us to examine more thoroughly the nature of indeterminacy in the systems we are engaged in changing through our human activities. This in turn requires us to explore the more subtle indeterminacies buried (sometimes as self-confirmations) in our 'natural' knowledge of those systems.

UPSTREAM DECISIONS ABOUT ENVIRONMENTAL EFFECTS

The shift of attention upstream has at least two major implications for the way that we think about regulatory policies and processes.

Firstly, the locus of decision making shifts more to the internal processes of industrial R&D, design and production, which introduces a range of complex organizational factors to do with how this behavior is influenced. It is currently unclear to what extent it should be conceived as a self-contained process subject to external regulatory signals, or as an open learning system within and between organizations, and in which new understandings and practical environmental criteria may become 'organically' embedded. Most of the research literature and policy thinking about regulation and environmental policy is framed in the former terms (Schot, 1992). This conventional thinking tends to 'black-box' industrial decision processes and technology generally. This may have been defensible when the focus was on 'end-of-pipe' regulatory mechanisms, but to treat upstream challenges new conceptual approaches are needed which are rooted in industrial–organizational processes of negotiation and commitment, with a fuller sense of both their constraints and flexibilities.

Secondly, as the centre of gravity for analysis and decision moves further upstream and more distant from environmental effects, greater levels of uncertainty are obviously introduced in the investigation of possible causal links between decisions and environmental consequences. Less obvious however, and just as important, is that the type of uncertainty also changes. This is most easily seen by referring to Figure 9.1, in which various stages of decision from upstream to diverse eventual environmental discharges are schematically portrayed.

The key point is that in trying to draw causal connections between an upstream decision option and downstream consequences of that option, the intervening uncertainties are better characterized as indeterminacies. They are not merely lack of definition in a determinate cause–effect system; the relationship between upstream commitments and downstream outcomes is a combination of genuine constraints which are laid down in determinate fashion, and real open-endedness in the sense that outcomes depend upon how intermediate actors behave. These intermediate actors include managers and workers such as

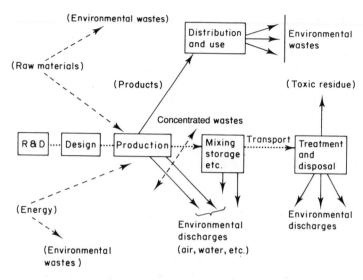

Figure 9.1 Production waste system (schematic)

plant operators, waste traders and other commercial agents, consumers, inspectors and other local regulatory actors; in any given case the significant actors and relationships, hence the variables affecting environmental outcomes, will be different depending on the system of production, waste generation and disposal, and the regulatory system in question.

Thus to illustrate, an industrial process generating more or less the same waste streams may present markedly different downstream environmental risks in the United States and the United Kingdom, because of significant differences in the regulatory cultures of these two countries. Even within the confines of a single system this is also true. Different levels of stringency of allowed discharges from point sources to air or water mean that different waste streams are produced in concentrated form for removal, treatment and disposal. A liquid toxic waste stream such as an inorganic acid may under the UK regulations be legally landfill-discharged by co-disposal with municipal garbage. The US regulations rule this out. Even in the same country the same industrial process will vary in the environmental disposition of its wastes depending on many contingent factors such as where it is produced, which company is involved, which waste disposal company (if any) it deals with, how prices for competing options are changing, and what opportunities exist for maximizing profits by exploiting recovery and recycle possibilities, or alternatively finding cheap disposal outlets in other countries with weak controls.

The distinction between uncertainty and indeterminacy is important because the former enshrines the notion that inadequate control of environmental risks is due only to inadequate scientific knowledge, and exclusive attention is focused upon intensifying that knowledge. As an aside here, existing interpretations of the potentially revolutionary precautionary principle do not seem to me to change this situation.

The extra concept of indeterminacy therefore introduces the idea that contingent social behaviour also has to be explicitly included in analytical and prescriptive frameworks. Of course behavioural regulation is already implicit in technical standards, but the full extent of contingency and indeterminacy, and the implications of this, are not recognized. This corresponds with the distinction I drew some years ago in the risk field, between what I termed 'intrinsic' and 'situational' risks from a given toxic waste (Wynne, 1987). The actual risks are a combination of the inherent toxicity, etc., of the chemicals composing the waste, and the ways various people actually treat it. This contingent 'treatment' also includes how relevant commercial actors define the material, since they have some freedom (which varies between regulatory regimes) to define it as goods not wastes (for example as raw materials for a recycling or energy plant), thus exempting it from regulation.

The type of indeterminacy so far discussed is the open-endedness in the processes of environmental damage due to human interventions. Risk frameworks have found these difficult to treat even for 'the human factor' in well-defined mechanical systems. In more extensive systems such as toxic waste life cycles a deeper tension is exposed between analytical knowledge of the risks which in standardizing risk situations inevitably implies the elaborate control and reorganization of social behaviour so as to conform with the standardized analytical models, and a realistic appreciation of the diverse situational forces and factors which defy such reductionist and deterministic treatment. The knowledge used to define such risks and to justify ensuing regulations is only confirmed if the social world can indeed be reorganized and controlled so as to reflect the assumptions built into that knowledge in the first place. Thus, for example the UK Government's assertion that co-disposal of toxic wastes with municipal garbage is safe, is based upon studies of several landfills in the 1960s and 1970s. Embedded in that body of risk knowledge is the fact that during those studies great care was taken with respect to the management of the sites and what went into them. The risk knowledge may be valid on a wider scale only if that condition, *inter alia*, is fulfilled on that scale. Whether or not it is fulfilled in future cases depends upon its being recognized as an indeterminacy in the system, and in the corresponding risk knowledge.

SCIENTIFIC AND SOCIAL UNCERTAINTY

When discussing the burden of proof for environmental decisions it is important to avoid the mistake of thinking that there is an objective level of uncertainty intrinsic to any piece of scientific knowledge at its current state or refinement.

The level of recognized uncertainty is itself a function of the perhaps sub-conscious perceptions of the role(s) of that knowledge. Another example is appropriate:

The scientific uncertainties about what happens chemically, physically and biologically in a landfill site are huge, and the opportunities for examining and reducing them are extremely limited. Thus the effects of putting a given waste into a site can only be approximately known, and again, they are not in any case determinate, but depend, *inter alia*, upon how the site is operated and managed. At which site a waste ends up, and in what condition, also depends upon many social unknowns and contingencies. In the US political culture the scientific uncertainties about what happens to a waste in landfills would be a hostage to fortune for regulators, who would have opponents exposing those uncertainties to insist that landfill was hazardous, that it was irresponsible to sanction it when its safety was so uncertain, and that it should be banned. Thus the social threat which exists in the extremely conflictual, mistrustful and adversary US regulatory culture, causes a scientific uncertainty to be accentuated and avoided, resulting in the US decision to phase out landfill of toxic wastes. Uncertainty underlying decisions is a social risk because of the institutionalized mistrust which pervades the US system. Social discretion is not regarded as an asset, unless of course one can monopolize it.

In the UK political culture on the other hand, the official attitude towards the same scientific uncertainties has been far more relaxed. The response has been that if things are uncertain they could therefore turn out better—there is no reason to assume the worst. For example, natural bacterial processes in the landfill may detoxify some chemicals so reducing the environmental risks; and if the risks depend upon sound operation and diligent waste handling, optimistic assumptions may be made unless strong evidence to the contrary exists. The point is that this official position has (at least until recently) been possible because the more consensual—and some would say complacent —UK political culture of environmental regulation has not experienced any social threat from exploitation by opponents of the technical uncertainties underlying such environmental policy decisions.

Thus uncertainties in the scientific knowledge for environmental protection decisions cannot be taken as objective shortfalls of adequate knowledge for full control of the effects. The extent of uncertainty seen in the scientific knowledge-base is itself a subjective function of complex social and cultural factors. Scientific uncertainty can be enlarged by social uncertainties in the context of its practical interpretation, and it can be reduced by opposite social forces (Gilbert and Mulkay, 1984).

I would like to give one further example of the deep ways in which indeterminacies can pervade the very detailed technical structure of scientific knowledge, before attempting to discuss the implications of this line of argument for environmental criteria. It is again drawn from the post-Chernobyl radioactive contamination issue in the United Kingdom, this time another aspect of the episode:

High levels of radiocaesium were discovered and then, against scientific predictions, found to persist in the fells and hill sheep of Cumbria, downwind and near to the Sellafield nuclear reprocessing plant. People soon began to question whether therefore the Government and its scientists had not secretly known all along that there was radioactive contamination in this area dating from well before the Chernobyl accident, either from Sellafield's routine emissions, from the 1957 Windscale reactor accident on the same site, from atmospheric nuclear weapons testing, or from some combination of these. Thus the question 'when did they know?' about the long duration of contamination of these hill soils and vegetation with radiocaesium became a highly charged one. Environmental groups critical of the Government's secrecy argued that its scientists had known since the early 1960s that radiocaesium persisted in acid peaty soils and remained available, unlike its behaviour in alkaline clay soils. They pointed to a paper published in *Nature* (Gale, Humphreys and Fisher, 1964) by a research team from the Harwell nuclear research establishment as evidence for their claim that the scientists had known all along that the radiocaesium would recycle into vegetation from the soil and thus maintain high levels of contamination in hill sheep.

The *Nature* paper reported measurements of the depth profiles of given surface deposits of radiocaesium after yearly time-intervals up to 4.8 years, in six different soil types, including alkaline clays and acid organic peats. Contrary to the assertions of environmentalist critics, it did not conclude that the behaviour of radiocaesium in terms of its depth distribution with time was any different between these soils. Thus it was arguable that the false scientific prediction of only short-term high levels was based upon an innocent, if mistaken, extrapolation from observed behaviour in lowland clay soils to the (peaty) Cumbrian fells. However, it is important to look more closely at the research and its relationship to the situation confronted in the post-Chernobyl emergency in the hill-farming areas.

The measurements of radiocaesium in the different soils were physical depth measurements. The authors observed that the mean depth from several measurements at each time interval in each soil type showed no significant differences among the different soils. The only difference was that the peaty soils showed a wider range of variance, but the mean was the same. Thus in terms of physical depth of radiocaesium as the key parameter, these soils were the same. On this basis the mistaken extrapolation could be said to have been reasonable, and the conclusion reached that the scientists had been wrong, but not conspiratorial—cognitively deficient but at least not morally so.

However, this approach, reasonable as far as it goes, omits another interesting dimension of the issue. The 1964 paper was clearly premised upon the assumption that the physical depth distribution with time was the main, even the only, parameter of interest. This corresponded with the assumption that the significant risks from such deposits of radiocaesium were from an external gamma radiation dose to a person standing on the surface. This would be mainly affected by the physical depth-distribution of the radiocaesium. Yet in the post-Chernobyl crisis a completely different exposure pathway became the focus of concern, namely the contamination of grazing sheep and thence humans who ate them. Thus the root uptake of caesium from soil into vegetation was the central factor, and this depended on its chemical mobility as well as its physical disposition. In terms of the chemical mobility parameter the acid peaty soils and alkaline clay soils were very different, since in the former caesium remains chemically free and mobile whereas in the latter it adsorbs on to the aluminosilicate molecules of the clays and is thus immobilized except for the relatively much slower processes of physical leaching of host particles. These chemical differences could indeed explain the wider range of variance (observed but not explored in the *Nature* paper) among the measurements in the acid peaty soil samples.

The example is outlined schematically in Figure 9.2. On the basis of a taken for granted social scenario of external gamma exposure as the controlling set of behavioural factors, the scientific knowledge about soils and radiocaesium was constructed from physical depth measurements, and chemical parameters were not considered. On this basis the soils were the same. Yet on the basis of the exposure scenario which unfolded after Chernobyl, the chemical availability of radiocaesium for vegetation uptake became central, without any scientist apparently realizing it at the time. As gradually became clear, on these grounds the soils behaved very differently. Sameness had switched to difference, within the same set of scientific observations. The very logic of science had been transformed, not by any new data, but by seeing from a different external perspective, namely a different scenario of human exposure.

This example illustrates how the detailed technical construction of scientific logics about environmental risks is not completely determined by the evidence from nature alone, but is partly open-ended depending upon what parameters are treated as the most significant. Usually, as with the *Nature* paper, such commitments are made without their authors realizing they have effectively

I   External γ-dose scenario

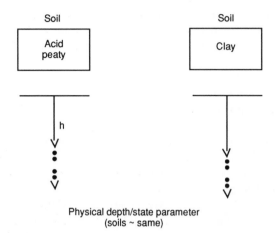

Physical depth/state parameter
(soils ~ same)

II   Food chain scenario

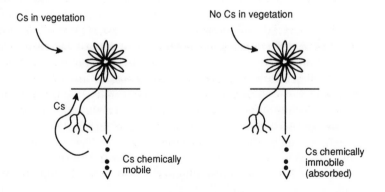

Chemical states parameter
(soils completely different)

Figure 9.2   Effect of different social scenarios of exposure on scientific logic

made such choices; they are simply part of the culture of the scientific research specialty. Yet the scientific knowledge is not fully determined by 'the facts' —what 'the facts' are has to be actively read into nature to some extent, in other words social mechanisms of closure around particular logical constructions have to occur. This is a further, more subtle and pervasive sense in which indeterminacies exist in the basis of authoritative knowledge about environmental risks.

CONCLUSIONS

The main point of this chapter has been to identify some less obvious issues for risk assessment and regulatory knowledge created by the policy shift towards preventive, or upstream strategies for integrating environmental criteria into decision making.

My argument is that moving attention upstream exposes not just more uncertainty, but fundamentally different ones, especially social indeterminacies, including indeterminacies in the 'controlling' scientific knowledge. Yet this point could be used as an argument against upstream regulatory strategies on the grounds of their infeasibility. My argument seems to imply that we cannot expect to find criteria for reasonable decision making of this kind. However this misses the main point, which is to treat these kinds of uncertainty and indeterminacy more seriously as potential sources of risk, and embrace them in a broader debate about the implications of societal commitment to such production processes.

The policy language of risk, as Donald Schon has noted (Schon, 1982), falsely reduces uncertainties to the more comforting illusion of controllable probabilistic processes. This conceals the dimension of ignorance behind practical policy and technological commitments based on a given body of scientific knowledge, and thus neglects important questions about the decreasing margins for error as such commitments in the form of environmental interventions increase in several dimensions at the same time. Thus, in another sense also, scientific uncertainty can be seen to be important not in itself, supposedly measurable on some objective scale, but as a function of (in relation to) the extent of technological or policy commitment riding on the body of knowledge concerned. As such commitments grow larger, we can tolerate less uncertainty; ironically as we discover more, the error costs rise alarmingly. Yet conventional risk-science is unable to help illuminate these, what we might call second-order risks.

The foregoing could be seen as a philosophical argument for the precautionary principle. However, even precaution in one direction throws up uncertainties and risks in others (Bodansky, 1991). Thus as defenders of environmental discharges are fond of saying, if we ban production which cannot meet the zero-discharge standards of strict precautionary principle advocates, what if we cannot feed people as a result? Long before that it would seem, consumers would be marching for pollution.

However, if we take the indeterminacy point seriously, we do not know how far new technologies and social practices can be developed in order to meet new constraints of sustainability, and new opportunities for conviviality. Also more circumspection about our interventions in nature would be engendered by recognition of the depth of ignorance and indeterminacy in principle, rather than concealment of this in the more controlled but artificial language of risk. The most important need is surely to develop 'regulatory' cultures which not only encourage but require greater public debate on the social benefits, costs and indeterminacies of different products and processes as well as on conventional environmental strategy questions. Only this more rounded approach to the environmental assessment problem can offer the possibility of overcoming what is otherwise a fundamental limitation of the risk-science paradigm, which is its intrinsic inability to see the full extent of ignorance and thus, second-order risk, underlying present technological commitments and trajectories. Indeed the dominant risk-science approach inadvertently conceals the extent of that ignorance, and thus blinds us to these more substantial kinds of ignorance and its consequences until they are upon us and we are forced into remedial modes of operation yet again.

All of this is relevant to the central issue in criteria for clean production decisions, because it should influence how we treat the issue of scientific burden of proof. With the advent of the precautionary principle the burden of proof appears to have shifted, but some more basic expectations still remain. Thus for example most formulations of the PP (certainly in the United Kingdom) accept the need to stop a discharge in the absence of full scientific proof of harm, if it is reasonably anticipated to be irreversibly harmful. However this still suggests that scientific proof is expected soon for such decisions. This may be a limited and mistaken way to view the problem because it appears to hold that the body of scientific knowledge remains qualitatively the same, whilst the threshold of acceptable risk is simply moved across the body of knowledge to a different position within that knowledge—as it were nearer to technology and further from nature.

However, the point of the example drawn from the radiocaesium-soil research knowledge was to indicate that 'when scientific knowledge knows what?' is more fundamentally open-ended, soft and thus more deeply problematic than this model recognizes. As we shift the normative rule through the body of scientific knowledge in this way, that body of knowledge itself may change. This is suggested in the different kinds of scientific knowledge produced on the one hand by conventional research recognized under assimilative capacity approaches to marine pollution regulations and on the other that underpinning the precautionary principle. The latter for example is much more ready to accept the use of composite variables such as 'stress' or 'immunocompetence', whose more holistic character is just what makes them scientifically suspect to conventional single cause–effect, precision-oriented research styles (Dethlefsen, 1988).

We cannot expect to leave the responsibility for defining the criteria of clean technology to environmental science and risk assessment, nor to any such technical disciplines acting alone. Nor can we even expect them to discover the different risks and benefits, for society to then exercise values and choices. The natural knowledge which those disciplines generate is already partly a reflection of our cultural values and identities. Thus to fully address the issue of values, behaviour and consumerist cultural identities which are increasingly acknowledged to be central factors in the environmental problem, will also require some willingness to wrest open the black boxes of 'natural knowledge' and consider their internal reconstruction. This implies institutional questions too. The preventive paradigm for environmentally sustainable technology is opening up a more radical shift in our relationship with scientific knowledge, and a correspondingly more radical challenge to society, than has yet been recognized.

REFERENCES

Bodansky, D. (1991). Scientific uncertainty and the precautionary principle, *Environment*, **33** (Sept. 1991), 4–5 and 43–44.

Dethlefsen, V. (1988). Assessment of data on fish diseases, in P. Newman and A. Agg (eds), *Environmental Protection of the North Sea*, Heinemann, London, pp. 276–285.

Funtowicz, S. and Ravetz, J. (1990). *Global Environmental Issues and the Emergence of Second Order Science*, Council for Science & Society, London.

Gale, H.J., Humphreys, D.L. and Fisher, E.M. (1964). Weathering of Caesium-137 in soils, *Nature*, No 4916, 18 January, 257–61.

Gilbert, G.N. and Mulkay, M. (1984). *Opening Pandora's Box*, Cambridge University Press, Cambridge.

Jasanoff, S. (1986). Contested boundaries in policy-relevant science, *Social Studies of Science*, **16**.

Kuhn, T. (1962). *The Structure of Scientific Revolutions*, Chicago University Press, Chicago.

Moltke, K. von (1987). *The 'Vorsorgeprinzip' in West German Environmental Policy*, Institute for European Environmental Policy, Bonn, London, Brussels.

Otway, H. (1985). Regulation and risk assessment, in H. Otway and M. Peltu (eds), *Regulating Industrial Risk*, Butterworths, London.

Schon, D. (1982). Risk and uncertainty, reprinted in S.B. Barnes and D.O. Edge (eds), *Science in Context*, Open University, Milton Keynes.

Schot, J. (1992). Constructive technology assessment: the case of clean technology, *Science Technology and Human Values*, **20**, (in press).

Wynne, B. (1985). Scientific uncertainty and environmental policy: towards a new paradigm, paper for UN World Commission on Environment and Development, Geneva, May 1985.

Wynne, B. (1987). *Risk Management and Hazardous Wastes*, Springer, London.

Wynne, B. (1988). 'Unruly technology: practical rules, impractical discourses and public understanding, *Social Studies of Science*, **18**, 87–103.

Chapter 10

Major Epidemics of the Twentieth Century: from Coronary Thrombosis to AIDS

Richard Doll
ICRF Cancer Epidemiology and Clinical Trials Unit
Gibson Laboratories
Radcliffe Infirmary, Oxford, UK

ABSTRACT

There has been a dramatic decrease in mortality over the last 100 years, particularly in the first few years of life. The rate of improvement, standardized for age, was practically constant from 1890 to 1950, slowed down from 1950 to 1975, and then speeded up again. Changes in society, medical knowledge, and biological organisms have contributed to the trend, some introducing new hazards as well as helping to prevent or cure disease. Those new hazards that have caused major epidemics (defined as having caused or threaten to cause more than 10 000 people to die or be seriously disabled) are reviewed. Most have been due to changes in personal behaviour made possible by increased affluence; others have been due to industrial pollution or to independent changes in biological organisms.

The most important have been the epidemics of lung cancer and coronary thrombosis. The first has caused nearly a million premature deaths in the last 50 years, amounting to 3.5% of all deaths in adults. It has been due principally to the increase in cigarette consumption and is now waning as cigarette consumption falls and the tar content of cigarette smoke is reduced. The size of the second cannot be estimated at all precisely as the previous incidence of coronary thrombosis is too uncertain; but it must be large. Factors that have contributed to it include increased cigarette smoking, reduced physical exercise, and an increased

Risk: Analysis, Assessment and Management. Edited by J. Ansell and F. Wharton.
© 1992 John Wiley & Sons Ltd.

prevalence of diabetes (due to increase consumption of refined carbohydrates). The most important are those that determine the level of blood cholesterol and the recent reduction in the total consumption of fat and the relative increase in the consumption of polyunsaturated fat explain most of the recent decrease in mortality.

In comparison, epidemics attributable to industrial pollution have been small, the most important being the 25 000 deaths from lung cancer, mesothelioma, and asbestosis due to the widespread use of asbestos. The epidemic of road traffic deaths may be most remarkable for the way it has been controlled. Despite the number of motor vehicles increasing more than 200-fold, the number of deaths due to motor vehicles has increased less than 20-fold and the death rate, which increased from 1909 to 1934, was lower in 1985 than at any time in the last 60 years apart from 1948 when the number of cars in use was restricted by the shortage of petrol.

Two epidemics have been due to changes in biological organisms. A change in the influenza virus enabled it to escape immunological control in 1918 and led to the greatest worldwide epidemic in modern history, with 140 000 excess deaths in Great Britain in two years and 10 million throughout the world. A virus similar to that which caused the epidemic now causes epidemics in swine. A change in a monkey virus is the likely origin of the organism that causes AIDS; it has not yet caused major mortality in Britain, but it is certain to do so unless an effective treatment is discovered as some 35 000 to 55 000 people are already thought to be infected, most of whom are likely to become ill. Until now the great majority of cases has occurred in male homosexuals and addicts who inject drugs intravenously, but experience in Africa and elsewhere show that the disease can also spread by heterosexual intercourse. Knowledge of the transmission rate and of the pattern of sexual behaviour in the community is too incomplete to enable any prediction to be made of the likely future spread of the disease.

This review has made extensive use of the vital statistics collected by the Registrars-General, the quality of which is due largely to the pioneering of an early Fellow of the Society (Dr William Farr). These have provided clues to the causation of the two big epidemics that held up the decline of the death rate and despite the rapid advance of laboratory medicine they will continue to be an essential component of society's armamentarium against disease.

INTRODUCTION

The 100 years that have passed since the Royal Statistical Society received its charter have seen dramatic changes in the life of that larger society that provides the data on which the Fellows of our Society can exercise their statistical expertise. Television, aeroplanes, and computers, to cite only three new features of life, have transformed society qualitatively, in a way that could not have been envisaged before they were introduced; but I doubt if any changes have been more important for the individual than the changes that have occurred in the annual risk of disability and death. For the most part these have been to our advantage. Some, however, have not and the path of progress has been interrupted by the occurrence of new hazards that have caused new epidemics of disease.

TREND IN MORTALITY

In comparison with the position 100 years ago, the risk of death has been substantially reduced. Standardized for age, mortality has been almost halved and the outlook at birth has been so altered that the odds, which used to be against surviving beyond 54 years, are now in favour of surviving to 77. The nature of this change is illustrated in Figure 10.1, which shows the proportion of individuals that would be expected to survive to each age in two cohorts of people (half of each sex) who were subject respectively to the death rates recorded in England and Wales in 1881–90 and 1982–84. The reduction in the numbers of deaths in the first few years of life is remarkable, the proportion dying in the first 10 years having been reduced by 95%. There is, however, much less change at the other extreme of life; for of those who reach three score years and ten the proportion who die within the next 10 years has been reduced by

Percent surviving by âge
England and Wales

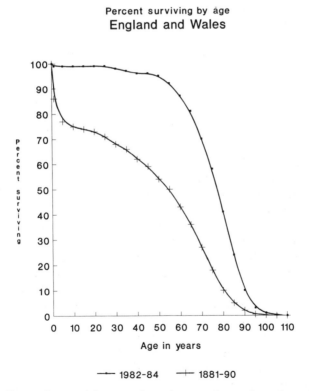

— 1982-84   —+— 1881-90

Figure 10.1 Proportion surviving at each age in two cohorts of equal numbers of males and females subject to the death rates current in 1881–90 and 1982–84

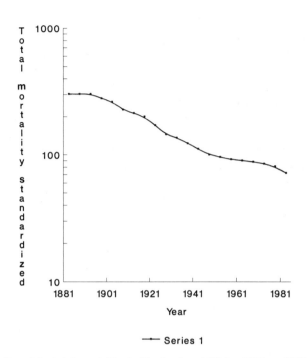

Figure 10.2   Trend in total mortality in England and Wales 1881 to 1985

only 35%; and even with current mortality rates only about 3 in 1000 infants can be expected to survive to celebrate their personal centenary.

The combined effect of these changes is seen in Figure 10.2, which shows the trend in total mortality with time, excluding only deaths abroad in the two world wars. Demographic changes have been allowed for by standardizing for sex and age in the way now used by the Office of Population Censuses and Surveys (1985): that is, by expressing the mortality in each quinquennium as a percentage of that which would have occurred if the mortality had been the same at each age and in each sex as it was in 1952. From the figure it appears that the rate of improvement was much the same from about 1890 to 1950 and again in the last 5 years, but that it slowed down for some 25 years after 1950.

The steadiness of the trend over such a long period and the slowdown are both surprising to clinicians who saw the profound effect that the introduction of sulphonamides and antibiotics had on the fatality of diseases due to bacterial infection and are aware of the many therapeutic advances that have occurred in the last 35 years. It appears, however, that even such large effects as were produced by the therapeutic revolution of the late 1930s and 1940s have been smoothed out and partly counter-balanced by the multiplicity of other factors that have influenced the incidence and fatality of different diseases, at different ages, and at different periods. These include changes in the biological organisms that cause disease, changes in industry and agriculture (which increased the gross national product and the production of food, introduced new chemicals, and modified the ambient environment), changes in the structure of society (which altered the distribution of wealth and the availability of medical care), changes in the average level of education, size of families, and personal behaviour, and changes in the genetic pool.

All these have contributed to the reduction in mortality and two at lease have done so without obviously causing more disease—namely, the improved standard of education and the reduction in family size. Most, however, have also introduced new hazards. Medicine, it must be admitted, falls into this latter category, although the harm produced has usually been small and quickly stopped. Two of the worst effects were caused by treating premature infants with 100% oxygen, which caused several hundred to be blinded for life in the late 1940s and early 1950s; and the prescription of thalidomide as a sedative for pregnant women, which caused some 3000 children to be born with serious congenital malformations in 1961–64. It is possible too that new treatments for asthma were responsible for the small epidemic of asthma deaths that occurred in the late 1960s and has recurred to a lesser extent in the last few years. I am, however, so prejudiced in favour of the general beneficence of medicine that the fact that the infant mortality rate in developed countries has been positively correlated with the number of physicians per 10 000 population (Cochrane, St Leger and Moore, 1978) seems to me more likely to reflect confounding than causality, and I have no reason to think that the practice of medicine has caused any major epidemic this century if, for our present purpose, we define a major epidemic as one that has caused, or threatens to cause, more than 10 000 people to die or to be severely disabled. That is, if we ignore the epidemic of disabilities (for example, the increased number of paraplegics condemned to a wheelchair life) that has been the tragic consequence of treatment designed to save life.

MAJOR EPIDEMICS

Epidemics on this scale have been due mostly to changes in personal behaviour made possible by the increased affluence that has resulted from industrial and agricultural developments and have most affected middle aged and elderly men. Some, however, have been due to industrial pollution or to changes in biological organisms over which we have no control.

In this chapter I examine only those epidemics that are peculiar to the last 100 years: that is, those due to new hazards, or to diseases that have been only newly recognized. I have therefore excluded many important conditions that have merely become more common due to an increased prevalence of old hazards. These range from poliomyelitis, which began to appear in more serious form because the improvements in sanitation resulted in postponement of exposure to the virus until later in life, through the alcohol-related diseases that have become more common with the doubling of per caput consumption of alcohol in the last 35 years, to the new phase of the old problem of drug addiction.

Of the new epidemics, two have been much the most important: namely, the epidemics of lung cancer and coronary thrombosis.

Lung Cancer

Lung cancer—or more strictly cancer of the bronchus—has been known to occur from time immemorial; but it was thought to be a rare form of cancer until the 1920s, when it began to appear more often as the certified cause of death and pathologists began to note more cases on autopsy examination. In the next 50 years, the death rate, standardized for age, rose inexorably each year as is shown in Figure 10.3. At first it rose more steeply in men than in women and it reached a peak in men in England and Wales in about 1973, when over 26 000 deaths (that is, nearly 9% of male deaths from all causes) were attributed to it. In women nearly 10 000 deaths (that is, 4% of female deaths from all causes) were attributed to it. In women nearly 10 000 deaths (that is, 4% of female deaths from all causes) are now attributed to it each year and the rise is still continuing. The enormous increase in mortality recorded since 1911 is, however, not all real. In part it is an artefact due to the improved methods of diagnosis that resulted from the successive introduction of chest X-rays, bronchoscopy, and open chest surgery, and the introduction of effective methods of treatment for pneumonia after the sulphonamide series of drugs began to be developed in 1936. Some of these cured the pulmonary infections that were produced by the early stages of the disease and allowed the cancers to grow large enough to be easily recognized. How much of the early increase in the mortality attributed to lung cancer was spurious and due to these changes and how much was real was debated hotly for many years (Doll, 1953); but it now seems likely that the true mortality rate in women was never much less than it is now in non-smokers (which is shown in Figure 10.3 and is some 32 times the rate that was recorded in women before 1920) and that the true rate in men was about 50% to 60% greater than the true rate in women: that is, a little more than the current rate in male non-smokers. On this basis the epidemic has been responsible for nearly a million premature deaths in the last 50 years, and has accounted for approximately 32% of all deaths in men and women over 25 years of age in this period.

New occupational hazards have contributed to the epidemic; but the overwhelming cause was the increase in cigarette smoking, which began about 100 years ago, gradually replaced pipe and cigar smoking, and increased the total

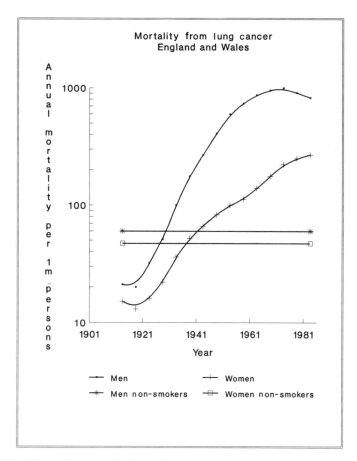

Figure 10.3   Trends in mortality from lung cancer in men and women in comparison with estimated mortality rates in non-smokers: England and Wales, 1911–15 to 1981–85, standardized for age

consumption of tobacco until, at its peak in 1973, adults were smoking on average 9.5 cigarettes a day. Pipe and cigar smoking did cause a few cases of lung cancer in men; but they were less effective than cigarette smoking per gram of tobacco consumed, because the alkalinity of the smoke enabled the nicotine to be absorbed in the mouth and made the smoke irritating and difficult to inhale. Cigarette smoke in contrast can be inhaled quite easily and, moreover, has to be inhaled before any material amount of nicotine can be absorbed. The bronchi have, therefore, been so intensively exposed that the consumption of 20 cigarettes a day has been found to increase the risk of developing the disease approximately 20 times.

Tobacco smoke, however, is only a weak carcinogen and hardly any cases are produced until smoking has been continued for 20 years. Consequently the effect of increasing consumption and of the change from pipes and cigars to cigarettes did not begin to show itself clearly until the 1930s and the peak mortality in men did not occur until the mid-1970s, by which time the vast majority of all male cigarette smokers at all ages had been smoking cigarettes all their smoking lives. Fortunately no such delay occurs before the effect of stopping can be seen, as tobacco smoke affects both early and late stages in the process of cancer induction. The incidence of the disease will, therefore, stabilize almost immediately smoking is stopped instead of increasing progressively with age. The reduction in smoking that has occurred among men in the last 12 years, combined with the introduction of cigarettes that deliver less tar, has consequently already produced a notable effect, as is shown in Figure 10.4. At all ages under 80 years the mortality in men has begun to decrease and it has decreased

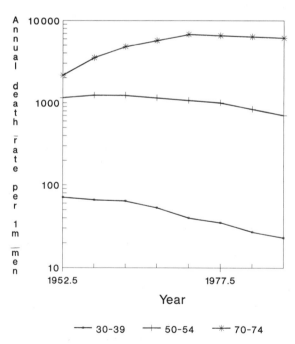

Figure 10.4 Trend in mortality from lung cancer in men in three age groups: England and Wales, 1950 to 1985

by more than 50% since the late 1950s in men under 50 years of age who, when they have smoked, have now smoked low tar cigarettes for most of their smoking lives.

In women, the epidemic is less mature, as it was only after the First World War that a substantial number of women began to smoke and the habit became steadily more prevalent until 1978 when the proportion of smokers and the per caput consumption per smoker were only slightly less than they were in men. The mortality rate is, therefore, still rising over 55 years of age and it is only under this age that the reduced tar delivery per cigarette has been able to cancel out the effect of increasing consumption (Figure 10.5). If the current trends persist much longer, lung cancer must be expected to displace breast cancer as the most common type of fatal cancer in women in England and Wales, as it already is in Scotland.

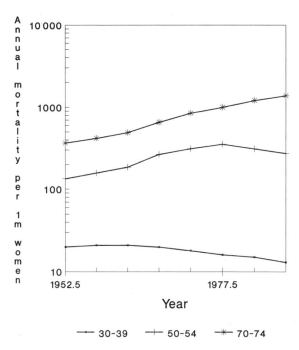

Mortality from lung cancer
England and Wales, women, by age

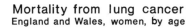

Figure 10.5 Trend in mortality from lung cancer in women in three age groups: England and Wales, 1950 to 1985

Coronary Thrombosis

The epidemic of coronary thrombosis (or myocardial infarction) has been at first sight both larger and more sharply defined. There is, however, great difficulty in determining the baseline from which the epidemic began. Pain like that produced by a thrombosis, but recurring frequently on physical effort and recovering quickly without subsequent evidence of a damaged heart, was first described as angina pectoris by Heberden in 1768 (see Heberden, 1772), and this is now known to occur when the coronary arteries are partially blocked by atheroma and temporarily unable to deliver enough blood to the muscles of the heart when effort requires more blood to be delivered. A few years later Jenner is recorded in the minutes of a local medical dining club as suggesting that sclerosis of the coronary arteries might have been the cause of death of men who died with anginal pain in the chest; but it was not until 1878 that Hammer provided a clear pathological account of a death due to thrombosis in the coronary arteries and not until 1912 that Herrick in Philadelphia recognized the condition as one from which recovery could occur. Nineteenth-century records show that angina pectoris was diagnosed frequently and that attacks were known occasionally to terminate in death; but it is difficult to believe that such a distinctive event as coronary thrombosis could have been missed consistently by the many percipient physicians of the period, whose expertise consisted primarily in clinical diagnosis and prognosis, if the syndrome had been at all common in their wealthy patients. We must, I think, accept that coronary thrombosis was much less prevalent 100 years ago than it is today, even if angina pectoris was not. This implies that the causes of the two conditions are in some respects different, which is not unacceptable as we know that at least one factor, namely, cigarette smoking, is more closely related to coronary thrombosis than it is to angina.

Clinical accounts by experienced cardiologists of the period (Mackenzie, 1913; Hutchison 1950; White, 1957) strongly suggest that some large increase in the incidence of coronary thrombosis did occur in this period. Their impressions are substantiated by coroners' records for part of Yorkshire over the period 1855 to 1926 and the autopsy findings at the London Hospital between 1907 and 1949. The former show that the number of sudden deaths that could be attributed to coronary heart disease each year began to increase early this century and was about six times as great in the 20 years from 1907 to 1926 as it had been in the preceding 50 years, despite very little change in the size of the population and the proportion over 65 years of age (Mackinnon, 1987). The latter, which were analysed by Morris (1951) and are of particular interest because the coronary arteries had been examined routinely since 1907, are summarized in Table 10.1. The increase in the number of cases of thrombosis or infarction could not be attributed to demographic changes in the population served, nor did it seem to be an artefact due to changes in hospital policy, and

Table 10.1 Necropsies with evidence of recent coronary thrombosis or myocardial infarction London Hospital 1907 to 1949 (after Morris, 1951)

Years	Average annual number	
	Men	Women
1907–14	1.4	0.2
1915–18	2.8	0.8
1919–23	5.0	0.8
1927–31	4.8	1.4
1935–39	6.2	1.8
1944–49	8.5	2.0

Morris concluded that the increase largely reflected a real increase in incidence. It is notable, however, that Morris found no evidence of an increase in the amount of atheroma in the arteries, which fits with an unchanged incidence of angina; but not with the idea that atheroma and thrombosis are causally related.

Mortality statistics for their part suggest that the epidemic has been enormous, for if all diseases of the coronary arteries are classed together, including coronary thrombosis with angina pectoris because angina pectoris is unlikely to cause death except as the result of a thrombosis, we obtain the picture shown in Figure 10.6, where the age standardized rates for both men and women are seen to have increased about 50-fold until the early 1970s, when coronary disease was responsible for 30% of all deaths in men and for 23% in women. Only during the two wars was there any check to the progressive rise.

It seems unlikely, however, that the whole of the increase shown in Figure 10.6 can reflect the true size of the epidemic, as the recognition of coronary thrombosis as a possible cause of death can have spread only slowly throughout the medical world, and it will have taken many years before all doctors became at home with the new term and used it to replace such non-specific diagnoses as myocarditis, myocardial degeneration, and cardiac failure or even apoplexy. Unfortunately it is impossible to make any sensible allowance for this as the categories used for classifying causes of death were too broad and too non-specific to be combined usefully until 1968. In that year the 8th revision of the International Classification of Diseases came into use and all terms that doctors are now likely to use to describe coronary disease are subsumed in one group (ICD numbers 410–414). One possible exception is the diagnosis of myocardial degeneration in the presence of arteriosclerosis, which was included with coronary disease after 1968 but was coded separately from 1950 to 1967 during which time its use as a certified cause of death progressively diminished. Deaths attributed to it can, therefore, be added to those attributed to coronary disease

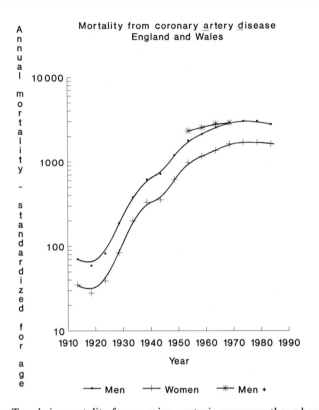

Figure 10.6 Trends in mortality from angina pectoris, coronary thrombosis and other coronary diseases in men and women: England and Wales, 1911-15 to 1981-85, standardized for age. Rates also shown with the addition of mortality attributed to myocardial degeneration in the presence of arteriosclerosis, 1950 to 1967.
Men + , rate for coronary artery disease plus myocardial degeneration with reference to arteriosclerosis

and the results obtained by so doing are shown for men in Figure 10.6. Even when this is done an increase continues to be observed.

That an increase did occur throughout the 1950s and 1960s is, I think, certain, because it was most marked in the age groups under 60 years in which the diagnosis would have been most precise. This is shown in Figure 10.7 in which deaths attributed to myocardial degeneration with arteriosclerosis have been added to those attributed to coronary disease in both sexes throughout the whole period. Nor can there be any serious doubt that the mortality rate has decreased in the last 10 years, because all other causes of heart disease, with which there is the remotest possibility of confusion, have decreased as well. What is less clear is whether the decrease is due to a decreased incidence of the disease or to improved treatment, which includes not only better treatment after

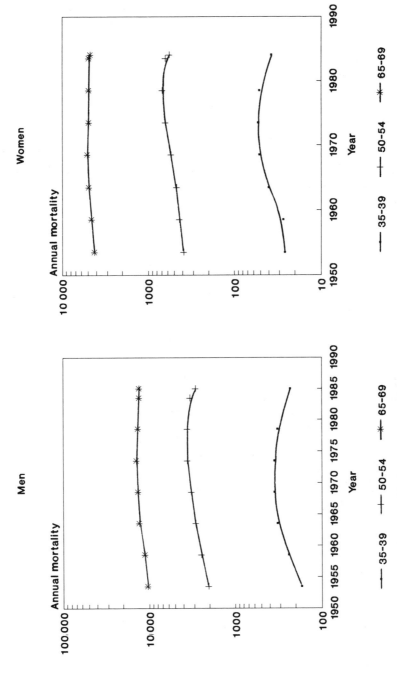

Figure 10.7 Trends in mortality from all diseases of the coronary arteries and myocardial degeneration in the presence of arteriosclerosis; England and Wales, 1950 to 1985 by sex in three age groups

a thrombosis has occurred, but operative intervention to improve the blood supply of the heart when premonitory symptoms occur. In other countries, where the fall in mortality has been greater and has gone on for longer (notably the United States, Australia, and New Zealand) about one-third of the fall has been attributed to improved treatment and the rest to prevention (Goldman and Cook, 1984; Beaglehole, 1986) and it seems probable that the same may have been true here, the fall having been delayed by 5 to 10 years by the ingrained conservatism of the British medical profession—a conservatism which, it must be said, has often been to their patients' benefit.

We cannot, unfortunately, assess the size of the epidemic in the same way as we did for the epidemic of lung cancer, when we used the current rates in non-smokers to estimate what the true mortality rate was likely to have been early in the century, because we are not sure what the quantitative effects of the most important causative factors are nor what their prevalence used to be before the epidemic began.

Some part of the increase is due to the increased consumption of cigarettes, which alone of tobacco products affect the incidence of the disease, possibly because the rate of absorption of nicotine from cigarette smoke is so much faster than from the smoke of pipes or cigars. Smoking, however, is important only at young ages, as is shown in Table 10.2, while the great majority of coronary deaths occur in the older age groups. Cigarettes can, therefore, have accounted for only about 20% of the mortality attributed to coronary thrombosis in men, and for less in women, even when the mortality rates were at their peak.

Other factors that may have contributed to the epidemic are the reduction in

Table 10.2 Relative risk of death from coronary heart disease, smokers compared to non-smokers, by age (after US Public Health Service, 1983)

Study	Relative risk at ages (years)				
	35–44	45–54	55–64	65–74	75–84
American Cancer Society in 22 states (cigarette smokers)	4.4	7.1	1.8	1.6	1.2
US veterans (cigarette smokers)	4.4	7.0	1.8	1.6	1.2
Californian study of industrial workers (smokers)	6.2	3.0	1.6	1.2	—
British doctors (cigarette smokers 15–24 a day	8.7	3.1	1.5	1.3	1.0

physical exercise, due to the progressive elimination of manual work, and the increased prevalence of diabetes, due to an increased consumption of refined carbohydrates; but the small effect of exercise in reducing risk and the low prevalence of diabetes mean that neither can have contributed much.

The greater part of the epidemic should be related somehow to changes in the level of blood lipids, for it is only the level of blood lipids that has been found to have a gross effect on the risk of the disease. International comparisons and cohort studies within countries both show that the risk increases with the level of blood cholesterol and, if allowance is made for regression to the mean in the measurement of blood cholesterol in the cohort studies, both also show, as Richard Peto (personal communication) has pointed out, that the risk doubles for every increase of 50 mg per ml. This implies that a reduction of the average level in Britain to that in China would reduce the risk by about five-sixths.

Not all cardiologists have accepted this conclusion; but its truth has been put beyond serious doubt by the results of the many controlled trials of the effect of lowering blood cholesterol by either diet or drugs. Not all trials appear to have led to the same conclusion and this has caused confusion among clinicians because they have failed to take account of the fact that results will differ by chance unless very large numbers of subjects are studied, if the differences expected are small and compliance with both the treatment and the control arms of the trials is as poor as it nearly always is. The results of all the 20 trials that have been properly conducted are, in fact, consistent with one another. Taken all together, they demonstrate, with a high degree of confidence, that the reduction of blood cholesterol of about 10% produces a reduction in risk of about one-sixth within an average of about two years: that is, about half the reduction that could be predicted from the epidemiological observations.

Unfortunately this is not the whole story, nor is medical opinion wholly agreed what the whole story is. It seems likely, however, that saturated fat in the diet increases the amount of blood cholesterol and its presence in the form of low density lipoprotein and increases *pari passu* the risk of the disease, while the polyunsaturated fats in fish and some plants tend to have the opposite effect. We can, consequently, attribute much of the recent decrease in mortality to the decrease in the amount of saturated fat and the increase in the ratio of polyunsaturated to saturated fats in the diet over the past 10 years that is illustrated in Figure 10.8, as well as to the reduction in cigarette smoking that has contributed to the decrease in men. But whether we can attribute the increase in mortality at the beginning of the century to dietary changes in the opposite direction is less clear. There is nothing to suggest that there was any gross increase in the per caput consumption of fat—except for the very poor (Michaels, 1966). Farming practices, however, have changed and the type of fat in animal carcasses may have been different.

I conclude that there has been a major epidemic of coronary thrombosis, which is now being controlled by changes in diet and cigarette smoking. The

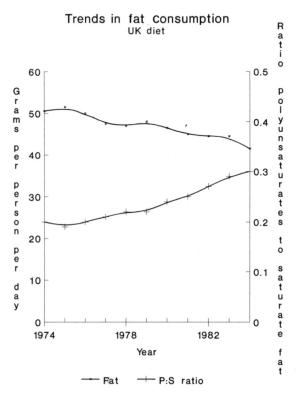

Figure 10.8 Trends in consumption of fats and in the ratio of polyunsaturated to saturated fat (P:S ratio): United Kingdom, 1974 to 1984

evidence, however, is incomplete and the size and origin of the epidemic are still uncertain.

Other Diseases Related to Smoking and Diet

Lung cancer and coronary thrombosis are not the only diseases that have been made more common by changes in smoking habits and diet; but no other disease has increased to anything like the same extent, the relationships observed between smoking and diet and other diseases have been complex and often confounded with other factors, and the changes of diet that have been related to those other diseases have often been more characteristic of the nineteenth century than the twentieth. I shall therefore leave them and pass on to consider epidemics that owe their origin primarily to industrial development.

Disease Due to Industrial Pollution

In comparison with the epidemics produced by changes in behaviour, these have been small—that is if we exclude the effects of coal smoke, with or without the accompaniment of sulphur dioxide, because it was not a new pollutant, but was prevalent long before the twentieth century began. The acute effects of the 1952 smog, which caused an estimated 4000 extra deaths in London and led to the Clean Air Act of 1956, were not evidently due to any new type of pollution. That they were so much more evident then than they had been previously, was, I suspect, partly due to the increased prevalence of cigarette smoking that had sensitized bronchi to the effects of the pollution and partly, perhaps, to the new antibacterial remedies that had diminished the impact of the normal winter risk of chest infection and so made the effects of the smog more prominent.

One type of industrial pollution has, however, certainly caused a substantial epidemic, mainly by contributing to the epidemic of lung cancer and partly by causing a small epidemic of what had previously been an extremely rare disease: namely, mesothelioma of the pleural peritoneum. This latter disease is nearly always due to exposure to asbestos, particularly to the blue and brown types; but it is difficult to estimate how many cases have been caused by asbestos as the disease was so rare that it was not classed separately until the 1960s and was not recognized as a cause of death in the International Classification of Diseases until the 8th revision which came into force only in 1968. A mesothelioma register has, however, been maintained in this country by the Health and Safety Executive since 1967 and some 6000 fatal cases, of which perhaps 90% are attributable to asbestos, have been recorded in it (Jones, Smith and Thomas, 1987). The disease commonly does not appear until 30 or 40 years after exposure has first occurred and it will, therefore, be many years before the preventive measures that began to be taken in the 1960s exert their full effect.

Studies of men occupationally exposed have shown that asbestos has caused about four or five times as many cases of lung cancer as of mesothelioma, so that the epidemic to date may have caused about 25 000 deaths, and the total is likely to be of the order of 50 000 all told (including both mesotheliomas and lung cancers and some 1000 deaths from asbestosis) before the account is finally closed.

Industrial chemicals and the industrial use of ionizing radiations have caused many other small epidemics of cancer within an occupational setting, but no industrial agent has caused any other epidemic of comparable size, despite the popular idea that industrial pollution has caused a great increase in the risk of cancer. That this idea should have been so widespread is, I think, understandable when one considers the explosive growth of the chemical industry after the Second World War, the discovery that thousands of chemicals are carcinogenic in animal experiments, the belief that in most cases carcinogenic chemicals exert an effect that is linearly proportional to dose down to very low levels without any evidence of a threshold below which no effect occurs, and the great prominence that cancer has come to have as a cause of death.

In fact, cancer has become more prominent only because so many other diseases have been largely eliminated or made less fatal while the mortality from cancer has hardly changed, as is seen in Figure 10.9 which shows the age specific mortality rates from cancer in 1931–35 and 1981–84. Apart from cancer of the lung and mesotheliomas, to which I have already referred, and the cancers related to the consumption of alcohol, the only cancers that have certainly increased in incidence to any large extent in young people (in whom the early effects of new hazards are most likely to be seen) are melanoma of the skin and cancers of the cervix and testis. The reasons for the increase of the first two do not appear to have anything to do with industry, the first being thought (but not proved) to be due to increased exposure of the untanned skin to sunlight and the second to increased exposure to venereally transmitted viruses, probably certain types of human papilloma virus. The reason for the increase in the incidence of the third (cancer of the testis) is still a mystery.

Other pollutants that are non-carcinogenic are less likely to have caused any serious effects, as the amounts released to the ambient atmosphere are generally far below the levels at which toxic effects are likely to appear, except possibly in the case of lead. When the Royal Commission on Environmental Pollution (1983) tried to evaluate the effects of lead pollution, other than the obvious effects of gross pollution of water supplies due to use of lead pipes in soft water

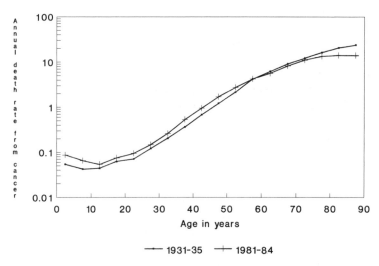

Figure 10.9 Mortality from cancer by age: England and Wales, 1931–35 and 1981–85

areas, it was unable to decide whether the correlation that had been observed between the body burden of lead in children and signs of mental impairment was 'a causal association ... or the effects of confounding factors, or both'. The Commission was, however, concerned that the amount of lead in the environment was steadily increasing and that the blood lead concentration in the United Kingdom was already about a quarter of that at which features of frank lead poisoning might occasionally occur. It consequently recommended that the dispersal of lead should be reduced whenever possible and its recommendation is now being put into effect. There is not any serious possibility that lead pollution has caused a major epidemic of mental impairment; but it was certainly wise to take steps to prevent it doing so in the future.

Road Accidents

Whether industrial development should also be held responsible for road accidents is a moot point. On the one hand, it is responsible, in the sense that without industrial development motor vehicles would not exist; on the other hand, motor vehicles would not do much harm unless they were driven without due care and attention. The potential for harm introduced by the car is enormous and its introduction has caused a major epidemic of serious injuries. The most remarkable feature of the epidemic may, however, be the extraordinary way in which it has been controlled.

In 1909, when road accident statistics were first collected on a national basis, there were 101 000 motor vehicles in Great Britain and 1070 fatal accidents occurred on the roads. Seventy-five years later the number of motor vehicles has increased 206 times to 20 million and the number of fatal accidents 4.8 times to 5135 (Department of Transport, 1986). This remarkable difference is due partly to the elimination of other forms of traffic, so that the deaths attributed to motor vehicles have increased 17 times, while those due to horses and horse drawn traffic, etc. (and the half-dozen due annually to steamrollers) have been eliminated, partly to the measures taken to reduce the risk of accidents, and partly to the advances in medical treatment that have ensured that when accidents do occur the risk of death is greatly reduced. The relative importance of these last two factors is illustrated in Figure 10.10, which shows (on a log scale) the trends in the numbers of motor vehicles, of people injured, and of people killed, all expressed as rates per million population per year. Rates are shown only for the period since 1926, as no tally had been kept previously of the numbers of injured and the records of vehicles and deaths were kept in a different form. Data for the years 1939-41 are omitted, as no figures are available for the numbers injured in the first years of the war. The rate of injury is seen to have grown less rapidly than the rate of vehicle ownership and in the last 20 years the rate has even fallen slightly while the rate of vehicle ownership has increased by 60%. In contrast to these trends, the death rate, which rose until

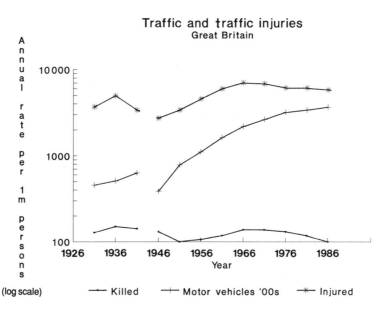

Figure 10.10 Trends in numbers of motor vehicles licensed and in numbers of injured and killed in road accidents, per million population: Great Britain 1926 to 1985

1934 and rose again after the war until 1966, was, in 1985, actually lower than it had been for 60 years, apart from 1948, when the use of cars was limited by the rationing of petrol.

Detailed figures for distances driven are available only for the last 12 years and these show that each vehicle is now driven further on average so that the numbers of injured and killed have been reduced even more in relation to the number of kilometres driven (by respectively 25% and 42%) than they have in relation to the number of vehicles (when they were reduced by 17% and 35%). Contrary to the belief fostered by sensational reports of motorway pile-ups, the rates of injury and death per million kilometres driven are 85% less on motorways than on A roads and even less in comparison with other roads (Department of Transport, 1986).

These surprising results, obtained partly by advances in medical treatment, partly by improvements in roads and vehicles, and partly by a long series of regulations to ensure that vehicles are properly maintained and less likely to be driven by incompetent or drunk drivers and that users are better protected by helmets or seat belts, have caused Britain to have one of the lowest rates of road death in the world, the rate of car user deaths per million kilometres driven being bettered only by Sweden and then only marginally. Even so road accidents in 1984 still caused 0·8% of deaths at all ages and 35% of deaths at 15–24 years of age. We should, moreover, note that 1% of the 350 000-odd injuries that occur each year leave some disability and that the advances in medicine, which have kept down the number of deaths, have resulted in an accumulation of human misery from injuries to the brain and spinal cord that are not recorded in the official statistics. We may never be able to eliminate road accidents altogether, but there is ample evidence to show that further reduction is practicable.

Influenza

Traffic accidents and the other epidemics that I have discussed have all arisen as a result of changes brought about by human activity. Humans, however, are not the only biological organisms that change. Micro-organisms continue to evolve and when changes occur in those that infect man new epidemics may result. The classic example is influenza, which is due to a virus that has a remarkable capacity to change its structure and particularly that of two important glycoproteins in its outer coat to which the human immunological system responds. Occasionally the changes are so great that the virus escapes the control of the immunological reaction produced by previous infections and new epidemics occur throughout the world. One such change occurred around the beginning of 1918 and caused not only the greatest worldwide epidemic in modern history, but also the most severe in that the fatality of the disease was particularly high in young adults in whom it approached 50%. Modern drugs would doubtless have saved many lives from the pneumonia that followed the infection; but many young people died within 24 hours from the initial damage to the lungs.

The disease probably originated in the military training camps in the eastern United States in March 1918, whence, a few weeks later, the first major wave attacked the US expeditionary force in French ports. From there, it spread throughout western Europe, causing a peak in the civilian population in Britain in June. This first outbreak was relatively mild, and the full virulence of the infection was not seen until the second and third waves struck in October 1918 and March 1919. In England and Wales 140 000 excess deaths were attributed to the disease in these two years and altogether it caused more than 10 million deaths throughout the world.

Epidemics since then have recurred every few years, due to a variety of different strains of the virus; but none has approached the virulence of the 1918–19 epidemic and none has caused more than one-fifth of the death rate in Britain, as Figure 10.11 shows, though the Asian flu of 1957 was equally ubiquitous (Stuart-Harris, Schild and Oxford, 1985).

At the time of the 1918 epidemic, the influenza virus had not been isolated and there are, therefore, no direct records of its molecular structure. Studies of antibodies against the influenza virus in the blood of people of different ages have shown, however, that nearly all people born before 1921 and very few of those born after 1926 have antibodies against a type of influenza A that now causes influenza in swine and it seems that the virus may have taken refuge in

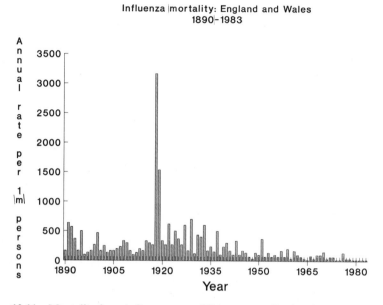

Figure 10.11 Mortality from influenza per million persons: England and Wales, 1890 to 1983

these animals. Swine influenza in the United States has persisted with very little antigenic change to the present day, which is why there was so much anxiety and a widespread campaign for immunization when a small outbreak of influenza occurred in an army camp in New Jersey in 1976 due to a virus whose antigenic characteristics were closely similar to those of the virus that causes the disease in swine.

AIDS

The other outstanding epidemic that has been the result of biological change in a micro-organism is the acquired immunodeficiency syndrome, or AIDS. The disease cannot yet be said to have caused a major epidemic in this country, as only 734 cases had been diagnosed by the end of March 1987; but it is certain to do so, as tens of thousands are already infected, a large proportion of whom must be expected to develop the disease, and very many more may come to be infected unless there is a major change in sexual behaviour, or a vaccine or some other method of prevention is introduced, or an effective treatment is discovered.

The disease was first recognized in the United States in 1981 and two years later the causal agent was identified: namely, the human immunodeficiency virus or HIV type 1 (Barre-Sinoussi *et al.*, 1983; Gallo *et al.*, 1984). The virus colonizes a type of T lymphocyte that plays an essential part in producing immunity against infection and probably also colonizes some of the nerve cells in the brain. The principle symptoms are, therefore, those produced by infection with organisms that normally live in comfortable symbiosis with man (including some than can cause cancer) and secondarily some degree of mental impairment. Left to run its natural course, the disease appears to be invariably fatal, with half the patients dying within one year and three-quarters within two.

The infection is now known to have been present in the United States in 1978 and several years earlier in tropical Africa. There is no evidence that anyone was infected before the 1970s and it seems probable that the virus is a new mutant, possibly derived from an organism that infects African monkeys. A different variety of the virus has recently been discovered in West Africa (HIV type 2) and it may be that the virus will show a lability comparable to that of the influenza virus.

Infection is now worldwide, but most of our knowledge about the clinical course of the disease and the mode of spread comes from the United States and tropical Africa, where infection has been present for longer than elsewhere, and we can estimate what is likely to happen in the United Kingdom only by examining what has already happened in these other places. American experience shows that the average incubation period before a sufficient proportion of the susceptible lymphocytes are destroyed for the disease to appear is four to five years, but no cohorts have been observed for long enough to be sure that no more cases will occur and it is consequently uncertain how long the average incubation period will prove to be and what proportion of infected individuals will eventually become ill. Estimates have ranged from 20% to 100%, with the weight of evidence tending to a figure near the latter, except perhaps for haemophiliacs who receive blood products in the course of medical treatment.

Until now, the vast majority of cases in the developed world have been in male homosexuals, drug addicts who inject intravenously, and patients who have received intravenous injections of whole blood or blood products. This is illustrated in Figure 10.12 which shows the cumulative number of cases in adults in the United States up to March 1987 in these three groups (with men who are bisexual or homosexuals and drug addicts classed as homosexuals), in heterosexually active men and women not in any of the three previous groups, and in an unclassified residue. The number in the last group, it will be noted, was reduced towards the end of 1984, by separating people who had received blood transfusions or blood products intravenously and those who were heterosexually active and again towards the end of 1986 by adding to the heterosexual group, people who were born in countries where heterosexual transmission is believed to play a major role.

From these data and observations on cohorts of men practising different types of homosexual behaviour it is clear that the principle modes of spread in

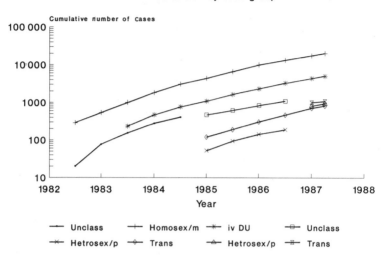

Cumulative number of AIDS cases
in adults USA by risk group

Figure 10.12   Cumulative number of AIDS cases by principal risk group: United States, 1982 to March 1987

the United States have been by the intravenous injection of infected blood and receptive anal intercourse. In Kingsley et al.'s (1987) study, for example, the rate of infection in homosexuals who were initially seronegative increased 16-fold with the number of partners if anal intercourse was practised receptively from 0.9% in men who had not received anal intercourse in the previous six months to 14.9% in men who had received it with five or more partners in the same period; but it only doubled with the same increase in the number of partners if anal intercourse had been practised insertively, as is shown in Table 10.3. In these data the rates have been standardized for the number of partners with whom the opposite aspect of anal intercourse was practised. For insertive anal intercourse

Table 10.3   Risk of infection with HIV by frequency and type of anal intercourse (after Kinglsey et al., 1987)

No. of partners in 6 months	Per cent seroconversion if anal intercourse	
	Receptive*	Insertive*
0	0.9	2.6
1	2.7	4.2
2–4	6.8	4.3
5 or more	14.9	5.2

*Standardized for number or partners with alternative practice.

alone a low seroconversion rate of 0.9% was observed, while no infection at all was observed in the small group of men whose sexual practice had been limited to fellatio or masturbation.

The spread of infection is, however, not limited to the two principal modes of receptive anal intercourse and intravenous injection. The experience of spouses of infected haemophiliacs shows that infection can be transmitted from male to female by vaginal intercourse and the results of case control studies of Haitian men in New York and Miami show that it can also be transmitted similarly in the opposite direction (Castro *et al.*, 1985). The spread of infection by vaginal intercourse in both directions is, moreover, confirmed by the high and approximately equal prevalence of infection in both sexes in parts of tropical Africa where rates of 10% have been observed in antenatal clinics and 60% in professional prostitutes and where anal intercourse and the use of addictive drugs intravenously are unusual or unknown.

To predict the number of people who are likely to become infected we need to know several epidemiological parameters that are as yet quite uncertain. In particular, we need to know the reproductive rate of the infection (that is, the average number of secondary infections produced by one individual in the early stage of the epidemic) and this is determined by the average rate at which new sexual partners are acquired, the probability that infection is transmitted per sexual intercourse, the frequency of sexual intercourse, and the average duration of infectiousness. For a sexually transmitted disease we also need to know the degree of heterogeneity in sexual activity that prevails in the population for, as Julian Peto (1986) pointed out, a small proportion of highly active individuals will be more likely both to acquire infection and to transmit it and their presence in a population will make the rate of spread much greater than it would be in a similar population in which the average number of new partners is the same, but spread equally throughout the whole population. In the long run, however, May and Anderson (1987) have pointed out that great variability in the average number of partners per unit time may result in a smaller proportion of the total population becoming infected than would be the case with less variability, as the highly active individuals will be eliminated from the population relatively quickly.

At present none of the requisite parameters is known except that the average rate of transmission per sexual act is certainly low (though it may vary from one individual to another) and that the duration of infectiousness is likely to be measured in years. To predict the size of the epidemic we have, therefore, to rely on: (i) estimates of the number of male homosexuals in the population (thought to be about 10 million at ages 16 to 55 years in the United States, a quarter of whom are exclusively homosexual); (ii) estimates of the number of addicts who are injecting drugs intravenously (thought to be about 12 million in the United States, half of whom inject one or more times a week); and (iii) the results of studies of the prevalence of infection in these groups, as judged by the presence of antibodies to HIV in the blood. Calculations based on these estimates led the Public Health service to estimate that there were about 1 to 1.5 million infected people in these two groups in the United States in mid-1986, at a time when some 19 000 cases had been reported in the corresponding categories, which suggests that the reservoir of infection was some 50 to 80 times greater than the number of reported cases.

The state of the epidemic in Britain in comparison with that in the United States is illustrated in Figure 10.13, which shows that the British epidemic is developing along the same lines as that in the United States, but nearly three years later and rather more slowly. For if we multiply the British numbers by 5, to allow for the difference in the size of the population, we see that we were 28 months behind the United States at the beginning of 1985 and 35 months behind at the beginning of 1987. The proportions of patients in the five risk categories in the two countries at the beginning of 1987 are shown in Table 10.4. In both countries, the vast majority of all patients (over 90%) were male homosexuals or

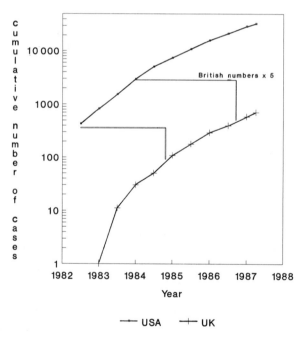

Figure 10.13 Cumulative number of cases of AIDS in adults: United States and Great Britain, January 1982 to March 1987

Table 10.4 Proportion of adult patients with AIDS in different risk categories: USA and UK, early 1987

Category of patient	Per cent of all adult patients	
	USA	UK
Male homosexuals*	73.4	89.0
Intravenous drug users	16.9	1.4
Persons who had received blood transfusions or i.v. blood products†	2.7	6.1
Active heterosexuals	3.8	3.3
Unknown	3.2	0.2
	100.0	100.0

*Including male bisexuals and homosexuals using drugs intravenously.
†Including haemophiliacs.

addicts taking drugs intravenously, though the proportion of addicts was much greater in the United States than here. If, despite this difference in the proportion of homosexual and drug addict cases, we use the same multiplying factor to arrive at the number of people currently infected, we obtain an estimate of between 35 000 and 55 000 in Great Britain to which, of course, we must add several thousand infected by other means including some 1000 haemophiliacs.

What the number will eventually be will depend critically on the relative ease of transmission by vaginal and anal intercourse and on the extent to which individuals modify their sexual behaviour. If the relative transmissibility is much the same and there is no change in sexual behaviour, the total may come to be measured in millions. Changes in sexual behaviour have, however, already occurred in homosexuals in both countries. In London (Carne *et al.*, 1987) questionnaires administered to 100 homosexual men 18 months apart revealed that by mid-1986 the median number of partners per month had been reduced from three to one and that the proportion having receptive anal intercourse with more than two partners a month fell from 27% to 8%. The use of condoms also rose (not, however, statistically significantly) from 13% to 25%. In a much larger American study of 2463 seronegative men, covering two six-month periods in 1984 and 1985 the proportion who had been the receptive partner in anal intercourse fell from 74% to 60% (Kingsley *et al.*, 1987). The changes may well have been much greater since, but whether adequate changes in sexual behaviour will occur in the rest of society soon enough to prevent a disastrous epidemic (in the absence of a vaccine or effective treatment) remains to be seen.

CONCLUSION

In introducing this review of the major epidemics of the twentieth century, I drew attention to the deceleration in the rate at which mortality was being reduced in the third quarter of the century. Some deceleration was almost inevitable, in view of the near elimination of deaths in the first 10 years of life. It would not have been so marked, however, without the new epidemics of lung cancer and coronary thrombosis, both of which have now begun to wane. How far the increase in the risk of these diseases accounted for the excess mortality over that predicted by extrapolation from the experience of the first half of the century is impossible to say, because the true extent of the increase in mortality from coronary thrombosis is too uncertain. It is, however, likely to have accounted for at least half the difference. No other epidemic has been of near comparable size and there is certainly no reason to attribute any major deterioration to general environmental pollution.

In reaching these conclusions, I have had occasion to make frequent use of the mortality statistics reported annually by the Registrars-General of the United Kingdom dating back more than 100 years. That we have figures for the whole of this century and figures, moreover, which, despite the vagaries of medical diagnosis are of some practical value in drawing attention to serious medical problems, is due primarily to the acumen, enthusiasm, and unremitting work of Dr William Farr. Civil registration of births, deaths, and marriages began in 1837 and two years later, in the same year that he was elected a Fellow of the then Statistical Society, Dr Farr was appointed Compiler of Abstracts in the Registrar-General's office with special responsibility for the compilation of statistical tables from the marriage, birth, and death registers. In the succeeding 41 years he created system and order out of nosological chaos so effectively that his tabulations and reports became a model for the whole world. Not content with this, however, he went on to show how examination of the Registrar-General's figures in the light of social conditions could be used to improve the health of the population as a whole and, in this he proved in Sir John Simon's words 'a master of the methods by which arithmetic is made argumentative'.

In these days, when the study of molecular and cellular biology is revolutionizing our approach to the therapy and prevention of disease, it is salutary to recall that clues to the aetiology of the two major epidemics that held up the decline in national mortality rates for 30 years were first obtained from the simple temporal and geographical comparisons of disease incidence that William Farr had made possible. Vital statistics may not play such an important part in the advance of medicine in the next 100 years as they have in the past; but they will still be needed to monitor the effect of national policies and to draw attention to the new problems that will almost certainly arise.

ACKNOWLEDGEMENT

This chapter previously appeared as a paper in the *Journal of the Royal Statistical Society, Series A*, **150**, 373-95 (1987) and it is republished with permission of the author, the editor and the publisher of the journal.

REFERENCES

Barre-Sinoussi, F. Chermann, J.C. Rey, F. *et al.* (1983). Isolation of T-lymphotropic retrovirus from a patient at risk for acquired immune deficiency syndrome (AIDS), *Science*, **220**, 868-870.

Beaglehole, R. (1986) Medical management and the decline in mortality from coronary heart disease, *Brit. Med. J.*, **292**, 33-5.

Carne, C.A., Weller, I.V.D., Johnson, A.M. *et al.* (1987). Prevalence of antibodies to human immunodeficiency virus, gonorrhoea rates, and changed sexual behaviour in homosexual men in London, *Lancet*, **1**, 656-8.

Castro, K.G., Fischl, M.A., Landesman, S.H. *et al.* (1985). Paper 6, International Conference on AIDS, Atlanta, Georgia, 14-17 April 1985.

Cochrane, A.L., St Leger, A.S. and Moore, F. (1978). Health service 'input' and mortality 'output' in developed countries, *J. Epidemiol, Comm. Hlth.*, **32**, 200-5.

Department of Transport (1986). *Road Accidents Great Britain 1985. The Casualty Report*, HMSO, London.

Doll, R. (1953). Bronchial carcinoma: incidence and aetiology, *Brit. Med. J.*, **2**, 521-7 and 585-90.

Gallo, R.C., Salahuddin, S.Z., Popovic, M. *et al.* (1984). Frequent detection and isolation of cytopathic retrovirus (HTLV-III) from patients with AIDS and at risk from AIDS, *Science*, **224**, 500-3.

Goldman, L. and Cook, E.F. (1984). The decline in ischaemic heart disease mortality rates: an analysis of the comparative effects Or medical intervention and changes in lifestyle, *Ann. Intern. Med.*, **101**, 825-36.

Hammer, A. (1878). Ein fall von thrombotischen verschlusse einer des kranzarterien des herzens, *Wein. med. Wchnschr.*, **28**, 97-102.

Heberden, W. (1772). Some account of a disorder of the breast, *Medical Transactions of the College of Physicians in London*, **2**, 59-67.

Herrick, J.B. (1912). Clinical features of sudden obstruction of the coronary arteries, *J. Amer. med. Assn.*, **59**, 2015-20.

Hutchison, R. (1950). Medicine to-day and yesterday. A retrospect, *Brit. Med. J.*, **1**, 72-3.

Jones, R.D., Smith, D.M. and Thomas, P.G. (1987). Mesothelioma in Great Britain 1968-1983. *Brit. J. Industr. Med.* (in press).

Kingsley, L.A., Detels, R., Kaslow, R. *et al.* (1987). Risk factors for seroconversion to human immunodeficiency virus among male homosexuals, *Lancet*, **1**, 345-8.

Mackenzie, Sir J. (1913). *Diseases of the Heart*, 3rd edn, Henry Frowde, London.

Mackinnon, A.U. (1987). The origin of the modern epidemic of coronary artery disease in England, *J. Roy. Coll. General Pract.*, **37**, 174-6.

May, R. and Anderson, R.M. (1987). Transmission dynamics of HIV infection, *Nature*, **326**, 137-42.

Michaels, L. (1966). Aetiology of coronary artery disease: an historical approach, *Brit. Heart J.*, **28**, 258-64.

Morris, J.N. (1951). Recent history of coronary disease, *Lancet*, **1**, 1-7 and 69-73.

Office of Population Censuses and Surveys (1985). *1841–1980 Mortality Statistics: Serial Tables*, HMSO, London.

Peto, J. (1986). AIDS and promiscuity, *Lancet*, **2**, 979.

Royal Commission on Environmental Pollution (1983). *Ninth report. Lead in the Environment*, Cmnd 8852, HMSO, London.

Stuart-Harris, C.H., Schild, G.C. and Oxford, J.S. (1985). *Influenza, the Virus and the Disease*. Edward Arnold, London.

US Public Health Service (1983). *The Health Consequences of Smoking: A Report of the Surgeon General*, US Government Printing Office, Washington DC.

White, P.D. (1957). Measuring the risk of coronary heart disease in adult population groups. 1. The cardiologist enlists the epidemiologist. *Am. J. Publ. Hlth.*, **47**(4), Part 2, 1.

Chapter 11

The Ethics of Risk Management

John Donaldson
Centre for Service Management Studies
Twyford, UK

ABSTRACT

The market economic principle of 'who benefits should pay' is usually taken to imply that 'who pays should benefit'. Both are ethical prescriptions as well as technical norms. This chapter considers the applicability of the rule, particularly in areas such as policies on monopolies and mergers, pollution, plant closures, administrative decisions affecting individuals, and the use of 'collective goods' such as roads. In these (and other areas) issues arise in which managers can influence the distribution of risks, and in which ethical rules and 'the facts' are often complex and easily entangled. Two possible approaches to their disentanglement are considered: the development of substantive decision-rules, laws and codes; and the use of procedures and criteria for improvement. It is concluded that in the areas considered, neither of the approaches provides a general procedure by which the distribution of risks can be justified, both are necessary, but taken together are not sufficient.

INTRODUCTION

Standard accounts of the distinction between risk and uncertainty, such at that provided in the *Penguin Dictionary of Economics* (Baxter and Rees, 1981) make a useful starting point:

> A decision is said to be subject to risk when there is a range of possible outcomes which could flow from it and when objectively known probabilities can be attached

---

Risk: Analysis, Assessment and Management. Edited by J. Ansell and F. Wharton.
© 1992 John Wiley & Sons Ltd.

to these outcomes. Risk is therefore distinguished from uncertainty where there is a plurality of outcomes to which objective probabilities cannot be assigned.

(Baxter and Rees, p. 393)

Viewed in these terms, economic and business activity contain both risk and uncertainty and, quite properly, much of managerial activity is devoted to controlling both. This insight is, it is to be hoped, both commonplace and uncontroversial. The ethical relevance arises not from the fact that managers (and others) seek to control risk and uncertainty, but from how it is done, and on what terms.

In economic terms, the principle and prescription 'who benefits should pay', and its converse, 'who pays should benefit' provide moral (ethical) underpinnings to the market system.

Both are technical norms from which elegant theorems can be devised as well as moral rules. This chapter considers the application of the principle (or rule), particularly in areas such as policies on monopolies and mergers, pollution, plant closures, administrative decisions affecting individuals, and other related areas, such as the uses of collective goods such as roads, and the safety of road vehicles.

In these and many other areas, issues arise in which managers can and do influence the distribution of risks. Ethical rules and 'the facts' are often complex and easily entangled. Two possible approaches to their disentanglement are considered: the development of substantive decision-rules, laws and codes; and the use of procedures and criteria for improvement. It will be suggested that in the areas considered, neither of the approaches provides a general procedure by which the distribution of risks can be justified: both are necessary, but even taken together are not sufficient for generating conditions in which the distribution of risks and uncertainties, and of the costs and benefits of them are adequately justifiable. What is meant by 'adequately justifiable', and what other elements are needed are open to discussion. A view of these is offered in the conclusion of the chapter, based on a 'pluralist' approach, that many basic principles inform useful approaches, but these principles can and do conflict, and are probably radically irreconcilable.

MANAGERS DO NOT SEEK RISK-FREE AND UNCERTAINTY-FREE ENVIRONMENTS

In the market sector, profit (or loss) is viewed as a reward for (or cost of) risk taking, and accrues to the risk takers, the shareholders. This does not mean that risks and uncertainties do not occur in non-market sectors such as public administration, only that the profit criterion is missing there, and is usually replaced by various proxies, from 'shadow pricing' to 'value for money' concepts. It is clear that managers to not seek to create a risk-free and uncertainty-free environment, and at the level of interests, it is not in their interests to do so. On the contrary, they often wish to convince competitors, actual and potential, that competing with them (e.g. by deciding to enter or remain) in a particular market is risky, and that the probability of the risked situation occurring is high. Similarly it is sometimes important to convince employees that the whole enterprise is at risk with a high probability of closure if a particular plant is *not* closed down. In such circumstances, the decision is often withheld from employees until the die is cast, at which point, alternative plans appear, with little chance of success. The point is not that it is immoral or unethical in general for managers to close plants, but that in the way companies are structured, the information on which all parties could base a rational decision is retained by managers. This is usually explained (justified) on a variety of grounds: the need to avoid alarm while options are considered; the need to avoid stock-market movements in response to rumours, management's right to manage in the interests of shareholders, and much else. Creating uncertainty in the eyes of fellow managers can enhance people's hand in 'micropolitical' games.

Some such activities are held prima facie to be against the public interest, as for example in the case of monopoly and restrictive practices. But we need to know whether, and if so why, it is thought that acting against anyone's interest, or the public interest, is immoral or should be regarded as unlawful. The general answer is that the economic and business systems are essentially value systems. Pursuing one's own interests against those of competitors is part of the game. It is true that in the long run, and on the whole, economic theory contends that everyone is potentially a gainer if the rules are adhered to, but that does not explain why one person should not gain at everyone else's expense. The explanation is the proposition that everyone has legitimate interests in a properly functioning economy, but 'legitimate' and 'properly functioning' are moral concepts. It can only work if people recognize that the notion of legitimate interests is a moral one. We take a legitimate risk if the production of the risk is done by a fair and acceptable system. It should be noted that it does not help to regard the system as derivable from the assumption that all participants pursue their maximum gain, subject to various constraints, such as their own budget. It does not help because the constraints cannot be assumed away: they are created, in large part (though not completely) by managerial activities in structuring, them; the constraints are no more than the risks and uncertainties created by a mixture of managerial activities and 'hard facts'. But since it is within the power of managers to influence both the 'hard facts' and other people's perceptions of what they are, the ethical issues cannot be safely left to any automatic mechanisms for adjusting between the interests of individuals, of which the market system is one among many.

The conclusion to this section is thus that managers seek to influence the distribution and perception of risks and uncertainties. This is not necessarily morally justifiable or unjustifiable, but no decision can be made on the matter until the ethical principles are spelled out. Only a pure market would be free of risk and uncertainty, and it is an abstraction, useful for analytical and prescriptive purposes, and only these.

ETHICS: WHICH PRINCIPLES APPLY?

In the context of this chapter, the relevant ethical issues concern which ethical principles should, logically, apply. On what principles should risks and uncertainties be managed, distributed and redistributed? Before attempting to address the question, it is helpful to consider Kant's distinction between rules of skill, counsels of prudence and moral (categorical) imperatives.

Broadly, the 'rules of skill' refer to technical matters. These would include the skilled operation of management tasks, from forward planning and policy analysis to technical matters relating to product design, estimating of potential demand, risk analysis, and the range of other management techniques available. The 'counsels of prudence' are concerned with estimating safety margins, the likelihood of cost estimates being too tight, the likely trouble if the top managers, or the employees find out what is 'really going on' (if it diverges from what is supposed to be).

The 'moral imperatives' refer to the principles that can support or override the decisions taken using the other kinds of analysis: managers can hold, and presumably have on occasions held, that although a particular decision (plant closure, takeover, production of a useless and possibly dangerous product) is technically possible, without any possibility of backfiring, and highly profitable (and thus in the interests of shareholders), it would nevertheless be wrong to proceed. Examples include fashionable, profitable and unnecessary operations in medicine that are no longer performed.

The principles, 'who benefits should pay', and 'who pays should benefit' are relevant here. The principles apply primarily to the market sector, but also apply to the public section ('value for money') but not so easily to charity payments, at least so far as the direct benefits are concerned. The recipients, by definition, cannot pay and the donors presumably do not wish to line up for their share of the free soup and soap.

SOME CASES

Pollution

Much of the contemporary discussion on environmental and pollution issues was foreshadowed in the 1960s by discussions of 'welfare economics' and the attempted construction of a 'social welfare function'. It was hoped that, for example, if a polluting factory were set up, the cost of cleaning up the pollution could be dealt with. This involved the expedient of finding the costs and benefits of fitting pollution control equipment, and, alternatively, putting a cash value on it, so that 'victims' of the pollution could pay to have the factory closed, or could receive compensation for putting up with it. Alternatively, the consumers of the factory's products could pay directly through the price mechanism if the firm were to be made to pay costs for technically cleaning up their product or production processes. The scale of the problem is now much greater than it was then, as is the recognition of the need to act. This chapter does not offer a solution to the problems of pollution and the 'environment', but it is worth noting some major features of the arguments:

- All parties now appear to agree that there is a problem.
- Disagreement exists on the degree and nature of the risks.
- This disagreement often shows up in a refusal to accept the neutrality or objectivity of the 'facts' adduced by the various parties. By way of a specific example, and anxieties about polluted water supplies appear to have led to a large increase in the consumption of bottled 'spring water', held to be 'pure' and 'natural'. Recent claims from some sources have held that the bottled water often contains as many bacteria, and sometimes more, than are found in public water supplies.

Thus the 'facts of the matter' are far from morally neutral. The ethical principles of 'who benefits should pay' can thus be seen to be difficult to put into practice in this case, even though they underpin the whole business and industrial system.

Road Transport

The law provides consumer protection in various forms. This can be taken as recognition that consumers, because of the technical complexity of many products, are not truly in a position to know what they are buying. The moral principle, *caveat emptor*, let the buyer beware, is not fully applicable. Thus complex goods are invested with a warranty by law: they must be fit for the purpose and of merchantable quality. A practice has developed in the motor-cycle supply industry in which vehicles are sold without warranty. Further, some vendors are refusing to sell warranties or to sell vehicles on credit cards (because a warranty is implied in their use), or to perform safety checks, because they also imply a warranty. This is done by the expedient of describing the vehicles 'as seen', or 'for spare(s) with 6 months' MOT'. The market, traditionally, is for inexperienced young people, whose maintenance knowledge on these high-technology machines is limited, as are, typically, their cash resources, and supply of tools and equipment. Spares are very expensive, requiring very long waits for delivery, and repair shops are expensive, few and overworked. Public transport is limited, especially outside the large towns, and highly congested in the large towns. The ethical principles in this case seem to be relatively straightforward: the machines are often very powerful, and their riders are highly vulnerable in the event of accident. Reliability and roadworthiness are thus imperative, but hard to come by.

One solution, apparently favoured by manufacturers, is that the machines should have a short life, during which they are highly reliable. Repairs in the event of accidental damage, however, become expensive in the same way as are repairs needed as a result of wear and tear.

Technically, it appears that minimum economic scale requires long production runs, if the initial purchase is to be within the reach of the potential purchasers. Long production runs generate the risk of flooding the market, hence it does not pay manufacturers to make the vehicles too long lasting or too easily repairable.

Thus, the realities—minimum efficient scale, the complexity of the machines, the shortage of public transport, the need to travel to work, especially among people too young to drive a motor car, but old enough to be expected to work—are 'hard' enough, but are consequences not so much of laws of nature or physics, but of decisions made by manufacturers and authorities. Here the risks concern much more than economic interests, but, as in the 'pollution' case, life itself. The ethical principles include at the least, the grounds on which risks and uncertainties are distributed, and the degree of responsibility attributable to the various parties.

Administrative Decisions Affecting Individuals

In *Key Issues in Business Ethics* (Donaldson, 1989), I described a case concerning the DHSS (now DSS). In that case, the salient features were that the institution made demands on the individual, and ended as judge and jury in its own cause, in that an adjudicator, employed by the institution was supplied with information by one side in a dispute, even though information was obtained from the other party. Whether both sets of information were used remains unclear. In terms of risk, the institution could be seen as ensuring that the decision was favourable to it, by means of a variety of techniques which structured the risk and uncertainties, provided incomplete and conflicting information, even to the point of saying that nothing could be done anyway, so the client was invited to accept improperly attributed blame, pay up, and receive unofficial sympathy.

Arrangements for examination boards in universities sometimes exhibit similar properties. For example, in some universities, appeals are heard by the board that made the decision in the first place. In others, an independent appeals board makes decisions. As might be expected, the appeals system produces many more changed decisions than the 'primary board' system. In the latter, the risks have effectively been transferred to the student: a true case of *caveat emptor*. In the 'appeals board' case, examiners feel under pressure to produce unfavourable decisions only when absolutely necessary, so as to avoid undue criticism from the appeals board. In the 'primary board' case, examiners frequently remind themselves that there are rules that they have always worked to; but that, nevertheless, they can make whatever decision they like, and that precedents do not count. In one case, pressure is on to reach publicly justifiable decisions, with a danger that standards may fall. In the opposite case, there appears to be a relatively harsh system.

Thus, the institutional arrangements distribute risks, both directly and indirectly. The moral principle, in my argument, is that of fairness and consistency of treatment: *caveat emptor* applies only when the buyer knows what is being bought, and what its implications are, and can thoroughly inspect the goods. Otherwise the institutional systems tend to distribute risk, uncertainties and costs to the weakest and most vulnerable parties in the transaction. Thrasymachus' principle in Plato's *Republic*, (ed. Lee, 1955) that 'justice is the interests of the stronger' may indeed still be descriptive, but it remains without much support in ethical theory.

A MODEL OF RISK DISTRIBUTION IN ORGANIZATIONS

It has been argued that managers do not and should not be expected to seek to provide a risk-free and uncertainty-free environment, but that the distribution of risk and the procedures by which it is done are subject to ethical evaluation. The general rules of 'who benefits should pay', and *caveat emptor* often require, for effective operation, that managers provide information which it is not in their interests to provide. The same applies to the principle of justice. They are not by any means unique in being in this position, but the effects of their actions can be far reaching. It is possible to identify some common patterns in what used to be called 'industrial dynamics'. These patterns identify paths which organizations take, indicating gainers and losers in the transactions. It is important to note that these patterns are consequences of policy and structure decisions made by managers, and profoundly influence the interests of the people who have to do with the organization, as well as raising the ethical principles discussed above, in ways illustrated in the case studies.

SOME SOLUTIONS

One line of approach is to identify those areas in which an undesired 'administered distribution' of risk exists, and to seek to redistribute the risks and uncertainties by formal means, involving laws, the courts, regulatory agencies, codes of practice, industry self-regulation. Recent examples include the legislation, deregulation and reregulation, institutions, codes and bodies (such as the Securities Investment Board) in the 1980s aimed at protection of investors.

Well-canvassed weaknesses of this approach are that industry self-regulation has the same inherent faults as the appeals procedures in what I have called 'primary boards'. Industry will tend to interpret issues in its own way. What happens may be impeccable, within the framework in which industry see things, but limited in relation to individual investors. Similarly, it is often held that professional codes exist mainly to protect the professionals, even though at least some protection must be given to clients if credibility is to be maintained.

A second line is to provide managers with training in the concepts and skills necessary to act in the spirit of the principles chosen. A problem with this is the experience of the 'sensitivity training movement' in the 1960s, in which highly sensitized managers returned to situations which were structurally constrained, and run by colleagues who did not have the skills which the 'trained' managers now possessed. The result was disappointment, frustration and abandoning of what in principle was a useful way forward.

SUMMARY AND CONCLUSION

To restate the problem: managers redistribute risks and uncertainties in ways which suit their own interests, and are targets for others who wish to do the same. The outcomes are influenced by ethical principles, such as those of 'who benefits should pay' and *caveat emptor*, as well as by law, general principles of justice, codes and training. In attempting to identify and codify principles on which this can be done in the light of changing circumstances, several problems occur. These include the inevitable entanglement of 'the facts of the matter' with the principles enunciated. The battery of means available for identifying 'sound distributions of risk', and of methods for achieving them is also entangled, and not least by the extent to which managers of public and private organizations are able to benefit from an ability to set the rules of the game, or at least some of them.

Finally, the ethical issues associated with the management of risk seem to me to demonstrate a capacity for improvement, but also a capacity for resilience, recurring in different guises over time, as is the case with environmental and pollution issues from the nineteenth century onwards. It remains uncertain whether the same is true for methods for alleviating the problems.

BIBLIOGRAPHY

The general literature on ethics and 'normative economics' appears to have little to say that bears directly on the subject. In advance of a systematic literature search, the following references may be helpful:

Baxter, R. and Rees, R. (1981). *Penguin Dictionary of Economics*, Penguin, Harmondsworth.

Donaldson, J. (1989). *Key Issues in Business Ethics*, Academic Press, London.

Donaldson, J. and Waller, M. (1980). Ethics and organization, *Journal of Management Studies*, **17**(1).

Mishan, E.J. (1981). *An Introduction to Normative Economics*, Oxford University Press, New York.

Plato *The Republic*—Chapter 5: on the theme of 'Justice'. H.D.P. Lee (ed.) (1955). Penguin, Harmondsworth.

Rawls, J. (1971). *A Theory of Justice*, Harvard University Press, Cambridge, Mass.

Sen, A. (1988). *On Ethics and Economics*, Blackwell, Oxford.

Velasquez, M. (1988). *Business Ethics—Concepts and Cases 3rd edn*, Prentice-Hall, Englewood Cliffs, NJ.

Chapter 12

The Irresponsible Management of Risk

Colin Boyd
Associate Professor of Management
College of Commerce
University of Saskatchewan

ABSTRACT

This chapter argues that managerial decision making about risk avoidance measures must go beyond such pure technical analysis into the domain of moral judgement about the ethics of tolerating uncontrolled risk in business operations. This judgement requires the board and senior management to discuss and specify those moral values that will guide and perhaps override the technical judgements of subordinates. The chapter illustrates the need for senior management level involvement by reference to two recent examples of irresponsible risk management—The London Underground King's Cross Fire and The Zeebrugge Car Ferry Disaster

INTRODUCTION

The horrible inevitability that human endeavours will produce unpredicted outcomes is reflected in the popularity of sayings such as 'The best laid plans of mice and men . . .' and the various versions of Murphy's Law 'If it can go wrong it will'. Most unexpected outcomes are of a trivial nature, at least as far as human harm is concerned. But there have been a sufficient number of major

Risk: Analysis, Assessment and Management. Edited by J. Ansell and F. Wharton.
© 1992 John Wiley & Sons Ltd.

disasters in recent years to bring the issue of risk management in business organizations to the forefront in the press.

The names in the litany of corporate disasters, Bhopal, Ocean Ranger, Piper Alpha, Challenger, King's Cross, *Exxon Valdez*, Zeebrugge conjure up a nightmare image of death and destruction. Governments have calmed public outrage at the carnage involved by insisting on disclosure of the background to each disaster via the mechanism of the public inquiry. These inquiries have consistently revealed a lackadaisical attitude to safety within the management structures of each firm involved. This pattern of irresponsible management of risk is illustrated by the following descriptions of the Zeebrugge Car Ferry Disaster and the London Underground King's Cross Fire.

THE ZEEBRUGGE CAR FERRY DISASTER

In September 1990 the trial for manslaughter of P&O Ferries and seven of its employees and managers started at the Old Bailey. The trial arose from the deaths of 189 passengers and crew on board the P&O ferry *Herald of Free Enterprise* that sank on 6 March 1987 outside the Belgian port of Zeebrugge. The ship had sailed with its bow doors open, and the sea had flooded in when the ship built up speed. Only luck prevented the loss of all 539 on board. The death toll was the worst for a British vessel in peacetime since the sinking of the *Titanic* in 1912. How did such a lamentable disaster occur?

At first sight, the sinking was caused by neglect by three employees on the ship. The assistant bosun, who was supposed to shut the doors, overslept, and thus failed to shut them. The First Officer, who had been involved with loading vehicles, waited until he thought he saw the assistant bosun approaching the door controls on the car deck, and then left to go to his assigned station on the bridge. The Captain, who should have overall responsibility for ensuring the ship set sail in a safe condition, did not check to see that the doors had been closed.

At the Court of Investigation into the sinking it became apparent that the cause of the disaster went far beyond the neglect of three employees on one particular evening. There were many contributory factors, all of which had previously been known by the senior management. Requests to correct various deficiencies that contributed to the disaster had consistently been ignored or rejected. The Report of the Court of Investigation (1990) described many of the firm's defects:

(1) *Crew and officer shift rotations* Senior officers had complained that the scheduling of shifts resulted in three crews intersecting with five different sets of officers, frustrating the development of stable working relationships.

(2) *Rotation of temporary deck officers and trainees* The *Herald of Free Enterprise* was used as a training vessel for new officers. In one five-month period a total of 36 deck officers had been attached to the ship, which usually sailed with four officers on board. A series of complaints were sent to management: 'The result has been a serious loss of continuity. Shipboard maintenance, safety gear checks, crew training and the overall smooth running of the vessel have all suffered . . .'

(3) *Ambiguous orders* On the Zeebrugge route the complement of officers was reduced to three, without altering the standing orders that described the tasks of each officer. As a result the loading officer was required to be on the car-deck supervising door closure at the same time as he was required to be on the bridge overseeing the ship's department from the dock. Written complaints about this conflict had been sent to senior management.

(4) *Commercial pressure to sail early* There was a sense of urgency to sail at the earliest possible moment. One memo sent to shore managers said: '. . . put pressure on the first (loading) officer if you don't think he is moving fast enough . . . Let's put the record straight, sailing late out of Zeebrugge isn't on. It's 15 minutes early for us.'

(5) *The negative reporting system* The Captain assumed that the doors were closed because he did not receive a report that contradicted this assumption. This negative system of reporting (as opposed to a positive reporting system that required confirmation of closure before assuming the doors to be closed) was the normal approved operating procedure for the company. Also, the company's standing orders did not refer to opening and closing the bow and stern doors.

(6) *Five prior instances of sailing with doors open* Before this disaster there had been at least five occasions when one of the company's ships had put to sea with bow or stern doors open.

(7) *Lack of job descriptions* The company received a request to provide job descriptions for ships' officers. A senior manager declined, saying that 'it was more preferable not to define the roles but to allow them to evolve'. The Report described this as 'an abject abdication of responsibility. It demonstrates an inability or unwillingness to give clear orders. Clear instructions are the foundation of a safe system of operation.'

(8) *No meetings for two and a half years* The Report noted that there was one period of two and a half years during which there was no formal meeting between shore management and ship-board managers. Management did not listen to the complaints or suggestions or wishes of the ship-board managers.

(9) *Passenger overloading* Captains had complained to senior managers about the overloading of passengers on ferries. One wrote that 'This total is way over the life saving capacity of the vessel. The fine on the Master for

this offence is £50 000 and probably confiscation of certificate. May I please know what steps the company intend to take to protect my career from mistakes of this nature?' The Report concluded that no proper or sincere effort was made to solve this problem.

(10) *Requests for door warning lights*   After a 1983 incident when a ship sailed with open bow and stern doors, a Captain asked for warning lights to be installed on the bridge to show the status of the bow and stern doors. The memo circulated among managers, who wrote the following comments: 'Do they need an indicator to tell them whether the deck store-keeper is awake and sober? My goodness!!' 'Nice but don't we already pay someone?' 'Assume the guy who shuts the doors tells the bridge if there is a problem.' 'Nice!' A subsequent request for warning lights produced this written reply: 'I cannot see the purpose or the need for the stern door to be monitored on the bridge, as the seaman in charge of closing the doors is standing by the control panel watching them close.'

(11) *Report of internal inquiry into prior sinking*   The company ignored the recommendations of an internal investigation into passenger safety follow-ing the sinking of the passenger ferry *European Gateway* in 1982.

(12) *Water ballast and the resultant instability of the ship*   In order to dock in Zeebrugge and unload both upper and lower vehicle decks the bow of the *Herald* had to be sunk down about 1.2 metres by pumping water into tanks in the bow. Captains complained about the effect of the weight of this water ballast on the ship's handling and safety. At full speed, or even reduced speed, the bow wave came three-quarters of the way up the bow door and the ship was difficult to manoeuvre.

(13) *Rejection of request for high capacity ballast pump*   A Chief Engineer made repeated requests to management to install a high capacity ballast pump that could pump all the water ballast out of the ship quickly prior to departure from the dock. The existing pump took 90 minutes to empty the tanks and thus the ship could not get back on an even keel until it was well out to sea. The new pump would cost £25 000. This cost was regarded by the company as prohibitive, and the requests were rejected.

Irresponsible Management in P&O Ferries

The Report of the Investigation into the Zeebrugge Car Ferry Disaster castigates the management of the ferry company. It states that

> A full investigation into the circumstances of the disaster leads inexorably to the conclusion that the underlying or cardinal faults lay higher up in the Company. The Board of Directors did not appreciate their responsibility for the safe management of their ships. The directors did not have any proper comprehension of what their duties were. All concerned in management, from the members of the

Board of Directors down to the junior superintendents, were guilty of fault in that all must be regarded as sharing responsibility for the failure of management. From top to bottom the body corporate was infected with the disease of sloppiness ...

With regard for responsibility for safety, the Report said that 'The Board of Directors must accept a heavy responsibility for their lamentable lack of directions. Individually and collectively they lacked a sense of responsibility. This left a vacuum at the centre.'

Although the Report condemned the company and its management, the judge at the Old Bailey trial did not consider that there was sufficient evidence to justify the charge of manslaughter against P&O Ferries and seven of its employees and managers. After 27 days of a trial expected to last 5 months, he instructed the jury to find the defendants not guilty.

THE LONDON UNDERGROUND KING'S CROSS FIRE

Shortly after the evening rush hour had passed its peak on Wednesday 18 November 1987 a fire broke out on a wooden escalator at King's Cross station on the London Underground. Fifteen minutes after the discovery of the fire it erupted into a flashover that engulfed the booking hall in intense heat and thick black smoke, killing 31 people and injuring many more. The public was horrified by this disaster, a manifestation of everyone's worst fears about being trapped and helpless in the labyrinth of passages that comprise the Underground system. The Government initiated a formal investigation into the causes of the fire, chaired by Desmond Fennell QC.

The Fennell Report (1988) revealed that the cause of the fire was probably a discarded smoker's match that had fallen underneath the wooded escalator where it ignited an accumulation of flammable debris. Smoking had been banned on the London Underground since February 1985, following a fire at Oxford Circus station. The ban was not strongly policed however, and it was common for a smoker to anticipate leaving the system by lighting a cigarette on the up-escalator at the destination station.

The direct cause of the fire was relatively simple. But the various indirect causes of the fire and the nature of the staff's handling of the fire at King's Cross drew particular attention. The Report strongly criticized a broad range of attributes of the management of London Underground (LU). The managerial defects that were considered to have contributed to the fire and the deaths included the following:

(1) *London Underground's attitude toward fires* LU regarded fires as every-day operational inconveniences. 'Management remained of the view that fires were inevitable ... their attitude towards fire (which they insisted

should be called "smouldering" and regarded as an occupational hazard) gave the staff a false sense of security.'

(2) *Detecting the fire* LU expected fires to be detected by passengers or staff. The alarm was raised by a passenger. Following procedure, one of the staff went to inspect. But he was not based at King's Cross and had received no fire training. He informed neither the station manager nor the line controller. Subsequent investigation showed evidence both of matches underneath the escalator, and of burn marks from many previous fires, each of which had self-extinguished without detection.

(3) *Extinguishing the fire* A manually operated water fog system was in place under the escalator. No member of staff knew that this fire extinguishing system existed, and hence no one knew how to operate it. In the ticket hall at the top of the escalator the main firefighting equipment was hidden behind a hoarding that had been erected to conceal construction work. The Report notes, 'Between 19.30 and 19.45 not one single drop of water had been applied to the fire which erupted into the tube lines ticket hall causing horrendous injuries and killing 31 people'.

(4) *Staff training* No one at King's Cross knew how to react to a fire. Only 4 of the 21 staff on duty had any kind of training in fire control and passenger evacuation. Their instruction was of the 'chalk and talk' variety, described as theoretical and outdated. No training records were kept.

(5) *Communication systems* The public address system was not used during the fire. The system did not go into staff areas or entrance passages or escalator shafts. There were no public telephones, although an emergency alarm system was available via several 'Help Points', an information system connected to the station operations room. No signs had been posted to show that this system was out of order.

(6) *Surveillance* No one was in King's Cross operations room that night, and much of the equipment out of order. Some of the eight TV monitors were switched off. All five cameras which covered the Piccadilly and Northern Lines were out of service, having been removed when modernization work had begun. Neither the station manager nor supervisory staff had been consulted about the removal of the cameras.

(7) *Staffing and supervision* The Report states that 'there was no effective control of King's Cross station by London Underground supervisors or staff at any time before the disaster occurred . . . their overall response was uncoordinated, haphazard and untrained'. During the fire, passenger movements were directed by London Transport police, who just happened to be in the station at the time. The station manager learnt of the fire 12 minutes after the alarm, being told of it by telephone by a manager at another station. Some staff members had been allowed to leave early, others were on a meal break in a room with no phone.

(8) *Cleaning of escalators* The escalator had not been cleaned properly in 44

years of operation. The debris that accumulated underneath the escalator was a flammable mixture of grease and dust.

(9) *The wooden escalator*   Many fires had occurred on this type of wooden escalator. Many fire cleats, designed to prevent the entry of burning materials, were missing. LU had decided not to install automatic fire extinguishers because of excessive false alarms, and because wooden escalators did not have enough life left to justify the expenditure involved. Some wooden escalators were expected to be in use into the twenty-first century.

(10) *No fire certification*   LU lacked fire certification. A fire certificate requires unobstructed, well-lit routes of escape in case of fire, available for use at all times. LU did not meet any of these requirements. LU had successfully argued that it did not need to conform to fire certification standards because its stations were not buildings.

(11) *Responsibility for safety*   Although there were managers within LU who were charged with health and safety responsibilities, none of them saw passenger safety as part of the job. Each thought that he or she was responsible for staff safety alone. Thus LU lacked plans for passenger safety, such as evacuation plans. Safety was not monitored by LU.

(12) *Organization structure*   LU's organization structure was such that there was almost no communication between the engineering division, which managed LU's physical assets, and the operating division, which operated LU's passenger services. Engineering had no responsibility to ensure that operating staff were trained in safety and evacuation procedures. Operations had no control over the state of physical facilities such as escalators. A 'no trespassing' rule existed between the two divisions. There was confusion over areas of responsibility. LU did not understand its own structure, and organization charts had to be prepared especially for the investigation.

(13) *Lack of responsiveness*   The poor shape of King's Cross was widely known before the fire, but nothing was done. 'The many recommendations had not been adequately considered by senior managers and there was no way to ensure they were circulated, considered and acted upon ... Safety officers felt they were "voices in the wilderness" ... one said he found the same problems of poor housekeeping and electrical wiring in escalator machine rooms for years. He reported his findings but could not ensure that any action be taken.'

(14) *Budget underspending*   The Report notes that while LU suffered from lack of funds, the lack of safe operations was not due to inadequate funding but to poor allocation of funds. For example, the escalator cleaning budget had been decreased, and yet each year lift and escalator capital expenditure was consistently lower than the budgeted figure. In 1987/88, this budget was underspent by £1.4 million.

Irresponsible Management in London Transport

The Fennell Report ascribed some of the underground's failings to a rotten system of management. The organization was internalized, and had a warped organization structure that ignored passenger needs. Lines of responsibility, it said, were blurred, and operational and engineering staff did not know what each other was doing. No one person at King's Cross was in charge.

There was no definition of responsibility for passenger safety in LU's structure. There was a lamentable lack of safety training for staff, and a lack of disaster preparation. London Transport had a general ethos which not only neglected issues of safety, but which encouraged a false sense of security by downplaying the importance of critical emergencies such as fires.

Within London Transport the organization culture was such that no outside ideas or criticisms were acted upon. This blinkered vision arose partly from incestuous recruitment and promotion within London Transport, and partly from the smugness that came from a fortunate record of no prior deaths from fires.

Following the publication of the Fennell Report the Chairman of London Regional Transport and the Chief Executive of London Underground resigned. There were no civil or criminal prosecutions arising from the case.

A RESPONSIBLE APPROACH TO RISK MANAGEMENT

The images of defective management portrayed in both of the above cases are remarkably similar. Both disasters occurred in the context of total awareness by some members of the organizations concerned of the potential for catastrophe. Their voices were ignored, the system being deaf to their pleas for the correction of glaring deficiencies.

A similar story is told by Roger Boisjoly (Boisjoly, 1987), in his recounting of the launching of the space shuttle Challenger 3. Boisjoly and other engineers pleaded with senior managers of Morton Thiokol not to launch the spacecraft at a low ambient temperature, because of the resultant brittleness of the O-ring seals on the external rocket pods. Their recommendations were ignored, with the well-known tragic results.

At first sight, then, the lesson of these disasters is that organizations should pay heed to whistle-blowers and pessimistic organizational soothsayers should never be ignored. Should the responsible manager implement a mechanism to facilitate whistle-blowing, to ensure that voices from the bottom of the hierarchy are heard at the top?

Unfortunately, it is clear that such a solution is unworkable in the kinds of organizations described above. No matter how smooth the whistle-blowing mechanism, such a piecemeal approach to risk management is all for naught if it operates in a culture that does not wholeheartedly support the idea of safety as a dominant objective. Similarly, it is irrelevant for scientists to invest time and energy in ever-more sophisticated techniques of risk analysis if the output of their studies is broadcast to senior managers who just do not care about safety.

As one commentator has noted 'A thread running through these disasters is the absence of management of the risk factor commensurate with management of other areas. It is virtually completely absent in the culture and priorities of most of our companies' (Jacques, 1989).

The solution is simple. A responsible approach to risk management requires that senior managers adopt and voice a collective moral stance with regard to safety. The adoption of such a stance should not be an artifice, it has to be a sincere expression of a set of values that will determine the ethos of the organization. Any shallowness in the expression of these values will quickly be tested in the organization, with the culture quick to adapt to the expression of priorities revealed by the pattern of decision making by senior managers.

The board of directors and the chief executive have the ultimate responsibility for the articulation of a value system which addresses safety. The board must place a priority on matters affecting safety, must define responsibilities for these issues, and establish a system to monitor safety performance. Safety and other issues related to social responsibility should be treated as equivalent to other components of commercial strategy, worthy of board-level review and incorporated fully into the corporate value system. The ideal is the exact opposite of the cases of the two disasters described above.

If senior managers do not begin to express a sincere commitment to the issue of risk management, then they run the danger that society will decide to change the rules of the game. The public's outrage at the degree of irresponsibility shown by management in the succession of recent disasters had led to calls to alter the degree of legal protection that managers have for acts carried out on behalf of their employers. If business executives do not express a responsibility for the care of those who are affected by their business decisions, then the criminal justice system may be redirected so as to hold them accountable for both their actions and, more importantly, their inactions.

BIBLIOGRAPHY AND REFERENCES

MV *Herald of Free Enterprise*, Report No. 8074 Formal Investigation, London: Her Majesty's Stationery Office, 1987.
For further analysis of this disaster see Boyd C.W. (1990). Ethical issues arising from the Zeebrugge car ferry disaster, in G. Enderle, B. Almond and A. Argandoña (eds), *People in Corporations: Ethical Responsibilities and Corporate Effectiveness*, Kluwer Academic Publishers.

For classroom use the author has written a case study entitled *The Zeebrugge Car Ferry Disaster (A) and (B)* and an accompanying Teaching Note. These are available from the European Case Clearing House, Cranfield Institute of Technology, Cranfield, Bedford MK43 0AL. In North America this case is published in *Business Policy: Text and Cases* by J.L. Bower, C.A. Bartlett, C.R. Christensen, A.E. Pearson and K.R. Andrews, Irwin, 7th edn, 1991, and in *Social Issues in Business: Strategic and Public Policy Perspective* by F. Luthans, R.M. Hodgetts and K.R. Thompson, Macmillan, 6th edn, 1991, and in *Good Management: Business Ethics in Action* by J. Gandz, F. Bird and J. Waters, Prentice-Hall, 1991, and in *Business and Society: Corporate Strategy, Public Policy, Ethics*, by W.C. Frederick, K. Davies and J.E. Post, McGraw, Hill, 7th edn, 1991.

For an investigation into the King's Cross Underground Fire, see Department of Transport, London: Her Majesty's Stationery Office, Cm 499,1988. *See also The King's Cross Underground Fire: Fire Dynamics and the Organization of Safety*, London: Mechanical Engineering Publications for the Institute of Mechanical Engineers, 1989.

Regarding the Challenger disaster see R.M. Boisjoly (1987). Ethical decisions: Morton Thiokol and the space shuttle Challenger disaster, American Society of Mechanical Engineers (ASME), Paper 87-WA/TS-4, ASME Winter Annual Meeting, Boston, December 1987. See also H.S. Schwartz (1987). On the psychodynamics of organizational disaster: the case of the space shuttle Challenger, *Columbia Journal of World Business*, **23**(1), Spring, 56–67. Also see Jacques, M. (1989), By disaster's light, our ills revealed, *Sunday Times*, 26 February 1989.

Risk Management: a Review

Jake Ansell
University of Edinburgh

and

Frank Wharton
University of Hull

ABSTRACT

In this concluding chapter we review the approaches to risk management described by contributors and identify common concerns, concepts and methodologies.

INTRODUCTION

In the opening chapter Wharton identifies some of the basic concepts and general principles associated with risk analysis, assessment and management.

It is acknowledged that risk perception is a fundamental problem in the increasingly complex socio-technical systems and that missed or misconstrued perceptions about the results of our actions are the greatest source of risk.

The basic paradigm for risk analysis is described although it is recognized that actual problems are often of a scale and complexity which make the analysis intractable without some form of simplification. The process of reduction is itself inherently risky and there are serious problems associated with the estimation of the probabilities and size of perceived potential outcomes.

Risk: Analysis and Assessment and Management. Edited by J. Ansell and F. Wharton.
© 1992 John Wiley & Sons Ltd.

In assessing risks there has been a shift in recent years from a reliance on statistical and economic models towards concepts drawn from psychology and a recognition that the evaluation of risks almost always involves the application of values of a political nature. In every sector of risk management there is an unavoidable need to incorporate subjective and judgement contributions. This inevitably raises moral and ethical issues.

Risks cannot be avoided or eliminated entirely and it is suggested that in all forms of risk management there are essentially three principles at play—the maximization of expected values, the avoidance of catastrophe and the discounting of remote possibilities.

RISK PERCEPTION

Carter and Jackson, writing specifically on the subject of risk perception, stress that it is the lack of perception which contributes more than anything else to systemic failure.

Their main interest is in the failure to perceive causal relationships which lead to catastrophic failures which in hindsight were apparently predictable. They also observe that accidents continue to recur even when the causality is already understood.

They argue that there should be more emphasis on the process of identifying possibilities and less on the estimation of probabilities. Readers are reminded of the difficulties in attempting to apply the concept of expected value when dealing with one-off events.

They see the problems of risk management arising from a tendency to attenuate knowledge and argue that a more deconstructionalist and pluralist approach might provide a better chance for all relevant information to be discovered and the possibility of identifying potential causes of systems failure improved.

In similar vein, Wynne argues that there is a fundamental limitation to the risk-science paradigm which is its intrinsic inability to allow for the full extent of the ignorance underlying present technological commitments.

Risk assessment is a scientifically disciplined approach developed originally to analyse risk and safety problems for well-structured deterministic systems such as chemical or nuclear plants, aircraft and aerospace technologies. It is now expected to deal with badly structured problems arising from, for example, the creation of toxic wastes and the use of pesticides and their potentially extensive environmental effects.

Risks and uncertainty can be taken into account but ignorance (e.g. about chemical reactions) and indeterminacies (e.g. about human reactions) clearly cannot.

A preventive paradigm for an environmentally sustainable technology would bring the focus of attention further upstream to research and development strategies and industrial process design and cause a radical shift in our relationship with scientific knowledge.

In fairness to the scientist, however, he or she cannot be expected to develop models which incorporate every conceivable variable and interdependence in a complex ecological system. Simplification is unavoidable and this necessarily means leaving out what is judged to be the less relevant information. Furthermore, whilst scientists have a responsibility to identify risks, it is for managers and politicians to decide what needs to be done about them.

BUSINESS RISKS

Investment Risks

Organizations in the private sector of industries can only survive in increasingly sophisticated and competitive economies if they continue to generate the necessary cash flows and confidence with which to maintain liquidity and deter predators. They must constantly reinvest in the development of new products and services and the use of new technologies.

The necessary capital investment decisions are fraught with uncertainty and risk. Ho and Pike in Chapter 5 review risk analysis practice in capital budgeting in the United Kingdom and the perceived barriers and benefits. The survey indicates that whilst there is a steady growth in the use of risk analysis methods, practice lags far behind theory and the methods used are relatively primitive.

Payback period is still the most commonly used criterion in capital investment appraisal. It is easily understood and favours projects with more immediate returns thereby reducing the risk of losses arising from medium-term forecasting errors.

Formal risk analysis is usually confined to some form of sensitivity analysis in which the effects on overall performance indicators of percentage changes in estimated parameters are considered.

The major limitations on the use of more sophisticated probability based approaches are said to be the lack of information about the likely component cash flows and managers' inadequate understanding of probability based approaches to risk analysis.

Ho and Pike express the opinion, however, that with the development of methods for obtaining probabilistic estimates of cash flows and the availability of user-friendly computer financial modelling packages, more sophisticated techniques for generating risk profiles such as Monte Carlo simulation are likely to be used more often in the future.

Other authors have pointed out that the return on investment in advanced manufacturing technologies is long term and many of the potential benefits are difficult to quantify. By concentrating on short-term appraisal criteria in an attempt to reduce risk, managers may well be jeopardizing the long-term future of the organization and missing opportunities which are in the best interests of the shareholders (Bromwich and Bhimani, 1991).

The problem may be exacerbated by the fact that bonus or incentive schemes for managers encourage investment in projects with short-term returns (Ashford, Dyson and Hodges, 1988).

Operational Risks

In their survey, Ho and Pike identify seven methods which might be used to reduce risks once a capital project has been undertaken. The most commonly used by the respondents (86.4%) would appear to be that of maintaining tight control. There is a risk that an inability to keep a capital project to its planned duration and budgeted cost could cause a project, which appeared to be economically viable on appraisal, to have disastrous consequences for the organization. Business failures are often attributable to one disastrous project (Slattery, 1984).

A 'risk engineering' approach to the planning and control of large-scale projects developed initially for North Sea oil and gas projects has been described by Chapman. A more comprehensive account has been published elsewhere (Cooper and Chapman, 1987). It parallels the approaches taken by both Ballard and Ansell.

Methods for estimating the overall reliability of networks of independent and dependent activities are reviewed including controlled-interval and memory procedures, Monte Carlo simulation and functional and numerical integration.

A four phase method for time schedule risk analysis is described which involves the identification of not only primary risks and responses but also secondary risks and responses. Extensive documentation is required. Risk/response diagrams are constructed and probabilities estimated. The final phase yields an assessment of the relative contribution of each activity to the total project time schedule risk. The associated cost risks can then be obtained.

This chapter indicates the need for an integrated approach from experts on every aspect of project planning and control including economic, financial, environmental and contractual issues.

Financial Risks

Another way of at least reducing the size of any potential hazard and thereby changing a potential catastrophe into a manageable risk is to purchase either personal or a commercial insurance against loss. The cost of the premium will exceed the expected value of the loss or there would be no incentive for the insurance company to cover the potential loss.

Thomas has observed that banking, finance and insurance companies are commercial organizations whose business it is to assess, manage and profit from perceived risks. The author briefly reviews the kinds of model used for risk analysis in insurance, portfolio analysis and option pricing before giving a more comprehensive account of the statistical techniques used by finance houses, banks, and credit card companies to determine to whom credit can be extended.

Thomas describes two types of decisions—whether to grant credit and whether to further extend credit. A number of different approaches are outlined but Chapter 4 concentrates on discriminant analysis which is the most widely used statistical methodology.

Discriminant analysis is also the basis used by some companies to assess the creditworthiness of potential customers and by investors to assess the financial viability of companies (Taffler, 1981).

Technological Risks

Technological innovation has great wealth-generating potential but it is also the source of numerous threats to man and the environment. The management of technological risks is largely a matter of safety engineering.

In Chapter 6 on industrial risk, Dr Ballard stresses the importance of the concept of safety by design. Unfortunately the publicity given to the results of inquiries following major disasters such as Seveso, Bhopal, Chernobyl and Piper Alpha gives the impression that procedures and policies developed in safety engineering are largely based on bitter experience and a process of trial and error.

Risk perception is again recognized as the first step in risk analysis and Ballard identifies some approaches including hazard and operability studies, failure modes and effect analysis and the use of hazard checklists.

From these types of studies it is possible to develop fault trees which are described by both Ballard and Ansell. Ballard emphasizes the diagnostic use of fault trees to expose design deficiencies, whilst Ansell concentrates on mathematical/statistical usage to estimates of probabilities and size of outcomes. Both authors accept that it is not possible to eliminate all risks and suggest that potential hazards are capable of being ranked in terms of their expected value, i.e. the product of probability and size. The problem of defining the acceptable risk level remains to be resolved as a judgemental issue.

The application of the principle of safety by design is Ballard's main contribution to the debate. This involves making plant and equipment as far as possible inherently safe (avoiding the use of toxic materials for example), building safeguards in the form of instrumentation, fire walls and stand-by systems, and, finally, establishing appropriate operating, incident, test and maintenance procedures.

In describing the scope and limitations of existing mathematical/statistical methods used in assessing the reliability of plant and equipment Ansell highlights the degree of simplification that is required so that a result may be obtained. This shows that at every stage of the analysis there has to be compromise to obtain a feasible model.

A major problem is again stated to be the identification of possible hazards and the importance of collaboration between design and reliability engineers at an early stage in the design of plant and equipment is stressed.

Among the problems inherent in these approaches is the difficulty of accounting for interdependence in reliability between components or processes and the lack of complete historical data on which to base estimates.

Evidently the key difficulties in technological risk management relate to risk perception, the estimation of perceived risks and the problem of defining what constitutes acceptable risk.

Transportation Risks

Lee points to the limitations of risk analysis in the anticipation and prevention of transport accidents due to the fact that they are often the result of a chain of events many of which would be 'unimaginable or foolish'.

His chapter concentrates on the need to control the seriousness of accidents when they occur by limiting their possible consequences and facilitating recovery. In the case of transport accidents the difficulties are exacerbated by the fact that not only do they occur randomly in time but the location and nature of the accidents are also to a large degree unpredictable. Providing planned responses to incidents of this kind is much more difficult than, say, preparing for the possibility of an explosion at a chemical plant.

The need for well-defined emergency command structures and procedures and for well-rehearsed operations is stressed.

Three recent and fatal transport accidents representing land, air and sea transport are described in detail—the Clapham Junction Rail Disaster, the Kegworth Aircrash, and the Thames Boat Disaster—with particular reference to the effectiveness of the emergency services. In all three cases and in Professor Lee's opinion the fire, ambulance, hospital and police emergency services performed well together due, it was felt, to advanced careful planning.

By contrast Boyd was not at all impressed by the performance of company management (as opposed to emergency services management) in relation to the prevention and response to two other transport disasters in the form of the King's Cross Underground Fire and the Zeebrugge Ferry Disasters.

Carter and Jackson are similarly unimpressed by the failure of management to perceive and prevent the sinking of the *Titanic*, the explosion of the space shuttle Challenger, and a railway accident involving an automatic level crossing.

HEALTH RISKS

In his review of the major epidemics of the twentieth century Sir Richard Doll draws attention to the dramatic reduction in mortality in the United Kingdom over the last 100 years but points out that the reduction might have been even more dramatic had it not been for the emergence of the new epidemics of lung cancer and coronary thrombosis both of which would now seem to be in decline. Epidemiologists have demonstrated that these diseases are largely attributable to changes in behaviour and diet. By comparison, mortality due to increased industrial pollution and traffic accidents has been relatively small.

Doll pays tribute to the work of Dr William Farr for having created in 1837 the system of registration of births, marriages and deaths for England and Wales which provided the source of data essential in identifying the aetiology of the two major epidemics of lung cancer and coronary thrombosis through simple temporal and geographic comparisons of their incidence.

Ware (1990) has observed that with the decline in mortality from fatal diseases there has been a change in the focus and methodology of epidemiology during the last 30 years towards research into the subtle effect of environmental and personal risk factors on chronic disease.

Many multivariate methods currently used were not available 30 years ago. The incentive for their development has been the need to quantify relatively weak and subtle associations between exposure and disease in the presence of other, possibly more powerful, risk factors.

RISK ETHICS

Donaldson's underlying thesis (Chapter 11) is that whilst managers should not be expected to provide a risk-free environment the principle of 'who benefits should pay' should apply in the distribution of risks.

He describes instances in pollution control, road safety and administrative decisions affecting individuals where this principle is clearly not applied. Whilst decisions are influenced by principles of justice, the law, codes of conduct, and training, there are difficulties in attempting to codify ethical principles not the least of which would be disagreement between interested parties as to the degree and nature of the risks involved.

Donaldson describes the problems of trying to have risks redistributed by formal means—legislation, regulatory agencies, codes of practice, etc.—and the difficulties facing the manager trained in the concept and skills of the principles when operating in an unsympathetic organization.

The need for organizations to create cultures and establish priorities which encourage a more responsible attitude to risk management is an argument strongly supported by Boyd.

Using detailed accounts of the London Underground King's Cross Fire and the Zeebrugge Car Ferry Disaster to support his case, Boyd argues that managerial decision making must go beyond the technical analysis of risk and into the domain of moral judgements and management ethics. Senior managers have a responsibility to consider moral issues and where necessary override the technical judgements of subordinates.

The view is expressed that unless executives accept responsibility for putting at risk those employed by the organization and those affected by its business operations, then public pressure is likely to force government to make them more accountable in law.

Unfortunately effective risk management will always exact a price and as Donaldson has pointed out the application of the principle of 'who benefits pays' is in practice somewhat difficult to enforce. As Wharton observed earlier there is always the difficulty of deciding where the balance should lie between a relatively safe society which tends to stifle initiative and opportunity and a freer society in which there are greater and perhaps inequitably distributed risks.

CONCLUSION

The basic concepts and general principles outlined in the first chapter have undoubtedly been in evidence in the wide variety of contributions contained in this volume.

The underlying problems of risk perception were discussed at length by Carter and Jackson and Wynne and are clearly acknowledged in some of the more technical chapters by Chapman, Ballard and Ansell. There has to be acceptance of the risk before one can assess it. Some possible remedies have been described of both a methodological and a technical nature although the difficulties are bound to increase as technology advances and socio-technical systems become more complex.

The main aim of the epidemiological methods described by Doll is to highlight increasingly weak associations between risk factors in our behaviour, occupation and environment and our physical well-being. There have been significant advances in recent years in methods of multivariate analysis arising from research into the risk factors associated with chronic disease. In describing the financial risks to companies engaged in the business of lending to individuals and organizations, Thomas outlines the use of other forms of multivariate analysis, particularly discriminant analysis, again to tease out those factors which make one individual or organization a greater risk than others.

Several authors including Ballard, Chapman and Ansell have discussed the use of various forms of decision tree or network analysis in risk analysis. A common problem would seem to be that of reducing such models to manageable size without omitting possible sequences of events or failures which might lead to disaster. Difficulties in estimation of low probabilities and in defining acceptable risks are evidence in all cases.

Lee and Boyd highlight the importance of being able to ameliorate the effects of low probability disasters by having in place well-established and practised routines for dealing with emergencies—a requirement which might have been usefully added to the general principles described by Wharton in Chapter 1.

The shortcomings of the classical economic approach to risk assessment are evidently well understood and perhaps account for the reluctance by managers to use the more sophisticated methods of capital investment appraisal and risk analysis described by Ho and Pike. An over-reliance on the criteria of payback period which in a simplistic way combines appraisal and risk analysis could, however, increase the risk of a failure to invest in advanced manufacturing technologies which have relatively long payback periods and unquantifiable benefits.

The inevitable impact of psychological and political factors on risk management were recognized either explicitly or implicitly in every contribution. In a world where every action by individuals and organizations may put at risk not only other contemporary individuals and organizations but also future generations it is inevitable that politics will have a serious role to play in reconciling conflicting value judgements and interests. Donaldson and Boyd have highlighted the moral and ethical issues involved.

Clearly man has begun to grasp the fact that in order for industrial societies to survive he must work hard to reconcile his behaviour with members of his own species, diminishing resources, and his environment (Ashby, 1978). We can expect an explosion of interest in risk analysis, assessment and management.

REFERENCES

Ashby, E. (1978). *Reconciling Man with the Environment*, OUP, London.

Ashford, R.W., Dyson, R.G. and Hodges, S.D. (1988). The capital investment appraisal of new technology: problems, misconceptions and research directions, *Journal of the Operational Research Society*, **39**(7), 637–42.

Bromwich, M. and Bhimani, A. (1991). Strategic investment appraisal, *Management Accounting*, March, 45–8.

Cooper, D.F. and Chapman, C.B. (1987). *Risk Analysis for Large Projects: Models, Methods and Cases*, John Wiley & Sons.

Slattery, S. (1984). *Corporate Recovery*, Penguin Books.

Taffler, R.J. (1981). Forecasting company failure in the UK using discriminant analysis and financial ratio data, City University Business School, Working Paper 23.

Ware, J.H. (1990). The role of epidemiology in the assessment of societal risk: a statistician's perspective, *Chance: New Directions for Statistics and Computing*, **3**(4), 41–7.

Author Index

Subject Index